TAX-SMART
INVESTING

The *Wiley Financial Advisor* Series

Advising the 60+ Investor: Tax and Financial Planning Strategies
   by Darlene Smith, Dale Pulliam, and Holland Tolles
Tax-Smart Investing: Maximizing Your Client's Profits
   by Andrew Westhem and Stewart Weissman
Managing Family Trusts: Taking Control of Inherited Wealth
   by Rob Rikoon with Larry Waschka

TAX-SMART INVESTING

Maximizing Your Client's Profits

Andrew D. Westhem and Stewart J. Weissman

A Marketplace Book

John Wiley & Sons, Inc.
New York • Chichester • Weinheim • Brisbane • Singapore • Toronto

Copyright © 1999 by Andrew Westhem. All rights reserved.

Published by John Wiley & Sons, Inc.

Published simultaneously in Canada.

This publication is designed to provide accurate and authoritative information in regard to the subject matter covered. It is sold with the understanding that neither the publisher nor the authors are engaged in rendering professional services. If professional advice or other expert assistance is required, the services of a competent professional person should be sought.

Library of Congress Cataloging-in-Publication Data:

Westhem, Andrew D., 1933–
    Tax-smart investing: maximizing your client's profits / Andrew Westhem and Stewart Weissman
        p.   cm.—(Wiley financial advisor series)
    Includes index.
    ISBN 0-471-33261-5 (cloth : alk. paper)
    1. Investments—Taxation—United States.   2. Finance, Personal—United States.   3. Tax planning—United States.   I. Weissman, Stewart.   II. Title.   III. Series.
HG4910.W384   1999
343.7305'246—dc21   99-19899

Printed in the United States of America

10 9 8 7 6 5 4 3 2 1

This book is dedicated to all the hardworking financial professionals who conscientiously serve their clients in the areas of investment planning, financial planning, and tax planning. Their efforts are appreciated not only by those clients but by the clients' loved ones as well.

Contents

Acknowledgments

We'd like to thank all the professionals, from all fields, who have made this book possible. That includes Stewart's staff, especially his wife and invaluable coworker Brenda, and Andrew's staff as well as his son David, who is an outstanding financial professional in his own right.

Thanks also to Donald Jay Korn for all of his work in preparing the manuscript; Samantha Hudson, our extraordinary publicist; Debra Englander, our outstanding editor at John Wiley; and Chris Meyers of Marketplace Books, for his invaluable assistance for the entire project.

We'd also like to thank Mark Skousen, Richard Band, Peter Dickinson, and Phil Springer of Phillips Publishing for their ongoing support, and Harry Dent for his inspiring insights.

Introduction

The bull market that dominated the 1980s and 1990s has brought smiles to the faces of many investors . . . and their advisors. Chances are, many of the clients with whom you've been working have managed to accumulate substantial amounts of wealth.

However, those clients probably aren't as wealthy as they think they are. That's because a not-so-silent partner is waiting to share in their profits: the IRS. What's more, many state and even local governments have their own tax collectors lined up for a cut of your clients' gains.

Suppose, for example, you've advised Dr. Jones to sponsor a tax-deferred retirement plan. At your suggestion, Dr. Jones has contributed regularly to the plan and invested wisely, building up a balance of $1 million.

Is Dr. Jones a millionaire? Not really. To get his hands on even $1 of that money, Dr. Jones will have to pay income tax to the IRS. If he were to withdraw all that money today, he'd effectively owe over $400,000 to the IRS. Depending on where he lives, the total tax bill could top $500,000.

Sue Smith is in a different situation, but taxes still play a role in her financial future. Sue has been investing regularly in mutual funds, outside of any tax-advantaged plan. Altogether, she has poured $100,000 into her funds, which are now worth $250,000. Those funds may be worth $250,000, but they're not worth $250,000 *to Sue.* If she wants to cash them in and use the proceeds to pay her children's college bills, she'll owe tax on a $150,000 capital gain. The exact amount she'll owe will depend on specific circumstances, but it's likely that at least $30,000 of her gains will go to the IRS: Her $250,000 mutual fund portfolio is worth no more than $220,000 to her.

The preceding examples are by no means unique. Virtually all investments have tax consequences, and those consequences can sharply reduce the amounts of money that investors get to enjoy. If you're going to do the best job of advising your clients, you need to know the after-tax as well as the pretax implications of your recommendations. In other words, the true value of an investment is how much it pays in *net gains*. The bottom line is the bottom line.

That's why we've written this book. We've spent years advising clients, especially the high-income, high-net-worth clients to whom the tax code is particularly important. We've discovered the tax traps that can snare the unwary—and we've managed to develop some sophisticated tactics for eluding those traps.

First, Talk the Talk

Throughout this book you'll learn the strategies we use to help our clients keep more of their investment dollars while paying less to the government. Before we begin, though, we'd like to spend a little time on a vital matter: client communications. You'll get the best results if your clients understand the principles behind tax reduction. Therefore you should be sure that your clients grasp these basic principles:

- *Ordinary income versus capital gains.* Most taxable income is *ordinary,* now taxed at rates of up to 39.6% (federal taxes alone). However, certain income is classed as *capital gains.* Generally, when an investor sells an asset (a stock, perhaps, or a house) any profit is considered a capital gain.

- *Long-term versus short-term gains.* Under a tax law passed in 1998, assets held more than 12 months are considered *long-term property.* Gains on the sale of such property generally are taxed no higher than 20%.

■ *Basis.* When investors report capital gains, the taxable gain is the amount they receive minus their *basis,* or cost for tax purposes. Keeping good records is an excellent way to track basis and make sure that excess taxes are not paid.

■ *Tax brackets.* Few investors really understand the concept of marginal tax rates. When you tell a client that he or she is in a "36% tax bracket," that means that the next dollar the client earns will be taxed at 36%. Similarly, a $1 tax deduction will be worth 36 cents (36%) in tax savings.

Clients need to understand that this is *not* an average tax rate: If they earn $200,000, their federal income tax will not be $72,000. In tax planning it is the *marginal tax rate*—the impact this investment will or will not make—that is most important.

■ *Effective tax brackets.* Although federal income tax brackets (ordinary income) are 15%, 28%, 31%, 36%, and 39.6%, those are not the true tax brackets for many investors, especially those with above-average incomes. Why not? Because of many technicalities buried in the Internal Revenue Code.

To cite a common example, taxpayers' itemized deductions are reduced for every dollar of income over a certain limit—currently that limit is about $125,000. Thus, if a client increases his or her income from $150,000 to $160,000, not only will income tax be assessed on that $10,000 at the taxpayer's marginal tax rate, but itemized deductions also will be reduced. *In effect, this is an extra income tax.*

Therefore, individual circumstances will determine a precise marginal tax rate. For those in the 36% bracket, the effective rate might be 37%; for those in a 39.6% bracket, the effective rate might be 41%.

What's more, that's only step 1 in determining a client's effective tax bracket. Step 2 is factoring in state and local income taxes when they apply. Making the calculation even more difficult, state and local income tax generally is deductible for federal tax purposes.

Here's a simplified example. You determine that a client's effective federal marginal tax rate is 41%. That client lives in a city where state and local income tax must be paid; the client's marginal rates for those two taxes are 8% and 4%—12% altogether.

However, the client gets a 41% federal tax deduction for every dollar paid in state and local income tax.

1. Multiply 41% times 12% to get 4.92%—that's the client's effective tax savings.

2. Subtract that 4.92% from 12% to get 7.08%, the effective additional cost to this client of state and local income tax.

3. Add 7.08% (state and local) to 41% (federal) to get a true effective tax bracket: 48.08% in this example.

You really don't need this type of precision to be able to advise clients. However, it is important that your clients be able to approximate their effective tax rates. Here, you might inform your clients that their effective tax bracket is nearly 50%. If they buy stock that pays a $1,000 annual dividend, their true benefit from that dividend will be around $500 after tax.

- *Alternative minimum tax.* If you think explaining effective tax brackets to clients is difficult, wait until you discuss the AMT!

  The AMT is an alternative tax system. Taxpayers start with their regular taxable income, as shown on their tax return, and add back certain "preferences" and "adjustments." (You really need to work with an experienced tax professional to do the actual calculation.)

  From this number, certain allowances may be subtracted. Then the result is multiplied by 26% (certain amounts by 28%) to get the client's AMT obligation.

  After going through this exercise, the AMT obligation is compared with the regular tax obligation. The client pays whichever amount is *higher:* The IRS always wins this game.

  For years, the AMT was a fairly abstract concept because few taxpayers actually paid it. However, that number is growing and is expected to reach into the millions by the early years of the twenty-first century.

  Advisors and clients alike need to understand the AMT and whether it applies to them. In some circumstances, tax advantages will be denied because an investor is in an AMT situation.

Again, it's not necessary that you or your clients memorize the AMT rules. However, it is important that your clients know how the AMT works, because investment decisions may be affected.

Once you've explained these fundamentals to your clients, you'll be ready to move on to the taxwise investment strategies explained in this book. Knowledgeable advisors appreciate the advantages of working with knowledgeable clients.

TAX-SMART
INVESTING

Roll Your Own

Directly Owned Stocks and Bonds

Despite the tremendous surge in mutual fund investing during the 1990s, some clients still prefer to buy individual stocks and bonds. This approach takes more effort, but it also keeps investors in control over their financial future. Moreover, as a planner you'll discover that owning securities directly is a much more tax-efficient way to invest.

Direct investments will not be suitable for every client. Some, especially those who are less sophisticated, prefer to turn over the responsibilities for stock and bond picking to a mutual fund manager. Nevertheless, it's likely that some of your clients will prefer direct investments, and they'll be relying on your guidance in this area. As you'll see, the tax advantages of the direct approach can be substantial.

Consider the example of John Smith, who invests $10,000 in ABC Mutual Fund in October 1999, instructing the fund to reinvest all distributions so he can build wealth over the long term. Most mutual investors choose the reinvestment option.

For years, ABC has done extremely well by investing in large, well-known companies: Coca-Cola, Gillette, General Electric, and so forth. One day after John invests, ABC's portfolio manager decides that these stocks are too expensive, so he sells them, taking huge profits.

As required by tax law, ABC distributes those profits to its shareholders, including John. On his $10,000 holding, he might receive a $2,000 distribution. Even if he reinvests that distribution, he has a $2,000 taxable gain and might owe around $500 in taxes—simply because he invested at the wrong time.

Now, consider what might have happened if John had bought Coke and Gillette stock directly. He could have held onto his stocks indefinitely without paying tax on any gains. True, John would owe tax on the dividends those stocks pay, but the dividends are so low (Coke is paying 0.8% as of this writing) that the resulting tax bill would be minimal as long as he buys and holds onto his investments.

Of course, John might want to sell some stock from time to time, which would generate a taxable gain. When that happens, he can sell the shares that would generate the least taxable gain; also, he can sell some losers to offset his winners and negate his tax bill.

Investing in individual bonds offers tax advantages, too. As we'll see in the next chapter, John can choose municipal bonds and earn tax-exempt income. Even if he prefers Treasury bonds, as many investors do, his interest income will be taxable on his federal return but exempt from any state or local income tax.

Best of all, investing in individual bonds keeps John in control. He can choose the maturities he wishes and the credit quality of the issuers. From a tax standpoint, John can decide to sell individual bonds at a loss if he wishes, and those losses may be used to offset gains he takes on his stocks.

In short, buying individual stocks and bonds gives John unmatched flexibility when it comes to his investments. That flexibility, in turn, leads to a great many tax-saving strategies. In the rest of this chapter, we'll look at some of those strategies.

The Beauty of Buy-and-Hold

The best strategy is the simplest one—buy high-quality growth stocks and hold onto them. In the 10 years through 1998, the Standard & Poor's 500 Index (which represents most of the value of the U.S. stock market) gained 18% per year. Thus, $10,000 invested in the stocks that make up the index in 1989 would be worth over $54,000 in 1998.

During that time, dividends on the S&P 500 stocks generally were 2% or 3% per year. Thus, investors would have owed about 1% a year in tax on the dividends they received. The other 15% or 16% of annual return came from *appreciation,* or rises in stock prices. As long as those investors held onto their stocks and refrained from selling, they would have owed no income tax at all on the gains they enjoyed.

The Buffett Formula

Professional investors know the value of buying growth stocks for the long term. Consider the example of Warren Buffett, perhaps the world's greatest investor. If one of your clients had entrusted Buffett with $10,000 in 1956 and reinvested all the profits that were generated, that client's stake would have grown to more than $80 million in the 1990s!

Buffett is so opposed to short-term trading that he once suggested a 100% tax on profits made on stock held for less than one year. "My favorite time frame for holding a stock is forever," he told *U.S. News & World Report* in 1994. Speaking to his local newspaper, the *Omaha World-Herald,* in 1986, he explained his philosophy this way: "We like to buy businesses. We don't like to sell, we expect the relationships to last a lifetime."

Buffett's company is Berkshire Hathaway, which is actually a holding company for all the stocks he owns for his own account and for other investors. Each year, Berkshire Hathaway's annual meeting is attended by experts from all areas of the financial markets, who analyze every word in Buffett's address to shareholders.

At the 1992 meeting, he illustrated his approach to investing with these remarks: "The really important thing is to be in the right business. The classic case is Coca-Cola, which went public in 1919 at $40 a share. The next year, after World War II, sugar prices changed dramatically and the stock went down to $19. You would have lost half your money if you had sold then."

On the other hand, an investor who had bought one share in 1919 and held on, reinvesting all dividends, would have held Coke stock worth $1.8 million. (That was in 1992; since then the stock has continued to move up.) "We have had depressions," Buffett told his audience. "We have had wars. Sugar prices have gone up and down. A million things have happened. How much more fruitful is it for us to think about whether the product is likely to sustain itself and its economics than to be questioning whether to jump in or out of the stock?"

A Perfect Ten

Nor is Warren Buffett the only great investor to favor a buy-and-hold approach to the market. Peter Lynch, who managed Fidelity Magellan mutual fund during the era when it posted legendary results, advised investors to look for "10-baggers," stocks that appreciate 10-fold for their investors. There's more money to be made that way than by taking profits (and paying taxes) every time a stock goes up a few points.

Coke, as mentioned previously, has been more than a 10-bagger, but so have many others, including Gillette and Disney, Microsoft and Intel. Cisco Systems provided investors with a 31% annual return from 1987 to 1997. That's a 15-bagger: A $10,000 investment would have grown to $150,000.

Are there more 10- and 15-baggers out there? Certainly. Harry S. Dent, author of *The Roaring 2000s,* predicts the Dow Jones Industrial Average will rise from 9,000 in 1998 to 35,000 in 2008. If gains such as these come to pass, many companies—particularly those in communications and technologies—will amply reward patient investors.

Marginal Notes

Can your clients really enjoy such stock market gains without selling shares? Certainly. If they own stock in top-rated companies, they have solid assets, respected by everyone. This increased net worth gives them credibility if they want to buy a house, open up a line of credit, or start a new business.

What's more, if your clients need to get their hands on some cash, they can borrow up to 50% of the value of those shares from their broker. Such loans are called *margin loans.* For example, if a client invested $10,000 in stocks and watched them grow to $50,000, his or her broker would lend that client up to $25,000. As is the case whenever anyone borrows, the loan proceeds can be received free of income tax.

Broker loan interest rates are normally reasonable, usually about the same as borrowers pay on a home equity line of credit. Can borrowers deduct that interest? Not if they spend the money to buy a new car or vacation in Hawaii. However, if they use the borrowed money for investments (as opposed to using the money for a week on Oahu), the interest will be characterized as "investment interest." Then the borrower can use the interest expense as a deduction to offset taxable income from dividends, interest, and capital gains.

A Capital Idea

If clients prefer not to borrow, they can sell shares. As long as they have kept good records, they can sell the shares that will generate the lowest taxable gain.

Suppose, for example, that Betty Anderson has invested $25,000 in Coca-Cola over the years, accumulating 1,000 shares. The stock now sells at $75, so her shares are valued at $75,000. She wants to sell $30,000 worth of stock (40% of her holdings) to cut her risk and help pay for her children's college educations.

Thus, Betty wants to sell 400 shares of Coke. Going over her records, she chooses the 400 shares that have the highest purchase price and directs her broker to sell those specific shares. (She identifies them, in writing, by the price she paid and the day they were bought.) She is careful to specify shares held at least 12 months because they qualify for a bargain 20% tax rate on long-term capital gains.

Suppose that Betty identifies shares with an average purchase price of $50 per share. (Altogether, her average purchase price is $25 per share.) She'll have a $25 capital gain per share, or a $10,000 gain on 400 shares. At 20%, she'll owe only $2,000 in tax. This leaves her with $28,000 to spend (more than her entire investment in Coke) as well as the $45,000 in shares she still holds.

An even better strategy would be for Betty to give the 400 shares to her two college-age children. If she and her husband make joint gifts, they can give away all 400 shares ($30,000 worth) and incur no gift tax. Then the children can sell the shares, pay only 10% in tax ($1,000) because of their presumably low tax brackets, and have $29,000 to spend for college.

Lop Off the Losers

If a client has invested in a diversified portfolio of, say, 10 different stocks, he or she may be able to sell without taking gains at all. Among those 10 stocks, some may be losers. When the client needs to sell stock in order to raise cash, he or she can sell those losers. Doing this year after year will "cut losses and let winners run," a proven strategy for winning big in the stock market.

This approach has tax advantages, too. Selling stocks at a loss obviously won't generate any taxable gains. What's more, taxpayers can deduct up to $3,000 worth of capital losses each year from their taxable income; excess losses can be carried forward to future years.

Suppose, for example, a client invested $10,000 in a stock that has since fallen in value to $7,000. Now he needs $7,000 to pay some bills that have accumulated. He could sell this stock and put his hands on that $7,000, tax-free. What's more, he'll get a $3,000 capital loss that could save him more than $1,000 in income tax. And the rest of the stocks in his portfolio—the winners—can stay untouched in hopes of further appreciation.

A Slice of Life

A portfolio of individual securities can be used for retirement income, too, even by clients who own low-dividend growth stocks. The trick is to slice off just enough capital each year to meet current needs.

Suppose that Ron Mason had invested in growth stocks all during his career, building up a $500,000 portfolio. Then Ron retires. He decides he needs $30,000 from this portfolio each year to supplement other retirement income. His growth stocks yield only 1% ($5,000 per year in dividends) so he decides to shift into bonds paying 6% ($30,000 per year).

This will be a costly maneuver, after tax. First, selling all of his growth stocks will generate a sizable tax bill. Assuming his basis in these stocks is only $200,000, selling them will produce a $300,000 gain. He'll owe at least $60,000 to the IRS, at a 20% rate, giving him no more than $440,000 to invest in bonds.

What's more, the interest generated by the bonds will be fully taxable. Even in retirement, Ron's tax bracket likely will be 28% or more.

After tax, Ron will wind up with nowhere near $30,000 per year—and he's locked himself into a no-growth portfolio of bonds.

What would be a preferable alternative? Ron can retain his $500,000 portfolio of growth stocks and slice off $30,000 worth each year by careful selling. As noted previously, he can specify the shares he wishes to sell, minimizing the taxable gains—or even taking some losses. Moreover, the capital gains he does realize may be taxed at only 20%, a lower rate than he'd owe on bond interest.

Best of all, Ron keeps his portfolio of growth stocks largely intact. The $30,000 worth of stock he sells in order to meet retirement living expenses may be offset by continued growth of the stocks retained in the portfolio.

'Til Death . . .

As we've seen, paying capital gains tax on appreciated securities is optional. Clients can convert stock market paper profits to cash by borrowing against them or by selling them—or they can simply leave stocks and stock funds alone. What if clients never need to cash in stock market gains? Well, then they can die holding those stocks and bequeath them to their heirs. The heirs, in turn, get a *step-up in basis,* a form of tax code magic that makes all the appreciated gains disappear.

Suppose, for example, that Charley Harris is a lifelong stock market investor, putting a total of $50,000 into shares of various companies. Charley dies on February 1, 2000, holding shares worth $200,000. In his will, he leaves all of those shares to his daughter Peggy. Thus, Peggy inherits shares with a *basis* (cost for tax purposes) of $200,000, the value on the date of Charley's death.

In January 2001, Peggy decides to sell those shares, now worth $220,000. Her taxable gain will be only $20,000 (her $220,000 selling price minus her $200,000 basis in the shares). All the appreciation (from the original $50,000 to $200,000) during Charley's lifetime escapes capital gains tax.

One other tax shelter may be available to Peggy. The executor of Charley's estate can use the day six months after Charley's death—August 1, 2000—as an *alternate valuation date.* That is, Charley's estate can be valued on August 1 rather than on February 1. If

Charley's stocks have gone up to $210,000 by August 1, for example, yet Charley's overall estate is not large enough to incur estate tax, then the executor can use the alternate valuation date, and Peggy's basis in the shares will be stepped up to $210,000. In this case, if she sells for $220,000, she'll have only a $10,000 taxable gain.

It's true that Charley could do the same with mutual funds as with individual stocks: hold them until death and leave them to Peggy, with a step-up in basis. However, if he invests in mutual funds he'll be paying tax each year on gains realized within the fund. With individual securities and a buy-and-hold strategy, Charley can avoid tax on capital gains altogether.

Sweet Charity

When clients invest in individual securities they have one more tax-saving strategy they can pursue: Give them away. Donating appreciated securities makes more sense than giving away cash.

Suppose, for example, one of your clients gives $1,500 to her alma mater's fund-raising drive each year. If she writes a check for $1,500, she is giving away $1,500 on which she has already paid tax—expensive dollars.

Instead, suppose this client is holding shares of General Motors that sell for $75 apiece. She could give away 20 shares of GM to her alma mater, the equivalent of the $1,500 cash gift. In fact, she can specify low-basis shares, perhaps 20 shares she bought some years ago for $30 per share.

Those shares might be selling for $75, but they're not really worth $75 to your client. With a $30 basis, she'd have a $45 capital gain if she sold them, owing $9 in tax at a 20% rate. Thus, those shares are worth only $66 to her, after tax, and giving away 20 shares is like giving away $1,320—20 times $66.

However, your client would get a full $1,500 tax deduction for her gift. The university, as a tax-exempt entity, can sell the shares and owe no tax. So your client gets a $1,500 tax deduction for a gift worth $1,320 to her, the school gets $1,500 to spend, and the IRS gets to hold the bag.

To implement this strategy, you or your client can call the charity that will be receiving the gift and get its brokerage account number.

Then call the broker holding the securities, explain what your client wants to do, and provide the account number. Follow up by fax or phone to confirm the transaction.

Again, your clients can do the same with appreciated mutual fund shares. However, with individual securities they can choose the company whose shares they wish to give away. For maximum tax advantage, they can donate the shares with the greatest unrealized appreciation.

A word of caution: Giving away appreciated securities is a great idea when clients are alive, but they shouldn't leave appreciated securities to charity when they die. Instead, advise them to give away assets from IRAs and other tax-deferred retirement plans, because this will save the heirs estate and income tax. Appreciated securities held until death should be left to the heirs for a step-up in basis, as explained previously.

Grand Finales

Investing directly in individual stocks presents outstanding opportunities for year-end tax planning. If your clients invest through mutual funds, they're at the mercy of the fund managers: They'll owe tax on whatever capital gains the fund distributes. If they invest in individual issues, they can initiate some sophisticated tax planning.

As mentioned, taxpayers can deduct up to $3,000 worth of capital losses each year. Therefore, the key to successful tax planning is to approach that $3,000 loss number each year. To do so, you and your clients should track all their capital gains and losses for the year, right into December. Then take the appropriate action at year-end.

Bill Thomas, for example, finds that he has net gains of $10,000 for 1999, as of mid-December. He figures he'll owe tax of around 25% on those gains (a mix of short-, intermediate-, and long-term gains), or $2,500.

Thus, Bill goes through his portfolio and sells enough losers to generate a $13,000 capital loss. Netting this loss with his gains, he'll wind up the year with a $3,000 capital loss. In Bill's 36% tax bracket, that means a tax saving of $1,080. Compared with the $2,500 tax bill he faced previously, selling his losers saved him $3,580 in tax.

What can Bill do with the money he received from selling his losers? He can spend it if he needs the cash. Otherwise, he can reinvest the proceeds. As long as he doesn't buy back the same stocks, he can reinvest right away. If he thinks the stocks he sold have good future prospects, he can wait 31 days and then buy them back. (Repurchasing them earlier would be a *wash sale,* so he couldn't take advantage of the tax loss.)

On the other hand, consider Carol Nixon, who goes through her records for 1999 in mid-December and discovers that she has $13,000 worth of net capital losses for the year. If she does nothing, she'll be able to deduct $3,000 worth of those losses, but the excess $10,000 will have to be carried forward, perhaps for many years.

At this point, Carol can take $10,000 worth of gains, tax-free. That is, she can sell securities for a $10,000 gain and pay no tax on those gains. She'll still wind up with a $3,000 net capital loss, fully deductible.

Again, Carol can spend her sales proceeds or reinvest immediately in similar securities. In this situation, though, she has yet another option: She can immediately buy back the same stocks she sold without losing any tax benefits. The wash sale rules apply to capital losses, not gains.

Why would Carol want to sell stock at a profit and immediately buy the same shares? Because that will increase her basis in the shares, resulting in a lower tax on a future sale.

Carol bought Microsoft stock several years ago for	$10,000
Her Microsoft stock is now worth	20,000
If she sells the stock, she'll have a taxable gain of	10,000
After using this $10,000 gain to offset $10,000 in capital losses, Carol buys the same amount of Microsoft stock for	20,000
Her new basis in Microsoft is not $10,000 but	20,000
The higher basis will mean a smaller taxable gain when she sells Microsoft some time in the future.	

The trick to successful year-end tax planning is to wind up with net capital losses of $3,000. If your clients buy their own stocks, they'll be able to manage this much more easily than if they invest through mutual funds. In any case, remind your clients to check previous tax returns to see if they have some capital loss carryforwards. If so, they can take gains, tax-free, to use up those suspended losses.

Swap Smart

If your clients hold bonds individually, they can do the same things as they can with individual stocks: take capital gains and losses with the goal of winding up each year with a $3,000 net loss. Indeed, during times when interest rates are rising—and bond prices are falling—they can use a popular tax-saving strategy called a *bond swap* with virtually no change in their portfolio.

Suppose, for example, one of your clients invested $50,000 in municipal bonds in 1997, when interest rates were very low. A few years later, interest rates move higher, and those municipal bonds fall in value to $45,000. Your client can sell those bonds for a $5,000 tax loss and buy $45,000 in different municipal bonds immediately.

It's true that investors can't buy back identical bonds. They can, though, buy bonds with the same yield, the same maturity, and the same credit rating—but from a different issuer. If investors buy back the same issuer's bonds, the new bonds must have a different maturity or interest rate.

Suppose a client sells $45,000 worth of New York Thruway bonds with a coupon of 5.375%, a 2027 maturity, and a yield to maturity of 5.4%, then invests the proceeds in $45,000 worth of Puerto Rico Electric Power Authority bonds with the same coupon, maturity, and yield to maturity. In effect, he's merely swapping one set of bonds for another with virtually identical characteristics. However, assuming he originally paid $50,000 for the bonds, he'll have a $5,000 capital loss that he can use toward achieving the goal of a $3,000 net loss. Assuming he has no other capital gains or losses for the year, he could then take a $2,000 gain elsewhere in his portfolio, tax-free.

The Preferred Approach

If your clients are interested in buying individual securities, there are other types of investments that merit your attention. For example, you might prefer to recommend *preferred stocks* rather than bonds. Preferred stocks, issued by corporations, typically pay generous dividends, and those dividends can't be discontinued as long as a common dividend is paid. They often yield as much as bonds, or a bit more, and they tend to be more *liquid* (easier to buy or sell) than corporate bonds.

What's more, preferred stocks offer a tax break, at least for corporate investors. Thanks to the *dividends-received deduction,* most corporations can deduct 70% of the dividends they receive from other corporations. Say Joe's Hardware, operating as a regular C corporation, invests in Con Edison stock and receives $1,000 in dividends this year. After the 70% deduction, Joe's Hardware will have only $300 in taxable income from its Con Ed dividends.

Although this tax break applies to all corporate stock dividends, it's a prime reason for buying preferred stock, because preferred issues generally pay higher dividends than common stock. (The holding period for preferred stock is longer, 91 days versus 46 days for common stock, in order for the recipient to qualify for the tax benefit.)

Thus, for taxpaying corporations, investing in preferred stock is better than investing in corporate bonds, because most of the yield won't be taxable. Investors can accept a lower nominal yield and still come out ahead after tax; a 7.5% payout from a preferred stock is equivalent to a 10.3% yield on a taxable bond, for a top-bracket corporation.

Since 1993, traditional preferred stocks have been joined by fully taxable preferred stock aimed at individual investors. This new type of preferred stock, deductible for issuers, does not qualify for the dividends-received deduction. Nevertheless, the yields appeal to buyers, especially individuals who wouldn't qualify for the dividends-received deduction anyway. Yields tend to be higher than the yields on Treasury bonds, corporate bonds, or banks CDs.

Issuers include well-known, financially strong companies such as Texaco, GTE, Transamerica, Cadbury Schweppes, McDonald's, SunAmerica, and Detroit Edison. To enhance liquidity, fully taxable preferred stocks generally are sold in increments of $25, or $2,500 for a round lot of 100 shares. Traded on the New York Stock Exchange, they may be easier to buy and sell than corporate bonds, which often have high transaction costs for individual investors.

Despite their popularity, there definitely are risks to go along with the higher yields of fully taxable preferreds. They're long-term issues,

*Preferred Stocks drawbacks
① must hold long time
② maybe called in*

often with 49-year maturities. If interest rates rise, prices can go down. There's no guarantee of a return of principal if investors sell prematurely.

What's more, these fully taxable preferred stocks may be called in by the issuer, generally in five years. Therefore, investors stand to lose if interest rates rise. But if interest rates fall, the issuers will call in the shares and issue new ones at the lower rates, so investors won't profit. Indeed, this dilemma confronts all investors who buy callable bonds.

Considering these pros and cons, should your clients invest in fully taxable preferreds? They're a viable alternative in any situation where clients would hold long-term debt. Fully taxable preferreds can be used in tax-deferred accounts, and they can be used by investors who want high current income. Low-bracket retirees may be suitable investors.

If clients are willing to take the risk of holding long-term fixed-income securities, they might as well be paid handsomely.

Switch-Hits

Another type of preferred stock is worth considering: *convertible preferreds.* As the name suggests, they can be converted into the issuer's common stock. Thus your clients have one foot in the stock market while the other foot remains in high-yield territory.

Convertibles come in two flavors: bonds and preferred stock. For investors, there is little difference between the two. In case the issuer goes bankrupt, though, the holder of a convertible bond would have a higher claim on corporate assets than the holder of convertible preferred stock.

Altogether, there are hundreds of companies with convertibles outstanding. Often, the convertibility *kicker* is what allows these companies to issue bonds or preferred stock at an acceptable (to the issuer) rate.

Thus, convertibles begin life as fixed-income securities, so they pay hefty yields. In the late 1990s, when common stock dividends averaged less than 2%, convertibles paid 6%, 7%, and more.

Once they have been issued, convertibles fluctuate in price in tandem with the underlying common stock. However, they tend to move in a narrower range—less downside risk, less upside potential. Wall

Street's rule of thumb is that convertibles climb 75% to 80% as much as the common stock and fall 50% as much.

Paying a Premium

Convertibles may seem complicated, but the underlying economics are straightforward. They have higher yields than common stocks, so investors pay more for a convertible than for an equivalent amount of common stock. This excess is the *conversion premium.*

For example, suppose XYZ common stock trades at $100 per share and pays a 1% ($1 per year) dividend. The company issues convertible bonds, each of which is convertible into 10 shares of XYZ common stock. The convertible bond pays $100 in interest per year.

If that's the case, investors have two ways to gain control of 10 shares of XYZ common: Buy one convertible bond or 10 shares of the common. If investors buy the bond, they'll receive $100 in interest; buy the stock and they'll receive $10 in annual dividends. Buying the convertible puts them ahead by $90 per year.

Therefore, if 10 shares of the underlying stock sell for $1,000, the convertible bond will sell for more. How much more? That varies widely.

The XYZ convertible might sell for $1,100, yielding over 9%. That's a 10% conversion premium. At that rate, the extra income ($90 per year) would make up for the premium ($100) in just over a year.

Suppose the convertible was priced at $1,500, yielding less than 7%. That's a 50% premium ($500) over the stock price, and it would take more than five years for the extra income ($90 per year) to make up for the extra cost.

Which type of convertible should you and your clients look for? That depends on the client's needs and risk tolerance. Generally, convertibles with low conversion premiums behave more like stocks, while those with larger conversion premiums act more like bonds.

Taking Stock

If your clients are in the market for convertibles, they should buy issues only if they like the underlying stock. They're probably better off paying premiums under 20%.

There are risks with convertibles, too:

- The interest or dividends paid by convertibles is fully taxable. Therefore, convertibles may be appropriate holdings for tax-deferred retirement plans.

- If interest rates rise sharply, sending both stocks and bonds into a tailspin, convertibles likely will take a steep fall.

- Some convertibles are callable at par. If an investor has paid a premium (say, $1,200 for a convertible with a $1,000 face value), he or she might suffer a loss if the convertibles are called.

- Some high-yielding convertibles cap investors' gains and require conversion within a short time period. They're often known as DECs, PERCs, or PRIDEs and are sold by major brokerage firms.

Thus, you need to do your homework before recommending convertibles to your clients. The *Value Line Convertibles Survey* is a good source for current data.

Junk Is Not Garbage

In addition to convertibles, your clients also might want to consider *junk bonds* for tax-deferred retirement plans. Junk bonds may offer better-than-bond yields and stocklike total returns.

In the late 1990s, junk bonds (sometimes known as *high-yield bonds*) maturing in 5 to 10 years yielded 8% to 11%, depending on how junky the bonds were perceived. That's much higher than the 6% yield your clients likely would receive from Treasuries of that maturity. What's more, the junk bond market returned 10% or more to investors every year from 1992 to 1997, much better than Treasury bonds performed.

The junk bond market has prospered for several reasons:

- *Strong demand.* Cash keeps flowing into high-yield bonds from mutual funds, pension plans, and individual investors.

- *Weak supply.* Issuance of junk bonds is down because banks are lending more to lower-rated companies, eliminating the need to issue bonds.

With demand up and supply down, prices of junk bonds have increased.

- *Increasing institutional acceptance.* High-yield bonds have become a mainstream investment. One firm (Drexel Burnham Lambert) is no longer in control of the market, so there is less perception that the game is rigged. Some pension funds and insurance companies now invest 15% to 20% of their portfolios in high-yield bonds.

Low Grade

Junk bonds are corporate bonds with low or no ratings, from agencies such as Moody's and Standard & Poor's. Bonds rated from BBB to AAA are considered to be *investment grade,* meaning that they're suitable for prudent investors. Bonds with lower ratings or unrated bonds are considered speculative, or "junk." With the latter type of bonds, investors run a greater risk of not receiving the promised interest payments or a return of principal.

Because junk bonds are riskier, they pay high yields to attract investors. Such high yields, in turn, make it relatively difficult for weaker companies to pay the promised interest. Therefore, junk bonds are very sensitive to the overall economy. When times are good—as they have been during most of the 1990s—chances are greater that the issuers' businesses are doing well, so they'll be able to meet their obligations. If the economy falls into a recession, more companies won't earn enough to make their interest payments. A weakening economy helped cause the junk-bond slump in 1989–1990.

Increasing merger activity is good for junk bonds, too: Many issues will shoot up in price when the issuers are acquired by stronger companies.

High-yield bonds are less sensitive to interest-rate movements than other types of bonds. Therefore, adding them to your clients' fixed-income holdings may actually reduce risk while increasing total return.

Junk bonds may work well for older investors who want to increase their current income and reduce their reliance on stock market appreciation. All investors are better off holding junk bonds inside a retirement plan, where the interest income won't be taxed until withdrawn.

Recap

- A buy-and-hold stock market strategy will result in very low tax obligations, year after year.

- If clients have children or grandchildren who are at least 14 years old, they can give these youngsters appreciated securities to sell and reduce the capital gains tax rate to 10%.

- Another way to cash in on stock market gains is to borrow against them, tax-free.

- If your clients don't need to cash in their gains, they can bequeath securities to their heirs, who'll owe no income tax on appreciation during your clients' lifetime.

 - Giving away appreciated securities to charity is better than giving cash.

- For the best tax results, your clients should try to offset gains with losses so they end each year with a $3,000 net capital loss.

CHAPTER 2

Marvelous Munis
The Allure of Tax-Exempt Bonds

Many tax-advantaged investments offer tax deferral or tax reduction. As explained in Chapter 1, investing in growth stocks permits your clients to defer the tax they owe on any appreciation and ultimately pay that tax at lower long-term capital gains rates.

In contrast, municipal bonds pay income that's *tax-exempt*. Investors don't owe any tax on that income, now or in the future. What's more, this tax exemption is firmly established by tax law and by decades of acceptability.

The purpose of this tax exemption is to give state and local governments an edge in the bond market. Suppose AT&T and the Salt River Agricultural Project both want to borrow money. If all things were equal, Salt River likely would have to pay as much interest—or even higher interest—as AT&T to sell its bonds. Thus, tax policy has been designed to give Salt River an edge. While the interest on AT&T bonds is taxable, Salt River's bonds pay interest that is exempt from federal income tax.

Naturally, tax-exempt interest is more desirable than taxable interest, so investors are willing to pay more for Salt River's bonds. Higher prices generate lower yields. Thus, while AT&T might have to pay 6.5% interest in order to get investors to buy its bonds, Salt River might have to offer only 5.2%. That results in tremendous cost savings for every state and local government across the country.

Investors get a good deal, too. A client who's in a top tax bracket will pay about 40% of interest income to the IRS. That 6.5% AT&T bond will yield around 3.9% after tax. Obviously, that client is better off with 5.2% from Salt River. The same is true in the 36%, 31%, and even the 28% tax brackets. Clients who pay 28% to the IRS will net 4.7% from their AT&T bonds, less than the 5.2% paid by Salt River.

The Bigger, the Better

Does that mean that you should advise every client whose tax bracket is at least 28% to buy municipal bonds rather than other types of bonds? Not necessarily. There are a few points to consider.

- Municipal bonds (*munis*) don't belong in tax-deferred retirement accounts. Bond interest that's paid inside IRAs, 401(k)s, and so forth, isn't taxed anyway, so why buy munis? Investors are better off with higher-yielding bonds.

  What's more, holding municipal bonds inside a tax-deferred account converts tax-exempt interest to taxable interest—a true tax disaster. All the money that comes out of a tax-deferred account is taxable, even if that money came from municipal bond interest.

- Munis have certain disadvantages when compared with Treasury bonds. Muni issuers may default on their obligations, for example. Investors have to pay commissions to buy and sell munis, and those commissions may be high for small transactions. Munis often are callable: If interest rates fall, munis may be called away from investors (redeemed prematurely), forcing them to reinvest at lower rates.

When does it pay to buy munis instead of Treasuries? That's a judgment call you and your clients have to make.

Suppose, for example, one of your clients has a total portfolio of $400,000 and you recommend a 25% bond allocation (that is, $100,000). Invested in 6% Treasuries, this client would earn $6,000 per year on those bonds; assuming a 36% federal income tax bracket, he'd net $3,840. On the other hand, if he invested that $100,000 in 5.2% munis, he'd net $5,200 per year.

Thus, on a $100,000 bond portfolio, this client would pocket an extra $1,360 per year, given the interest rates mentioned. Is that worth assuming the credit risks, call risks, and liquidity risks of munis? You and each of your clients must decide. Generally, the larger the amounts involved and the higher a client's tax bracket, the more it pays to buy munis. A client who's investing only $25,000 in bonds is probably better off in Treasuries.

Controlling Factors

Assuming some of your clients decide to put their bond money into munis, they have still more choices to make. Should they invest in municipal bond mutual funds (there are literally thousands from which to choose), or should they invest in individual bonds? That's mainly a matter of each client's personality.

Municipal bond funds offer diversification and professional management. Some clients will prefer to invest in one fund and go on with their lives. They'll likely wind up with a respectable flow of tax-exempt income and a stable asset in their portfolio.

On the other hand, buying municipal bonds directly will provide more control. Some clients prefer to know exactly which bonds they're holding, how they're rated, and when they mature. These clients will have more flexibility in implementing bond-swap strategies, as explained previously. Moreover, buying individual bonds will probably generate higher yields over the long term: When investors buy a municipal bond fund they pay about 1% a year to manage assets yielding around 5%, which eats substantially into returns.

Remember, though, that the muni market is not for novices. There are countless bonds out there, many of which have not undergone close scrutiny by securities analysts. To help your clients buy individual bonds successfully, you may want to establish a relationship with a reputable broker who represents a firm with extensive research capabilities. Shop around before making any commitments: Bond dealers typically offer better prices than stockbrokers.

State Capital

Whether your clients buy munis directly or through a fund, they'll also have to decide whether or not to invest locally. Typically, when investors buy munis issued within their home state they'll escape state and local income tax as well as federal income tax. If they invest in out-of-state munis, those tax-exempt bonds become taxable if they're subject to state and local income tax.

Suppose, for example, you have a client who lives in a state with a 10% income tax. She buys a municipal bond yielding 5% from a neighboring state. That interest would be exempt from federal income tax but subject to her state's 10% tax, so she'd owe 0.5% in tax, bringing her net yield down to 4.5%. She'd pocket more with an in-state bond yielding only 4.6%.

Theoretically, diversifying a bond portfolio makes sense. If your clients invest solely in bonds issued by one state, and that state runs into financial distress, you may find those bonds will be downgraded, devaluing the bonds—and damaging your relationships with your clients.

As a practical matter, though, most investors who live in states with income tax prefer in-state municipal bonds, which are double or even triple tax-free. Why buy tax-exempt bonds if they wind up paying tax on them?

If your clients buy local bonds, how can they reduce the risks of loading up their portfolios with bonds from one state? They can buy high-quality bonds (rated A or better by the major agencies) and hold them until maturity. This assures investors of getting their money back at maturity. Generally, they should look for bonds with maturities of no more than 10 years. Longer-term bonds usually don't yield much more than 10-year bonds, so there's no reason for investors to expose themselves to all the unknowns of holding bonds for 20 or 30 years.

If you have clients who are investing in individual bonds, advise them to buy munis when such bonds are first issued, because commissions are lowest then: Investors will pay institutional rates. Give the broker advance notice and ask to be notified when a new issue becomes available. Advise clients who have bought munis to plan to hold them until maturity, because investors will likely take a beating trying to sell small lots on the secondary market.

Another way to reduce the risk of holding munis from only one state is to buy an in-state municipal bond fund and simply hold on. A state may have its downs, but it will have its ups, too. With this approach, investors are trusting the skill of the portfolio manager to keep the tax-exempt cash flowing, good times or bad.

Fund Finding

If your clients decide to buy municipal bonds through a bond fund, what should you suggest they look for? Many clients will want a *single-state fund,* specializing in the bonds of their state, so they can avoid state and local income tax as well as federal tax. However, if they live in a state such as Florida, with no income tax, it doesn't make sense to buy a Florida muni fund: They're better off with a fund buying municipal bonds from around the country.

Whether clients are buying single-state or national funds, they'll have many to choose among. Their best bet probably is to begin at home: Start with the mutual fund family (Fidelity or Vanguard, for example) that they've been investing with. If you and your clients are comfortable with a certain fund family and it has a fund in the desired category, that's probably the best choice.

What if a fund family doesn't have, say, a New Jersey muni fund? Then you and your clients will have to shop around among the various New Jersey choices. Go on-line to do research over the Internet or visit your public library for references; Morningstar Inc., based in Chicago, is a popular source of mutual fund information. Look for a fund with a low expense ratio rather than the highest current yield: Over the long-term, efficient bond funds tend to have greater returns.

Moving Violations

Buying in-state municipal bonds or a single-state fund may be fine if your client is a physician who'll practice in the same town for 40 years, but not everyone has that sort of career. Moves from state to state are common for many people. And, of course, many retirees relocate to sunnier climes.

If your clients move after buying in-state munis, they may owe income tax to their new state on what will now be out-of-state bonds.

Even states without an income tax (Florida, for example) may impose an *intangibles tax* on out-of-state munis. They can avoid such taxes by selling their old munis and buying new in-state issues, but that will mean incurring transactions costs—on the buy side and the sell side— and perhaps capital gains tax as well.

Such clients may, in many cases, be better off holding their old munis until maturity, especially if their new home is a low-tax state. Moreover, if you're advising clients who expect to move to a different state at some time, tell them to keep short- and intermediate- rather than long-term bond maturities. After they mature, your clients can buy bonds issued in their new home state if they wish.

Social Insecurity

Ironically, there are situations in which tax-exempt municipal bonds are not tax-exempt, even from federal income tax. Social Security recipients who own municipal bonds or bond funds may find that municipal bond interest will increase the tax on their Social Security benefits, effectively making that interest taxable.

To determine whether a client's Social Security benefits will be taxed (up to 85%), you have to calculate his or her *provisional income,* which is the total of the following:

1. Adjusted gross income (AGI) as reported on the client's federal income tax return

2. Tax-exempt interest income from municipal bonds and municipal bond funds

3. One-half of the client's annual Social Security benefits

For example, with AGI of $20,000, tax-exempt income of $5,000, and $12,000 in annual Social Security benefits, a client's provisional income is $20,000 + $5,000 + $6,000 = $31,000.

On a joint return, taxpayers can have provisional income up to $32,000 without having to pay any tax on their benefits; for single filers the threshold is $25,000. Over those amounts, up to 50% of benefits can be taxed. If clients' provisional income is greater than $44,000 on a joint return or $34,000 filing singly, up to 85% of their benefits will be taxed.

Without going through all the math, the practical result is that if provisional income falls below $32,000 on a joint return or $25,000 filing singly, Social Security benefits won't be taxed. If provisional income is over those limits, though, municipal bond income is effectively being taxed. In those circumstances, why should clients accept 5% from a municipal bond when they could be earning 6% from a Treasury?

In general, after your clients start receiving Social Security benefits you should consult with them about their holdings of munis or municipal bond funds. You may find that it makes sense to recommend that they move out of munis into Treasuries or some other type of taxable bond.

A Painful Alternative

Whether or not clients are receiving Social Security benefits, their municipal bonds may be subject to tax because of a bizarre product of the federal government called the *alternative minimum tax* (AMT). In essence, the AMT is an income tax that's calculated in a different manner than the regular income tax. Each year, taxpayers are supposed to calculate their tax obligation both ways and pay whichever tax bill turns out to be *higher,* the AMT or the regular tax.

Thus, if Joe Green owes $70,000 on his AMT and $80,000 on his regular tax, he pays his regular income tax. But if Alice Brown owes $90,000 on her regular tax and $100,000 on her AMT, she pays her AMT. The IRS always wins in this game.

Why are the totals different in the two tax systems? The AMT calculation starts with regular taxable income and is increased by certain adjustments. Fewer itemized deductions are allowed for AMT purposes, no deduction is allowed for personal exemptions, and a number of tax preference items are also added back to taxable income. Addbacks include the bargain element of incentive stock options, state and local taxes, and home equity interest; the resulting sum is considered AMT income. AMT tax rates (26% and 28%) are lower than regular tax rates, which go up to 39.6%, but they're levied on larger amounts of income.

Up to now the AMT has not been a major issue for most taxpayers: Only 856,000 returns were subject to the AMT in 1998, according to the Congressional Joint Committee on Taxation. Unfortunately, the same Congressional committee has estimated that the number of taxpayers paying the AMT will increase more than 10-fold by 2008, so that 8.8 million taxpayers will wind up in the clutches of the AMT.

What does all of this have to do with municipal bonds? Back in the 1980s, a federal tax law change created a class of "AMT munis." That is, the interest on some "private activity" municipal bonds used to finance state and local infrastructure projects is subject to the AMT.

In the municipal bond market, AMT munis carry slightly higher yields than truly tax-free munis of comparable quality and maturity. Because of the higher yields, such munis have become extremely popular. As long as investors pay regular income tax rather than the AMT, they can pocket the extra yield without having to worry.

However, for taxpayers who are subject to the AMT, the interest on such bonds becomes taxable rather than tax-exempt. Thus, investors in AMT munis might be paying tax on a 5.1% yield rather than paying no tax on a regular muni with a 5.0% yield.

The solution to this problem lies in monitoring your clients' portfolios. If they're not paying the AMT now and they hold short-term munis, there's not much to worry about. However, if they're buying long-term munis, perhaps to help pay for a child's education, they definitely should be careful about AMT bonds. That applies to *zero-coupon munis* (munis where all the interest is deferred) as well as to regular munis. Municipal bond issuers are required to disclose whether the interest is subject to the AMT, so you should read the related documents before advising your clients about investing.

What's more, many municipal bond funds hold significant amounts of AMT bonds, because such holdings push up their yields. For example, in 1998, Dreyfus's General Municipal Bond Fund reported that 42.6% of its assets were in AMT bonds, while Federated Municipal Opportunities Fund was at 46.4%. If your clients invest in a fund with 46% AMT holdings, then 46% of the income dividends they receive will be subject to the AMT. Again, funds are required to disclose their holdings of AMT bonds, so you need to screen your clients' investments thoroughly. Generally, investors should be particularly wary of "high-yield" muni funds, which may hold large amounts of AMT bonds, while "tax-free" muni funds must keep their AMT exposure below 20%.

Borrowing Trouble

Another tax point to keep in mind: No interest—not even mortgage interest—will be deductible if the loan proceeds are used to buy municipal bonds or municipal bond funds. So, if clients are tapping a home equity line of credit or a brokerage firm margin account, tell them to be sure not to use that money to invest in munis or muni funds.

Safety Belt

For the closest thing to absolute safety that the muni market has to offer, ask about *prerefunded bonds.* Suppose a municipal bond issuer sold 30-year bonds eight years ago, paying 7% interest. Now, it wants to replace those bonds with a new issue paying 5%, slashing its interest expense. However, its 7% bonds can't be called in for another two years.

Often, issuers in such situations will sell the new issue at 5% and just park the proceeds in Treasuries. When the old issue can be called, the Treasuries will be sold to raise the cash. Therefore, the old issue is virtually default-proof: It's backed by Treasuries. Generally, such prerefunded issues are short term, paying relatively high tax-exempt yields (considering their credit quality and their short maturities).

Recap

- The higher a client's tax bracket, the greater the appeal of municipal bonds.
- If clients have a relatively small amount to invest in bonds, they're probably better off buying Treasuries than munis.
- Buying individual municipal bonds gives investors more control, while buying through mutual funds provides convenience.
- If clients live in a state with an income tax, they'll probably prefer to buy bonds issued in that state or a single-state muni fund.

- After clients begin to receive Social Security benefits, they may be better off selling their munis and investing in higher-yielding taxable bonds.

- Many clients should avoid municipal bonds that pay interest subject to the alternative minimum tax (AMT), as well as muni funds with a heavy AMT exposure.

Defer and Conquer

For Employees: Make the Most of 401(k)s and IRAs

Your clients who work for corporations are likely to be eligible to participate in a 401(k) plan. Most companies, large and small, now offer 401(k) retirement plans to employees; people who work for nonprofit organizations have similar 403(b) plans, while government employees have "thrift savings plans."

For each type of plan, the principle is the same. Participants elect to defer some income now, deferring income tax as well. Earnings also grow, tax-free, until money is withdrawn from the plan. Growth within each employee's account depends to a great extent on investment acumen: The better the decisions, the more income for retirement.

In other words, it's critical that clients make the most of their tax-deferred *defined contribution plans,* as these vehicles are known. Here's how they can add more feathers to their nest.

Match Point

As the *New York Times* reported in 1998, 85% of large companies and 75% of small companies offer some type of employer match to employee contributions. Typically, the match is 50 cents for each dollar invested, up to 6% of salary.

Suppose, for example, that Doug Anderson has a nominal salary of $60,000 per year. If he contributes 6% ($3,600) to his 401(k) this year, his employer will put another $1,800 into Doug's account, for a 50% match. Therefore, Doug should contribute at least $3,600; if he doesn't, he's passing up free money.

Should Doug defer more than $3,600? As of 1998, workers may be able to contribute up to 25% of their wages to a 401(k), up to $10,000 per year, depending on the terms of their plan. Going beyond $3,600 might be a good choice for Doug, depending on how much he needs to live on and how much he can afford to invest. Another option for Doug is to invest his next $2,000 in a Roth IRA (see page 36) rather than in his 401(k).

Know Where to Hold 'Em

Deciding how much money to put into the plan, of course, is only half the battle. Participants then have to determine how to allocate their money among the various investment choices.

Most 401(k) plans offer some type of conservative fixed-income choice in addition to various mutual funds. Clients' decisions will stem, in large part, from the overall shape of their investment portfolios.

Suppose, for example, that Doug Anderson is married, with two small children, and his wife is a full-time homemaker. Doug contributes $3,600 per year to his 401(k) (to get the maximum employer match), but that's really all he can afford to invest. Thus, his entire investment portfolio is held inside his 401(k) plan.

In this situation, Doug's investment strategy for his 401(k) is fairly straightforward. He should keep his account diversified between stocks and fixed-income investments, but he should emphasize stocks, which likely will provide greater long-term returns. His equity allocation might be anywhere from 60% to 80%, depending on his age and his personal risk tolerance. The younger he is and the more he can stomach riding an investment roller coaster, the more he should commit to the stock funds offered in his 401(k).

In or Out?

On the other hand, consider Jennifer Jordan, who participates in the same 401(k) plan. Jennifer has a greater income as well as some inherited wealth, and her children are grown. Thus, Jennifer not only has a 401(k) account, she also has a brokerage account for additional investments. While her 401(k) is tax-deferred, Jennifer owes tax each year on income generated by her brokerage account.

In her situation, then, Jennifer must look at her overall portfolio—both her 401(k) and her brokerage account—and decide which investments go where. Suppose, for example, she decides to allocate 25% of her portfolio to bonds. If she decides to invest through municipal bonds or muni funds (see Chapter 2), those bonds belong in the brokerage account. However, if she decides instead to hold Treasury bonds, corporate bonds, or junk bonds, she should invest in a bond fund inside her 401(k), where the bond interest can compound, free of current income tax.

Her bond allocation, in turn, will affect her equity holdings. Suppose, for example, Jennifer decides to hold her bonds as munis, outside of her 401(k) plan. That means that she can load up her 401(k) account with stock funds. On the other hand, suppose she decides to hold bond funds inside her 401(k) plan: That will mean less room there for stock funds, so more stocks will be held in her brokerage account.

How should she decide which stocks go where? If she wants to hold a mix of individual stocks and stock funds, the individual stocks should go in her brokerage account, for more flexibility, while the funds are held in her 401(k) account. Indeed, most 401(k) plans don't have individual stocks on the menu of investment selections.

Yet another possibility is that Jennifer will invest solely in stock funds, not individual stocks. If that's the case, she should start by looking at her 401(k) plan. Some plans, especially those offered by small companies, offer only a few stock funds. In that situation, Jennifer should pick one or two stock funds that look most attractive and put her money there.

Chances are, the best funds in a small 401(k) plan will be funds emphasizing large-company stocks. Jennifer should put her money into those funds and use her brokerage account to hold small-company funds, international funds, and specialty funds, rounding out her portfolio.

The situation probably will be much different if Jennifer works for a large company. At such companies, 401(k) participants often have dozens of choices. Here, Jennifer should hold the "exotic" funds inside the plan, where their capital gains distributions will be sheltered. Outside the plan, in her brokerage account, she can hold tax-efficient large-company funds, including index funds, as we'll explain later in the book.

A Few Good Funds

Employees of large companies not only have many selections in their 401(k) plans, they may be able to switch among them 24 hours a day, by phone or via the Internet. Therefore, participants in these plans may be tempted to make many short-term moves—they might shift into Asia one week, into South America the next week. Often, 401(k) holdings are a topic of conversation in the company lunchroom, and employees may rearrange their portfolios based on those discussions.

The results of such attempts at market timing are usually disastrous. Clients who invest this way are driving by looking in the rearview mirror, buying the latest hot funds. They're better off investing in a few good funds, then holding on. Performance should be reviewed every six months rather than every week or every day. Clients should give their investments some time to grow.

Overexposed

Some 401(k) plans will match employees' contributions with the employer's stock rather than cash. In the example of Doug Anderson, who contributes $3,600 from his pay to receive the $1,800 match, that $1,800 might be in shares of his employer's stock: 30 shares, for instance, if the stock sells at $60. Moreover, there may be restrictions forbidding 401(k) participants to sell any of that stock before age 50, for example.

If that's the case, clients may wind up with an investment portfolio that's too heavily weighted in one stock and thus exposed to a fall in its price. Therefore, they should lighten up where they can. If they also hold stock options for their employer's stock, they should exercise some of those options and sell the shares, thus reducing their vulnerability to a decline in that one stock. And, once they reach the age where they can sell shares within the 401(k) plan, they should start a program to gradually unload some every month or every quarter.

Lone Danger

Ideally, the money saved in 401(k) accounts will accumulate until the owners' retirement, when your clients will use those funds to supplement their income. What if your clients need to take money out before then? All withdrawals from 401(k) plans are fully taxed. In addition, withdrawal before age 59½ carries a 10% penalty tax.

A less taxing strategy is to borrow money from the account. Many 401(k) plans permit participants to borrow as much as $50,000—sometimes even more if the money is used to buy a house. (However, the owner of a closely held company may be prohibited from borrowing from the plan.)

Borrowing from a 401(k) has several advantages. The loan proceeds are tax-free. Your client will pay back the loan—interest and principal—to him- or herself rather than to a bank or some other lender. And there's generally less hassle borrowing from one's own 401(k) plan than from an unrelated party.

With all those advantages, what's the downside to borrowing from a 401(k)? The key disadvantage to 401(k) loans is that they hurt returns: Clients may be better off over the long term leaving money in the plan and borrowing from another source. Money borrowed from a 401(k) will not be sitting in a stock fund and earning 10%, 15%, or more per year.

There may be tax concerns as well. Loans from 401(k) plans need to be repaid on a schedule, so payments will probably be withheld from the client's paycheck. If the client leaves the company, the loan needs to be repaid; if he or she doesn't have the cash, the loan will be treated as a distribution, subject to income tax and possibly an early withdrawal penalty before age 59½.

So how should your clients regard 401(k) loans? If they have to borrow money for an important purpose, such as funding their children's education, they may prefer to borrow from their own retirement account and repay that account. But they should not borrow frivolously—they shouldn't strip their 401(k) so they can take a vacation, for example. Loans from a 401(k) should be taken with care and repaid scrupulously.

Haste Makes Waste

As of 1999, employees can defer up to $10,000 per year to contribute to a 401(k). However, highly compensated executives need to be careful they don't reach the maximum too fast and thus lose out on some matching dollars.

Suppose, for example, Ed Sawyer, who earns $120,000 per year, participates in a 401(k) plan that will match contributions 100%, up to 5% of pay. Ed should be able to receive a $6,000 employer match, or 5% of $120,000.

However, if Ed contributes $1,000 per month, he'll reach the $10,000 maximum after 10 months of contributions. Because he's earning $10,000 per month, the company's 5%-of-pay match will be $500 per month—after 10 months, he'll have received a $5,000 match, not a $6,000 match.

Ed's monthly compensation	$10,000
Employer's monthly 5% match (5% × $10,000)	500
Total match after 10 months (10 × $500)	5,000
Expected annual match (5% × $120,000 salary)	6,000
Shortfall	1,000

Instead, Ed should contribute $833 per month over 12 months. If Ed extends his contributions throughout the year in this manner, his employer will match $500 per month throughout the year, bringing the annual match to the expected $6,000. The trick, then, is to spread out 401(k) contributions in order to get the employer match all year long.

Roll Right

What will your clients do with their 401(k) accounts when they retire? They have several options, but in most cases they'll be best served by rolling the balance into an Individual Retirement Account (IRA). Such a rollover maintains the tax deferral and keeps your client in charge of investing retirement money.

There's a catch, though—often the case when one is dealing with the IRS. If an employee doesn't know the rules, the employer will automatically withhold 20% of the retirement plan balance when it's rolled into an IRA. If your client has accumulated $400,000, for example, that's $80,000.

That $80,000 will be refunded when your client files a tax return for the year, but *only if he makes up the difference.* That is, if a client has $80,000 withheld, he'll have to replenish the IRA with $80,000 in cash in order to maintain the tax-free rollover. If not, that $80,000 will be considered taxable income—and your client will get socked with an additional 10% penalty tax if he's under age 59½.

To avoid this, an employee should ask the former employer specifically for a *trustee-to-trustee transfer.* Money will move from the old 401(k) account directly to the new IRA without the employee ever touching a penny of it. If that's the case, none of the money will be withheld and the employee won't have to come up with extra cash to keep the retirement plan intact.

Separating IRS from IRA

After your clients have rolled over their 401(k) into an IRA, they can invest the money as they'd like; inside the IRA, the money will build up, tax-free. If they need the money for retirement income, they'll owe tax on any withdrawals. However, in that situation they may well be in a lower tax bracket than they were during their working years. Thus, not only will they have deferred income tax for many years, enjoying a tax-free buildup, they will have shifted income from years when they owed, say, 36% in income tax to years when they owe only 28%.

Your clients may find that they need to withdraw little or no money from their IRAs because they have enough income from other sources. If that's the case, they naturally will want to extend the tax deferral as long as possible, letting money build up inside the IRA. However, tax laws require participants to start withdrawals after reaching age 70½. If they don't take out the required amount, they'll pay a *50% penalty* on the shortfall.

How much are retirees required to withdraw? Typically, they'll name a beneficiary and take out just enough to allow their IRA to stretch over a joint life expectancy. For example, suppose your client starts the "required minimum distributions" at age 71, when his spouse is 70. Their joint life expectancy is just over 20 years, so they'll need to withdraw about 5% of the money from the IRA that year. Naturally, if they withdraw 5% but their IRA grows by, say, 10% that year, the overall balance will continue to expand.

This is a complicated subject, so clients should consult with a tax lawyer or a CPA. The bottom line, though, is that if they don't need all the money in their IRA they can stretch it out for many years, providing tax-free buildup for the client, the client's spouse, and their children.

John Smith dies at age 69 in 1999 with $642,000 in his IRA. His son Tom, 36, inherits. Tom can spread the distributions over his 46.4-year life expectancy. In 2000, for example, Tom is required to withdraw only 2.1552% of the IRA balance. Assuming the IRA earns more than 2.1552%, it will continue to grow.

Even assuming a conservative 7% growth rate, the IRA will double in about 16 years. Meanwhile, Tom will receive an increasing stream of cash for the next 33 years.

Altogether, Tom can pull out more than $1 million by the time he's 61 and still have $1.8 million in the account. At that point, Tom's minimum distributions will be over $90,000 per year. (If the IRA earns over 7% per year, the results will be even more impressive.) (See Appendix B for an in-depth example.)

The Roth Revolution

There's another route clients can take when it comes to IRAs: *Roth IRAs*. Actually, there are two types of Roth IRAs to consider.

First, there are annual Roth IRAs. Most people can contribute $2,000 per year to a Roth IRA as long as their incomes are moderate (under $95,000, or under $150,000 on a joint return). Contributions are nondeductible. However, after reaching age 59½—with a minimum holding period of five years—all the money that comes out of a Roth IRA will be tax-free.

That's certainly worth pursuing, especially for young people. If teenaged children or grandchildren start Roth IRAs and contribute $2,000 each year until they're earning enough to reach the income limits, they'll probably build up a substantial amount by the time they reach age 60.

Second, your clients might be able to convert a regular IRA to a Roth IRA. If they do, they'll have to pay all the deferred income taxes. After the conversion, if they pass the five-year, age 59½ barriers, their IRA will become a tax-free investment account.

Suppose, for example, a client has accumulated $400,000 in a 401(k) account. When he retires, he rolls it over to an IRA. Then, he converts this IRA to a Roth IRA.

He'll pick up $400,000 in taxable income from the conversion, so he might pay up to $160,000 to the IRS. However, from that point on all your client has to do is hold onto the account for five years. Then he can leave the money in the Roth IRA as long as he wants or take out tax-free income whenever he needs money.

The catch? Roth IRA conversions aren't available if adjusted gross income is $100,000 or more. Thus, some retirees may be shut out.

Also, coming up with the cash to pay the tax bill can be a painful experience. Your clients are much better off paying the taxes from other funds and leaving the IRA intact, but not everyone will be able to do so, especially if those taxes have to be paid in one year.

One strategy to consider is to borrow the money to pay the tax, perhaps drawing on a home equity credit line. The interest on $100,000 worth of such debt is deductible, so clients can get tax-free cash and deduct at least some of the interest payments. In the meantime, the money in the IRA can continue to compound, tax-free.

Recap

- Most employees now have the option to defer taxable compensation via a 401(k) plan or similar program.
- If an employer provides matching contributions, your clients should contribute at least the full amount that will be matched.

- Although clients should not borrow from a 401(k) account for trivial purchases, such loans may be better than borrowing from a third-party lender.

- When clients retire, they'll likely roll their 401(k) account into an IRA.

- With careful planning, clients can stretch out their IRAs to the next generation, providing an incredible amount of wealth for the family.

- Roth IRAs, first available in 1998, provide an opportunity to receive tax-free investment income.

CHAPTER

4

Lapping Up the Lion's Share

For Employers: Choosing among Retirement Plans

Your clients who are self-employed or who own their business probably sponsor retirement plans. Such plans help attract skilled workers, motivate them to produce, and encourage them to stay with the company. Therefore, it's in your client's interest to offer a plan.

At the same time, being a plan sponsor has its costs. Contributions to the plan come from money the company could use to expand the business—or to pay the owner a bonus. There are expenses incurred in administering the plan, not to mention the time involved. If the company contributes $100,000 per year, for example, and only $25,000 goes into the owner's account, the plan is going to have to provide a *lot* of employee motivation to make it worthwhile.

Thus, it's only natural that your clients will want a substantial amount of those contributions to go into their own retirement accounts and perhaps the accounts of any co-owners. Fortunately, there are several acceptable techniques for accomplishing those objectives.

Bulking Up Benefits

One way to swell a business owner's retirement fund is to adopt a *defined benefit plan,* a real pension plan that promises to pay certain amounts in retirement. With a defined benefit plan, the company may contribute (and deduct) very large amounts to the owner's account.

With a defined benefit plan, the amount of a pension for which a participant can qualify depends on career earnings and length of service with the company. For highly compensated owner-executives, annual pensions might be $100,000 or more.

In order to provide a business owner with a pension of $100,000 per year, there must be a substantial amount in the owner's account. Depending on the assumptions that are used, your client may need to build up a fund of $1 million, $1.5 million, or more in time for retirement.

Therefore, if your client is in her 50s or 60s, getting ready to retire in a short time, she might have to contribute $50,000, $60,000, or more per year to a defined benefit plan in order to reach her goals.

Unfortunately, defined benefit plans are expensive to administer: They lock the company into fixed contributions even in bad years, and they may require high contributions for certain employees. That is, your client's company may have to contribute surprisingly large sums for an old employee who has been with the company for many years, even if that employee is a relatively low-paid worker. Tougher tax rules also have dimmed the allure of defined benefit plans.

Such plans typically assume earnings of 5% or 6%: The lower the assumption, the more the company can contribute. During the 1990s, though, many defined benefit plans have increased 15% to 20% per year or more, thanks to the strong stock market. In those cases, defined benefit plans may be *overfunded* (that is, there's more money in the plan than is currently needed), so further contributions are not permitted.

So, what's the bottom line on defined benefit plans? If your client is 50 or older and has a much younger crew of low-paid employees, a defined benefit plan may be worth the cost.

Uncharted Course

Many small companies and self-employed individuals, though, will find defined benefit plans too expensive. If defined benefit plans are out, what's in? *Defined contribution plans.*

With such plans, there is no set pension that will be paid to the retiree. Instead, the plan rules determine the amount that's contributed each year. Those contributions will build to a greater or a lesser amount over the years, depending on how the funds are invested, and the retirement benefits will be contingent on the amount that's accumulated.

Defined contribution plans may take two forms: money purchase or profit-sharing.

- A *money purchase plan* is similar to a defined benefit plan in that the employer is committed to contribute a certain percentage of employees' compensation to the plan each year.

- A *profit-sharing plan* gives the employer the flexibility to contribute more or less (or even nothing at all) each year.

Frequently, employers will combine a money purchase and a profit-sharing plan. This provides both commitment and flexibility while permitting business owners to contribute the maximum $30,000 per year to their own accounts.

If your clients are self-employed, they can establish noncorporate retirement plans (informally known as *Keogh plans*) that are essentially the same as corporate plans. A hybrid money purchase and profit-sharing Keogh may enable them to contribute up to $30,000 a year to the plan without locking them into such a contribution year in and year out. That $30,000 is the maximum for employees under a defined contribution plan, too.

Tilting the Playing Field

While defined contribution plans have many advantages, there are some weaknesses. Often, a large portion of the plan contributions must go to employees' accounts rather than to the owners.

To see how expensive such a plan might be, consider a business with two owners who draw sizable salaries, four senior executives who also earn six-figure incomes, and four junior staff members. Assuming that this company chooses a standard profit-sharing plan paired with a money purchase plan to allow a $30,000 contribution to each owner's account, it would have to contribute the same percentage of

TABLE 4.1 Plan Contributions

	Age	Compensation	Contribution	Percentage of Compensation
Owner 1	53	$160,000	$30,000	18.75%
Owner 2	61	160,000	30,000	18.75
Employee 3	40	158,326	29,686	18.75
Employee 4	33	100,000	18,750	18.75
Employee 5	24	100,000	18,750	18.75
Employee 6	50	100,000	18,750	18.75
Employee 7	27	38,000	7,125	18.75
Employee 8	29	33,919	6,360	18.75
Employee 9	35	30,000	5,625	18.75
Employee 10	25	24,000	4,500	18.75

eligible compensation for everyone. Thus, to maximize the owners' retirement accounts, the plan contributions might appear as shown in Table 4.1.

Although the owners' compensation is actually far greater than $160,000, that is the maximum amount (in 1999) that may be taken into account for qualified plan purposes.

Altogether, the firm has to contribute $169,546 in order to place $60,000 into the owners' accounts. Only 35.39% of the contributions go to the two owners.

Fortunately, the IRS has approved some techniques that channel more to the owners' personal account and less to rank-and-file employees.

Integration

One such technique is integration with Social Security. With an integrated plan, the company contributes a higher percentage of pay for those earning more than the Social Security wage base ($72,600 in 1999). Lower-paid employees receive a higher percentage of their pay in Social Security benefits, so integration can be used as an offset.

TABLE **4.2 Integrated Plan Contributions**

	Age	Compensation	Contribution	Percentage of Compensation
Owner 1	53	$160,000	$30,000	18.75%
Owner 2	61	160,000	30,000	18.75
Employee 3	40	158,326	29,647	18.73
Employee 4	33	100,000	17,352	17.35
Employee 5	24	100,000	17,352	17.35
Employee 6	50	100,000	17,352	17.35
Employee 7	27	38,000	5,844	15.38
Employee 8	29	33,919	5,217	15.38
Employee 9	35	30,000	4,614	15.38
Employee 10	25	24,000	3,691	15.38

The effect of such integration is to somewhat reduce the contributions made on behalf of employees, as shown in Table 4.2. Even after integration, though, it will cost $161,070 to put $60,000 into the owners' retirement accounts. Only 37.25% of the contribution goes to the principals.

Age Weighting

A more sophisticated way of skewing benefits is to adopt an *age-weighted* profit-sharing plan. If your client and any co-owners of the company are significantly older than their employees, much greater contributions may be made to their accounts.

In some instances, a 50-year-old executive might be entitled to a contribution equal to 20% of pay, while a 25-year-old receptionist might be entitled to a contribution equal to 3% of pay. The IRS may consider this fair because the receptionist's contribution has 25 more years to compound, tax-free. At retirement age, the benefits, based on percentage of earnings, likely will be roughly equivalent.

Therefore, age-weighted profit-sharing plans are based on equivalent future benefits, rather than equivalent contributions. Because most employers tend to be older than their employees, these plans favor owner-employees. The basic age-weighted plan might look something like the one shown in Table 4.3. This plan has several obvious advantages. Total costs are way down (to $68,739) while the share going to the owners is way up (to 66.54%). In companies where there is one principal shareholder, or two principals of roughly the same age, such plans may be ideal.

Nevertheless, there can be problems:

- If a company has two or more principal owners, the younger ones may get a smaller retirement plan contribution than the oldest owner. In the preceding example, it's highly unlikely that the 53-year-old co-owner will accept a plan that provides him with half the benefit the older owner receives.

- Lower-paid but older employees may be entitled to a disproportionately high retirement plan contribution. While a 25-year-old employee might get only a 3%-of-pay contribution, a 50-year-old employee might be entitled to nearly 8% of pay as a contribution, more than the company would like to spend.

TABLE 4.3 Age-Weighted Plan Contributions

	Age	Compensation	Contribution	Percentage of Compensation
Owner 1	53	$160,000	$15,736	9.83%
Owner 2	61	160,000	30,000	18.75
Employee 3	40	158,326	5,374	3.39
Employee 4	33	100,000	3,000	3.00
Employee 5	24	100,000	3,000	3.00
Employee 6	50	100,000	7,851	7.85
Employee 7	27	38,000	1,140	3.00
Employee 8	29	33,919	1,018	3.00
Employee 9	35	30,000	900	3.00
Employee 10	25	24,000	720	3.00

Cross-Testing

To address these concerns, *cross-tested* or *new comparability* plans have been created. These plans are age-weighted by groups of employees, not by individuals. The *average* age is the yardstick.

An owner-executive group (which might consist of one person) may be entitled to most of the contributions, while an employee group, with a younger average age, gets smaller contributions. In general, as long as the average age of the owners' group is at least five years greater than the average age of the other groups, sharply higher payments can be made on behalf of the owner-employees (see Table 4.4).

With this plan, total contributions are reduced to $77,528, of which 77.39% goes to the two owners. Compared with the original standard plan, the owners receive the same amounts while contributions to the entire plan are reduced by more than 50%.

If age-weighted and cross-tested plans have a flaw, it's the expense. A company will need to work with a qualified benefits pro and an attorney to set up and maintain these plans.

Start-up costs might be $4,000 to $5,000, plus another few thousand dollars each succeeding year for administration. Nevertheless, that

	Age	Compensation	Contribution	Percentage of Compensation
Owner 1	53	$160,000	$30,000	18.75%
Owner 2	61	160,000	30,000	18.75
Employee 3	40	158,326	4,750	3.00
Employee 4	33	100,000	3,000	3.00
Employee 5	24	100,000	3,000	3.00
Employee 6	50	100,000	3,000	3.00
Employee 7	27	38,000	1,140	3.00
Employee 8	29	33,919	1,018	3.00
Employee 9	35	30,000	900	3.00
Employee 10	25	24,000	720	3.00

TABLE 4.4 Cross-Tested Plan Contributions

might be a reasonable amount to spend, considering the extra benefits for your client and any other owner-executives.

No Complaints

What about employee morale? Will workers be upset if a company provides such a skewed plan? Probably not. Today, with so many self-funded plans—such as 401(k)s—employees tend to appreciate any profit-sharing plan because the employer makes contributions. As corporate profits go up, contributions generally increase, so employees have an incentive to perform well.

In addition, with an age-weighted plan an employee's contribution may increase each year as that employee grows older, which can help with employee retention.

Many small companies offer 401(k) plans with a supplementary profit-sharing plan to increase retirement benefits for the principals. An age-weighted plan can supplement a 401(k) plan and bring the top executives up to the maximum contribution, regardless of how much the rank-and-file employees contribute to the 401(k).

Keep It Simple

At the other end of the spectrum, some employers prefer less expensive and less complicated plans, even if that reduces tax-deductible contributions to their own account. Such employers can select simplified employee pension (SEP) plans, sometimes known as SEP-IRAs because they resemble IRAs.

To establish a SEP, a client merely fills out a form (much shorter than the lengthy plan and trust documents required by profit-sharing plans, defined benefit plans, etc.). Because a SEP is not a qualified plan, no trust fund is involved.

What's more, the setup form does not have to be filed with the IRS. No annual reports need be filed, either, although a copy of the SEP form must be provided to each covered employee. Altogether, SEPs are easier and cheaper to set up and maintain than are other employer-sponsored plans.

SEPs are flexible, too. Contributions may be anywhere from zero up to the maximum each year, which is 15% of compensation. The math is a little different for self-employed individuals, working out to about 13% of self-employment income. In either case, though, the maximum SEP contribution is $24,000 per year (as of 1999).

With all of the advantages of SEPs, what's the downside? Deductible SEP contributions are limited to $24,000 per year rather than $30,000. SEP accounts do not enjoy the creditor protection enjoyed by qualified plans. What's more, the company may have to contribute on behalf of workers it would like to omit, including part-timers and former employees.

In 1997, the Savings Incentive Match Plan for Employees (SIMPLE) was added to the tax code. Although SIMPLE plans may have some advantages over SEPs, they effectively limit employers' contributions to their own accounts to $12,000 per year, so they might not appeal to many business owners or professionals.

Responsibility Knocks

Deciding which retirement plan to sponsor is just a first step. As mentioned, a company can contribute up to $30,000 per employee in a defined contribution plan, perhaps more in a defined benefit plan. Many small businesses will contribute hundreds of thousands of dollars per year to retirement plans.

Then what? That money isn't just stashed under a mattress. It might be placed in a bank account, invested in GE stock, or used to buy an office building. In essence, the money has to be invested by someone, and that person has to choose among countless possible investments.

If your client's business or professional practice sponsors a plan, your client has a *fiduciary responsibility*. That is, your client has an obligation to every plan participant to invest that money prudently. If companies invest foolishly, not only will the owners' retirement funds be depleted, but they could be sued by unhappy plan participants.

Unfortunately, there is no precise definition of what it means to be a *prudent investor*. Certainly, a fiduciary can't invest all of a company's retirement plan money in penny stocks or silver futures. Similarly, keeping everything in Treasury bills won't pass the test, because that's a strategy guaranteed to produce a low return.

Instead, a fiduciary should invest most retirement fund money in the stocks of established companies and high-quality bonds. Your client will probably be better off emphasizing stocks, which have produced excellent long-term returns, and using bonds for current cash flow as well as portfolio stability. Many institutions have stock-bond ratios around 60-40 or 70-30.

If you're an investment advisor, you can help such clients pick out a diversified portfolio of individual securities or invest through mutual funds, perhaps no-loads. As the plan grows larger—to more than $500,000 or $1 million—you may be able to help your client hire a money manager with a good reputation to make the investment decisions.

Pile on the Paper

Even if clients hire professional money managers, they still have a fiduciary responsibility. That means every investment decision has to be made with the idea that they'll be able to justify it, if questioned, 5 or 10 or even 30 years in the future.

Your clients should put everything in writing. Before they buy anything for the plan they should dictate a memo that explains current market conditions and why they're buying this particular stock or bond. If they're buying on the advice of an investment advisor, the advisor should put those recommendations in writing.

Best of all, the company should have a formal "investment policy statement" for its plan. This policy might state, for example, that the basic strategy is to keep 60% to 70% of the portfolio invested in equities, at least half of which will be in stocks of companies in the S&P 500 (which is made up of America's largest corporations). The policy might also state that up to 10% of the portfolio can be invested in more speculative issues, which will enable the plan to pursue the occasional stock tip.

On the bond side, the investment policy might state that the plan will invest only in bonds issued by government agencies or in corporate issues rated A or better by an independent service. Your client should distribute a copy of the overall policy to all plan participants and follow that policy when investing.

If your clients decide to hire a professional manager, they shouldn't hire a niece or nephew who just earned an MBA. Instead, you can help your client do some research into prospective managers and keep a record of the search. You and the client can interview a few likely candidates and choose the one who seems to offer the best record and competitive fees. In addition, you and your client should have a formal review with the manager at least once a year to be sure everyone is satisfied with how the plan is being handled.

A popular strategy today is *indexing:* holding a mix of stocks designed to mirror a particular portfolio. A client might, for example, decide to hold one-third of a retirement plan in an S&P 500 index fund, where the management expenses will be very low. Why pay an investment pro to invest in GE, Coke, or IBM?

Then that client might hire a money manager or use mutual funds to invest the rest of the plan's equity allocation in small-company stocks and international stocks, where stock-picking expertise can be critical. For bonds, a plan probably can buy Treasuries directly or use a low-cost, high-quality bond fund.

Showing the Way

Some of your clients may offer employees a plan—such as a 401(k)—in which each participant makes his or her own investment decisions. In that case, your clients haven't discarded fiduciary responsibility. On the contrary, the federal government holds employers responsible for educating employees.

Again, you can help your client set up the plan, perhaps with cooperation of a *third-party administrator* who specializes in employee benefits. Again, your client should keep records explaining the choice of a particular plan. You (or someone you bring in) can supply participants with educational materials and provide some guidance on their investment selections.

What if your clients offer employees a retirement plan such as a SEP-IRA, in which each employee chooses where to invest the amount that's contributed? Your client's fiduciary responsibility probably will be fulfilled by having you (assuming you're an investment advisor) meet with each participant at least once a year to provide some direction. The better informed the employees are, the better the choices they'll make and the less chance your client will wind up facing trouble in the future.

Recap

- Sponsoring a retirement plan for employees can be expensive, so your clients who are employers may want to establish a plan that can skew benefits toward their own account.

- Several such plans are available, and the added benefits your clients will receive may be worth the cost.

- Another alternative for employers is to offer a low-cost, simplified retirement plan for all employees.

- Whichever type of plan is chosen, the funds contributed must be invested wisely for the best long-term results.

- Clients who sponsor a retirement plan for employees assume a fiduciary responsibility to ensure plan money won't be mismanaged.

- If your clients invest plan money on their own, they should keep a paper trail showing that they invested prudently.

Putting the Tax Collector on Hold

Fixed Annuities for Tax Deferral

Every Monday, the *Wall Street Journal* runs an "Annuities Watch" article, reporting on these increasingly popular investments. Tens of billions of dollars are poured into annuities every year (an estimated $122 billion in 1997 alone), in no small part because of tax advantages. Moreover, in the late 1990s innovative *equity-indexed annuities* have gained favor by offering a combination of stock market upside, guaranteed minimum returns, and tax deferral.

For all the excitement about annuities, though, the terminology can be confusing, if not misleading: Some annuities will never pay an annuity. The primary definition of the word *annuity* refers to a regular stream of payments. Many retirees take their pension in the form of an annuity—they get a monthly check from their former employer, generally for the rest of their lives.

However, some newspaper and magazine articles don't focus on this type of annuity. Instead, they refer to a contract that may be acquired, chiefly from insurance companies but also from other financial institutions. (In this chapter we'll refer to insurance companies as the issuers of annuities, even though banks have become very active in this market.) When your clients invest in annuities, they pay money now in return for more money tomorrow.

One type of annuity, the *immediate annuity,* calls for investors to pay a sizable amount to an insurer in return for a stream of payments that starts right away. An immediate annuity might pay out for an *annuitant's* lifetime or for a certain number of years.

Suppose Joe Carson pays $10,000 to Dependable Insurance Company in return for a 10-year immediate annuity. Dependable might agree to pay Joe $110 per month. If so, then $10,000 worth of the annuity payments would be a tax-free return of Joe's own capital: Joe is getting a portion of his own money back with each payment, so he doesn't owe any tax on that portion. The remainder is taxable, and Joe might net around $100 of each $110 monthly payment, after tax.

Patience Is a Virtue

Immediate annuities have their uses, but most people are thinking of their opposite—*deferred annuities*—when they ponder annuities as tax-favored investments. A deferred annuity means that your clients pay today and collect tomorrow. In the interim, their accounts can grow without any income tax being due.

Joe Carson in the preceding example might pay $10,000 to Dependable Insurance for a deferred annuity rather than for an immediate annuity. He might pay $25,000, $50,000, or even more. If so, he's buying a *single-premium deferred annuity,* or SPDA, because one payment is enough to make an investment in full.

Alternatively, Joe might pay $1,000 per year for his annuity. He can pay more in some years, less in others. In this manner, he acquires a *flexible-premium deferred annuity* (which has no commonly used acronym). As the name suggests, this arrangement allows him to build up his contract over time, at his own pace. SPDAs are much more common than flexible-premium contracts, with the average outlay around $30,000.

Whether investors make one up-front payment or stagger their outlays over time, they'll enjoy the same benefits from a deferred annuity. The money invested will compound, tax-free, inside the annuity contract. If Joe's annuity calls for a 5% return, for example, his $10,000 will grow to $10,500, with no tax obligation. Each year the contract keeps growing, tax-free. After 25 years, his $10,000 might be worth $40,000.

The point of this buildup is to increase the money that will be available during retirement. Suppose, for example, Joe invests $10,000 in an SPDA when he's 40 years old. The following 25 years, until he's 65, are likely to be Joe's peak earning years. If he put his money in the bank, he'd owe the IRS 31%, 36%, even 39.6% of all the interest he receives. Inside the annuity contract, he pays 0% all those years.

At 65, after Joe retires, his income drops and he falls into a 28% tax bracket. Now he can draw on that $40,000 in his deferred annuity to help supplement his pension, Social Security benefits, and so forth, and pay less tax on the money as it comes out.

While a deferred annuity may be an excellent vehicle for supplementing retirement income, it's a disaster as an estate planning tool. If a client dies with a deferred annuity in the buildup stage, the heirs will owe income tax and possibly estate tax as well. Altogether, 75% might go to the IRS and 25% to your client's heirs.

Exit Strategies

If clients invest in deferred annuities, they should plan on using them for retirement rather than dying with them. To tap the money in their accounts, they have two choices:

- Annuitize.

- Don't annuitize.

Both have their pros and cons.

When an investor annuitizes a contract, he or she is essentially converting a deferred annuity into an immediate annuity that will pay periodic income. Suppose 65-year-old Joe Carson wants to annuitize a $40,000 deferred annuity contract. Dependable Insurance might offer him $300 a month for the rest of his life.

Assume Joe originally invested $10,000 in the annuity and he has a 20-year life expectancy when he annuitizes the contract. Over the next 20 years (240 monthly payments) Joe will get a partial return of his original investment with each check.

Joe's life expectancy is 20 years, or	240 months
Over the next 240 months, Joe will get back his $10,000 investment at a monthly rate of	$ 41.67
Joe's monthly income stream will be	300
With a $41.67 tax-free return of capital, the taxable portion of each payment will be	258.33
If Joe's tax rate is 28%, he'll owe	72.33
From each $300 payment, he'll keep	227.67

What happens after 20 years? Joe will have recovered all of his money, so ongoing payments will be completely taxable. (Some older annuities permit this partial tax exemption to continue as long as the payments go on.)

In our example, Joe annuitizes when he is 65 years old, with a 20-year life expectancy. What happens if Joe lives until he's 90? Until age 95? Until 110? The payments will keep coming in, $300 every month, to the benefit of Joe and the frustration of the insurance company.

Now look at the flip side. Suppose Joe annuitizes at age 65 and dies at age 66, after collecting just 15 of the $300 payments, for a total of $4,500. That's it—the insurance company gets to keep the remainder of Joe's money.

This may be an acceptable arrangement for Joe. If he has no dependents and is merely concerned about receiving income for his own retirement, he might embrace this kind of deal, which is called a *single-life annuity.*

More Safety, Less Income

Many people, though, are not willing to play the life expectancy lottery with an insurance company. They have other options available when they annuitize:

■ *Joint and survivor annuity.* This arrangement covers two people, usually a married couple. Such annuities will keep paying as long as either annuitant is alive.

Suppose Joe chooses a joint and survivor annuity with his wife Linda, who is 60. Between the two of them, their life expectancy is 30 years rather than 20, so the insurance company will make smaller monthly payments. Instead of $300 per month, they might receive $200 per month, partially tax-free for 30 years.

■ *Period-certain annuity.* This is a single-life annuity with the guarantee that payments will be made for at least, say, 10 or 15 years. Suppose Joe chooses a 15-year period-certain annuity and dies after receiving income for five years. In that case, a beneficiary named by Joe will receive payments for the next 10 years. The annuity payments might be set somewhere between those of a single-life and a joint-and-survivor annuity: If the former pays $300 a month and the latter pays $200, a period-certain annuity might pay $250 per month.

There may be other types of annuity payout options, but they're essentially variations on those described here. Whichever option your clients choose, there are tax advantages to annuitizing a deferred annuity. Each payment received is partially tax-free until life expectancy is reached. Moreover, a single-life annuity won't be subject to estate tax. (With survivor or period-certain annuities, the value of ongoing payments will be calculated and included in the decedent's estate.)

Despite the tax advantages, annuitizing a contract isn't for everyone. In our example, Joe has spent 25 years building up a $40,000 value in his contract. (Many annuity contracts will have a much greater value.) The day after he annuitizes, all he has is a monthly income stream.

What's more, his income stream is locked in when he annuitizes. Receiving $300 per month in 1999 might seem adequate, but that same $300 will likely buy a lot less in 2009 or 2019.

Withdrawal Gains

If Joe doesn't want to annuitize, he has several alternatives. He can keep the annuity in place, without annuitizing, and withdraw money from the contract whenever he wishes. The money that he doesn't withdraw will continue to grow, tax-free. Most annuities don't require investors to annuitize before age 85.

Thus, using periodic withdrawals rather than annuitizing provides more flexibility, extended tax deferral, and access to capital in case of an emergency. What's the downside? For one, many annuity sellers impose charges if buyers withdraw money from an annuity, especially in the early years. (A discussion of surrender charges follows.)

Surrender charges, though, generally disappear over time. A more serious concern—unfavorable tax treatment—remains a threat. Under a change in tax law passed in 1982, all annuities purchased after that date are taxed on a last-in, first-out (LIFO) basis: Earnings are taxed first, principal second.

Joe's annuity investment was	$10,000
His account now is worth	$40,000
If he withdraws money from the contract, he'll owe tax on the first	$30,000

After Joe has stripped out all the earnings and brought the contract's value down to $10,000, he'll be able to withdraw tax-free returns of principal. (Before the change in tax law, annuity withdrawals were first in, first out, so Joe could have taken out up to $10,000, tax-free.) Moreover, withdrawals before age 59½ are subject to a 10% penalty tax.

At first glance, this is a significant drawback. With a withdrawal strategy, investors will owe tax on the money that's pulled out of an annuity, while annuitizing provides a partial tax shelter.

In reality, though, the difference is likely to be minor. For a deferred annuity to pay off (that is, for the value of the tax deferral to outweigh the cost of the fees paid to the insurer), it's necessary to have a lengthy period of tax-free buildup: at least 15 years, ideally much longer. Over that time period, earnings are likely to grow substantially. In that situation, annuitizing won't provide very much tax shelter.

Consider Joe's single-life annuity in the preceding example.

Joe's single-life annuity pays	$300 per month
Joe's net income is	$228 per month
Alternatively, Joe could withdraw	$300 per month
In a 28% tax bracket, his tax bill will be	$84 per month
After tax, Joe's withdrawals will yield	$216 per month

The difference—$12 per month—may seem like a modest amount to pay for increased flexibility.

The bottom line is that you have to crunch the numbers in order to advise your clients, but don't ignore the possibility of using withdrawals rather than annuitizing. As you can see, it's possible to build up and then spend down a deferred annuity without ever receiving an annuity!

While you're crunching the numbers in order to help clients make their decisions, don't advise them to meekly accept an offer from the current insurance company. When it comes to paying out annuities, insurers make different assumptions and provide different payouts.

In our example, Dependable Insurance might offer Joe and Linda $200 per month for a joint-and-survivor annuity. Reliable Insurance might look at the same facts (the amount of the contract, ages of the annuitants) and offer $220 per month. In some instances, the differences between the high and low payouts might be 30%! So it pays to shop around (or to ask a life insurance agent for help). If a client wants to switch from one insurance company to another, the tax code permits tax-free exchanges of annuity contracts.

However, clients should not switch insurers solely to get the highest rate. Companies in financial distress might offer high returns in order to attract money and stay in business. The danger is that these companies won't be able to maintain the promised payments, or perhaps any payments at all. You want to be confident that your clients' insurers have the financial strength to keep operating well into the next century, paying out all the benefits that have been promised. As a rule of thumb, look for an insurer that has been in business at least 75 years and has more than $3 billion in assets. Ideally, your clients will choose companies with top ratings from independent agencies: AAA from Standard & Poor's, A++ from A.M. Best, and A+ from Weiss Research.

Better Than a Bank

Up to now, our discussion has focused on deferred annuities in general. If the idea of saving for retirement on a tax-deferred basis appeals to your clients, they have yet another choice to make: Should they invest in a fixed or a variable annuity? In the remainder of this chapter we'll cover fixed annuities; variable annuities are described in Chapter 6.

You can think of a *fixed annuity* as a tax-deferred bank account, but with higher returns. These vehicles are inherently conservative investments, so investors shouldn't expect huge returns. However, clients whose retirement plans include bank certificates of deposit, money market funds, corporate bonds, or Treasury securities can think of fixed annuities as a tax-favored alternative.

A fixed annuity goes up in value every day. As a general rule, people who buy fixed annuities tend to be less tolerant of investment risk and more concerned about safety. As one adherent puts it, "No one has ever lost capital in a fixed annuity."

As the name suggests, a fixed annuity pays a fixed return. However, the return is not fixed for the life of the contract, as it is when a client invests in a 30-year bond. Instead, a fixed annuity pays a certain interest rate for a certain period of time, just as a bank CD does. When the time period is up, a new rate will be set. Generally, the interest rates on fixed annuities are a bit higher than the rates offered by banks; typically, investors can lock in a higher yield if they're willing to commit to one rate for several years.

High Tease

When it comes to fixed annuities, it's not always what's up front that counts. Many fixed annuities are sold on the basis of a high yield that's guaranteed for one year. After that initial guarantee period, interest rates will be set and reset. Some insurers use first-year annuity rates as a come-on, then drop rates sharply. If hefty surrender charges are in place, investors may be boxed in. Annuities with lower up-front yields may have looser strings around them. Some companies, for example, allow investors to bail out with no surrender charges if the follow-up rate ever falls below the initial rate. Another point to consider is the guaranteed minimum rate: Some contracts set a minimum of 4.5%, while others (often those with high initial yields) set their minimums as low as 3%.

What's more, some annuities offer attractive first-year yields (and even follow-on yields) on the condition that investors annuitize the contract with the same insurer. Thus, investors are tied to the same insurance company for decades. Any extra yield may not be worth the long-term loss of flexibility.

A.M. Best, an insurance industry research firm, has published a survey of fixed annuity contracts five years after they were sold. In this survey, companies that ranked 75th or 76th (out of 93) in first-year yields wound up near the top in five-year contract value, while the companies with the fattest initial yields were at or near the bottom over the long term.

You and your clients can deal with a potential bait-and-switch problem in several ways:

- *Demand a bailout clause.* Here, the insurer permits the investor to switch to another annuity with no surrender charges if the fixed annuity interest rate drops below a certain level.

- *Go long.* Another strategy is to invest in a fixed annuity with a longer-term guarantee period, perhaps six or seven years. As long as the guarantee period equals or exceeds the period during which surrender charges are in effect, clients can hold on until maturity, then shop for the best deal available at that time. Matching the guarantee and the surrender period means that investors don't have to trust an insurance company's board of directors to set renewal rates fairly.

   Locking in a long-term guarantee on a fixed annuity will pay off if interest rates fall, because investors will be receiving an above-market yield. On the other hand, if rates rise, they will be locked in to below-market yields. Suppose one of your clients buys a seven-year, 6% fixed annuity in 1999 and interest rates shoot up in 2001. He'll still have five years left of 6% returns while other investors might be earning 8%.

- *Stay short.* CD annuities protect investors against rising interest rates, because their rates are set for a short period, usually one year. After that year, investors can shop around again, either renewing the contract or choosing another fixed annuity with more favorable terms. If there's a switch to another annuity, no surrender charge will be due.

- *Study history.* Before recommending a fixed annuity, ask the insurer what it's paying on similar contracts sold 5 or 10 years earlier. If longtime investors are getting less than the base rate for new subscribers, your client can expect to be lowballed down the line.

- *Climb a ladder.* Investors can minimize interest-rate risk by staggering maturities. For example, instead of buying one annuity for $50,000, they might buy five annuities for $10,000 apiece, to mature in one, two, three, four, and five years. This locks in some rates for up to five years. However, if rates rise, the maturing annuities can be reinvested at higher rates.

  Another form of laddering is to put, say, two-thirds of a client's fixed annuity money into a six-year contract, locking in today's rates, and the remaining one-third into a one-year annuity, allowing the client to take advantage of rising rates in the future.

- *Bet on the bull.* Instead of setting rates arbitrarily, equity-indexed annuities pay a return that's pegged to a stock market index, such as the S&P 500, but with a guaranteed minimum rate in case stocks turn sour. Such annuities might provide 75% to 95% of the return of the S&P 500, with a 3% guaranteed return no matter what the stock market does. Equity-indexed annuities are particularly popular in banks, where conservative depositors are being urged into the stock market by this "can't-lose, can-win" appeal.

- *Link your client's fate to an index.* Index-linked annuities pay a rate that rises or falls with an inflation index. If inflation increases and the cost of living goes up, so will your client's annuity yield.

- *Buy a bonus.* As opposed to bait-and-switch annuities, bonus annuities are promoted as investments with rates that will be in place for only one year. First-year bonus rates might be 8% to 9% when standard rates on fixed annuities are 5% to 6%. These are attractive for investors who bought a fixed annuity a few years ago and now want to switch: A bonus rate in the first year can offset the surrender fee, which might be 3% or 4%.

Sweet Surrender

When you weigh annuities, you should also evaluate withdrawal features—the amount investors are allowed to take out of the contract before incurring surrender charges. They might be allowed to withdraw up to 10% of the account each year, for example, but owe a 7% fee on excess withdrawals in the first year of the contract. Surrender charges may start as high as 9% and be in place as long as 10 years.

Many fixed annuities now permit monthly interest withdrawals. In addition, investors may be able to withdraw up to 10% per year, free of surrender charges. What's more, this privilege may be cumulative.

For example, if a client buys an annuity and waits three years, he or she may be able to withdraw 30% of the account balance without owing any surrender charges. If that money is rolled into another deferred annuity, no income tax will be owed. If your client does not roll over the withdrawal to another annuity, income tax will be due, but no penalty tax will be due if the withdrawals are made after age 59½.

In addition to surrender charges, some fixed annuities have *market-value adjustments* (MVAs) that penalize investors who withdraw when interest rates have increased. In a typical MVA, the account is retroactively credited with a lower interest rate than had been promised.

For example, suppose your client invests $50,000 in a 10-year fixed annuity with a 6% interest rate. Two years later, interest rates are up a point, to 7%, and your client wants a higher return. In some fixed annuities, an MVA and a surrender charge would knock down the net surrender value to $50,500, giving the client only a $500 (1%) gain after two years. Some fixed annuities with MVAs guarantee at least a return of principal, no matter how sharply interest rates rise.

Although MVAs are obviously intended to protect the insurance companies that issue fixed annuities, they do have some benefits for investors. For one thing, annuities with MVAs tend to have higher yields than those that don't. If interest rates go down, investors can get an even higher yield credited to their annuity. On the other hand, if interest rates go up, the MVA penalizes them only if they cancel the contract.

Split Decisions

One sophisticated use of a fixed annuity is in combination with a fixed-term immediate annuity: This parlay may be superior to municipal bonds.

Suppose, for example, John Smith is thinking about investing $50,000 in 5% municipal bonds, which would pay him $2,500 in interest every year, tax-exempt. Instead, John might invest $35,000 in a six-year, 6% fixed annuity. At the end of that time, his $35,000 will have grown to $50,000.

With the other $15,000, he might buy a six-year immediate annuity that pays $3,000 a year, most of which is a tax-free return of principal. The bottom line is that John winds up with a $50,000 fixed annuity (instead of $50,000 in municipal bonds), as well as significantly higher income during this period.

Split annuities, as they're known, are not easy to put together, but they may pay off if you do your homework and work closely with your clients.

Recap

- Deferred annuities are usually purchased with a large single premium, with $30,000 being the average investment.

- Earnings on the premiums can build up, free of income taxes, inside a deferred annuity.

- Deferred annuities are meant to provide retirement income.

- Deferred annuities should not be kept intact until death because the heirs will owe income tax and possibly estate tax as well.

- If investors withdraw money from a fixed annuity before age 59½, they'll owe a 10% penalty tax as well as income tax.

- Most deferred annuities also impose surrender charges for withdrawals during certain time periods, which might last up to 10 years.

Hanging Up on the IRS
Permanent Life Insurance as a Tax Shelter

Tax shelters come and tax shelters go. Back in the 1980s, thousands of investors poured billions of dollars into movie deals, cattle deals, lithograph deals, and other deals that were even more exotic, hoping for immense tax advantages. Then the tax code changed, in 1984 and 1986, and the aforementioned shelters disappeared.

Nevertheless, some tax advantages seem impervious to change. The basic tax benefits enjoyed by permanent life insurance, for example, have long been established in the tax code. What's more, whenever a politician indicates an interest in cutting back on these advantages, an army of influential insurance agents—from every Congressional district in the United States—rises in protest, and such revision is quickly forgotten.

Nothing is certain in this life, but you'd have to rate the retention of life insurance tax breaks as the closest thing to a certainty you're likely to find.

A Preference for Permanence

To understand the rationale behind these tax breaks, you need to know how permanent insurance works. In essence, there are two types of life insurance:

- *Term insurance.* These policies provide pure insurance—no more— for a given period of time. As people grow older and the likelihood of their mortality increases, they pay more for term insurance. If they reach a point where they don't need life insurance, they can simply stop paying further premiums and the coverage will cease.

- *Permanent insurance.* These policies combine pure insurance with an investment account, usually called the *cash value*. With permanent insurance, people pay much more than they'd pay for a term policy. Premiums generally are fixed, though: They don't rise over time.

With permanent insurance, a large portion of the premium goes into the cash value, where sizable amounts may build up. At some point in time, the money in the cash value may be tapped to help pay the premiums. For example, Bob James may buy a permanent policy calling for him to pay $5,000 per year in premiums. As he grows older, the cost of pure life insurance will increase. Eventually, he may reach the age where pure insurance would cost $6,000 per year. If so, the additional $1,000 needed for term insurance will come from the cash value.

Thus, cash value policies are designed to stay in place "permanently," hence the name. The traditional form of permanent life insurance is referred to as *whole life insurance.*

Since the 1970s, though, whole life has largely been supplanted by *universal life* (known in the industry as *cannibal life*), which offers flexibility as well as cash value buildup at current interest rates. Recently, some insurers have begun to offer universal life policies in which the cash value will grow either at a given interest rate or at a portion of the stock market's growth, whichever is higher.

Income Tax Immunity

All types of permanent insurance offer these tax advantages:

1. *No taxation of "inside buildup."* Generally, cash values grow from year to year. This growth is not subject to income tax.

2. *No taxes on policy loans or withdrawals.* As mentioned, the cash value is designed to provide a source of funds to pay expensive

premiums as the policyholder grows older. However, policyholders generally are allowed to tap the cash value via withdrawals (up to the amount of premiums paid) and loans. They can do so without owing income tax.

The money that's withdrawn or borrowed will reduce the insurance proceeds that the beneficiaries receive at the policyholder's death. The same is true of the interest on policy loans: Unpaid interest will compound and reduce death benefits.

Therefore, policyholders need to be very careful with loans and withdrawals—they can take out only a certain amount from the policy. If they withdraw too much, the policy will lapse, triggering an obligation to pay the deferred income tax on the cash value.

3. *No income tax on the death benefit.* At the policyholder's death, the beneficiaries won't owe any income tax on the insurance proceeds. They may owe estate tax in some circumstances, but that can be avoided with careful planning.

Ace in the Hole

In order for life insurance death benefits to avoid estate tax, the policyholder must have no *incidents of ownership* in the policy. That is, the policy must be owned by another individual or by an irrevocable trust. If the policy is held by a trust, the cash value and the death benefit will be protected from creditors and from squandering, so that's what insurance professionals generally recommend.

Permanent life insurance usually is bought for one of two purposes:

1. *Family protection.* The proceeds can support the policyholder's survivors.

2. *Estate liquidity.* If clients have substantial net worth (in excess of $650,000 per person in 1999), estate tax eventually will be due, at rates of up to 55%. Life insurance proceeds can be used to satisfy that obligation and keep other assets intact.

Although these are the main reasons for buying permanent life insurance, the aforementioned tax advantages make these policies attractive investments in some situations. America's largest companies, for example, use permanent life insurance to provide deferred compensation to their key executives. The cash value can build up without any reduction for income tax; when it comes time to pay the deferred compensation, money can be withdrawn or borrowed from the cash value.

Similarly, your clients might want to consider permanent life insurance as a possible source of future income. Policies should be bought primarily for family protection; however, in case there's a future need for cash, permanent life insurance can provide tax-free income.

Nothing for the IRS

To see how the benefits of permanent life insurance can work, let's look at a hypothetical example. Mike Harris buys a permanent life insurance policy at age 50 to provide for his spouse and children in the event of his untimely death. For the next 15 years he pays premiums of $10,000 per year, or $150,000 altogether.

By the time Mike retires at age 65, his children are living independently, thus reducing his need for life insurance. By that time, Mike's cash value is in the neighborhood of $250,000 to $275,000, assuming 8.5% annual growth and tax-free inside buildup.

At that point, the cash value of the policy may be large enough so that Mike can stop paying premiums. (As insurance agents like to put it, the premium "vanishes.") At this point in his life he'd like some supplemental retirement income, so he starts withdrawing $20,000 per year, tax-free. Note that his annual income from the policy is twice as large as the annual premiums he paid.

Mike continues to make withdrawals until he has withdrawn $150,000, the amount of the premiums he paid. After that, he borrows $20,000 from the policy each year. The policy loan premiums, like the withdrawals, are tax-free.

While Mike pulls out $20,000 per year from his policy, the balance—at least $230,000 in our example—continues to grow, free of income tax. Thus, the cash value is likely to remain undiminished or even increase.

Mike might continue to follow this procedure for 20 years, until age 85, pulling out a total of $400,000, tax-free. If Mike dies then, his ben-

TABLE **6.1 Using a Life Insurance Policy for Investment Income**

Mike's premium payments	$150,000
Tax-free cash to Mike	$400,000
Income tax–free insurance proceeds to Mike's beneficiaries	$300,000
Total income tax–free return on $150,000 investment	$700,000

eficiaries might receive about $300,000 in insurance proceeds, again without owing income tax. (See Table 6.1.)

As you can see, Mike and his beneficiaries may effectively receive decades of investment income without paying income tax. Mike can use the policy to provide income during his retirement; he can also provide his loved ones with a large chunk of cash at his death.

There are, however, a few cautions to keep in mind before you tell your clients to run out and put all of their savings into a permanent life insurance policy. First, as mentioned, the example assumes that Mike earns 8.5% per year inside his insurance policy. If interest rates stay low, as they have in the late 1980s and 1990s, Mike may not earn that much. On the other hand, if interest rates return to the levels of the 1970s and early 1980s, Mike might earn even more.

In truth, no one really knows what interest rates will do next year, let alone over a 35-year period such as the one described in our example. All such scenarios are projections; the actual outcomes are sure to be more or less desirable than the illustration.

Moreover, there's a relatively new form of permanent life insurance known as *variable life,* which we'll describe in Chapter 9. With variable life, policyholders can invest their insurance premiums in the stock market. That would have been a very good strategy from 1982 to 1998, but a poor choice during the 1966 through 1981 period.

What's more, a long holding period (35 years in this example) is necessary to make permanent insurance a good investment. These policies have steep initial costs, especially sales commissions, so clients should plan on waiting at least 10 years and probably longer before starting to tap the policy. The longer the wait, the greater the benefits of tax-free compounding and the smaller the impact of up-front selling costs.

Even after a long waiting period, though, policyholders need to withdraw and borrow with care. In the preceding example, taking out $20,000 per year provides Mike and his family with outstanding results. However, if Mike had pulled $30,000 per year from the policy, he would have drawn down the cash value to the point where he would have had to contribute more cash to avoid a lapse. Taking as much as $25,000 per year might have been dangerous.

If you think your clients may want to tap their life insurance cash value some day, you might decide to recommend variable life insurance, which permits policyholders to enjoy stock market growth. Other clients, though, will feel more comfortable buying universal life insurance.

With universal life, policyholders don't need to make any decisions regarding how premiums will be invested; instead, they'll ride along with the insurance company's investment portfolio. The cash value will go up each year, no matter what the stock market does, and your clients probably will get a return that's equivalent to the yield on high-quality bonds.

Thus, universal life may appeal to clients who don't want to gamble with their family's life insurance needs. Typically, premiums paid for universal life insurance will buy more insurance—a greater death benefit—than would be the case with other forms of cash value insurance. If we do enter into another period of higher inflation and rising interest rates, universal life will probably be a good choice.

Seeing, Not Believing

No matter what type of cash value insurance your clients buy, the agent likely will show an illustration. That is, your clients will get to see detailed printouts showing how the policies will perform in the future. For example, after 10 years of paying annual premiums of $3,208, there will be $35,012 in cash value.

These illustrations are generated with such precision that clients are likely to take them literally. After 10 years, what will the cash value be? Why, $35,012, of course.

In truth, insurance policy "illustrations" are projections or forecasts or, more accurately, estimates. They show what will happen if certain events take place, although those events are almost certain *not* to take place.

In the example of Mike Harris, for instance, it is assumed that his cash value will grow by 8.5% per year each year for 35 years. In reality, of course, his cash value will grow by differing amounts every year. If he chooses variable life, the cash value may actually decline in some years. Similarly, policy illustrations show overhead costs remaining fixed over the life of the policy while in fact those costs may vary.

Thus, policy illustrations are just what-if scenarios that need careful monitoring. In fact, clients who buy cash value policies should ask for updated illustrations every few years so they can check on performance.

Few permanent life insurance policies are sold on the premise that premiums will be paid indefinitely. Instead, premiums are expected to be paid for a certain number of years, after which the cash value may be so great that no further payments need be made.

Sometimes this works: Policies bought in the early 1970s benefited from the rising interest rates of the following years. On the other hand, "vanishing premium" sales pitches can be a trap. In the 1980s, many consumers bought policies expecting to pay premiums for only six or seven years. Instead, investment yields dropped and the premiums needed to be paid for 10 or 15 years or longer. Many policyholders were sorely disappointed when they were told to keep paying.

Thus, if you or your clients are shown a policy illustration, ask what investment return is being assumed. Then ask the agent to rerun the illustration at a yield that's a point or two lower—5% instead of 6%, for example. That will provide some idea of how long premium payments will need to be paid and will keep your clients from being misled by the illustration illusion.

Recap

- Term insurance is pure insurance, while permanent insurance includes an investment account known as the *cash value.*

- Increases in a policy's cash value are not subject to income tax.

- Policy loans and withdrawals are tax-free as long as they're not used to excess.

- Insurance policy proceeds are not subject to income tax.

- It's possible to use a permanent life policy's cash value as a source of tax-free funds in retirement.

- Policy illustrations are meant to demonstrate possible outcomes, but the numbers are not guaranteed.

CHAPTER

7

Gains without Pain

Dodging the Mutual Fund Trap

Pick up any business publication—indeed, virtually *any* publication—and you're bound to read about the wonderful results posted by mutual funds in the 1980s and the 1990s. Through the end of 1998, for example, the average mutual fund holding U.S. stocks had gained 19.07% per year for the prior three years, 16.99% per year for the prior five years, and 15.60% per year for the prior 10 years, according to Morningstar, Inc., Chicago.

To put that in perspective, if a client had invested $1,000 in the average stock fund at the beginning of 1989, by the end of 1998 that $1,000 would have grow to $4,262. A $10,000 investment would have grown to $42,620.

There's only one thing wrong with those marvelous numbers: They're unreal. Those statistics, as with virtually all statistics about mutual funds, ignore the impact that taxes can have on results.

Indeed, Morningstar, one of the leading authorities on mutual fund performance, calculates a "tax-adjusted return" for mutual funds. According to Morningstar, the average mutual fund returned around 13.5% per year for the past 10 years to investors in the highest tax bracket. At that rate, $1,000 would have grown to $3,548 and $10,000 to $35,480 in 10 years, after tax.

There's certainly nothing wrong with seeing money grow from $10,000 to $35,480, but that return is 18% lower than the pretax number. Longer term, the tax bite can be even more painful: Reportedly, Vanguard's popular S&P 500 index fund would have cost a top-bracket investor 36% of its pretax return to taxes during the first 20 years of its existence.

Although most investors are not in the highest federal tax bracket, most investors do have to pay state and perhaps local income taxes. Thus, investors in high-tax states and cities may wind up losing an even greater portion of their returns to income tax.

Dividends Are a Drop in the Bucket

Why do investors lose so much of their mutual fund returns to taxation? The pass-through of dividends accounts for some of the tax burden. Someone who invests in General Electric, for example, will receive a quarterly dividend. Whether that dividend is spent, saved, or reinvested in more GE stock, the investor will owe tax on that dividend.

The same is true for mutual fund investors. Say a fund invests in GE, Exxon, Citicorp, and so forth. All of those companies pay dividends to the fund—which owns the shares of these companies—and the fund, in turn, passes through quarterly dividends to its investors. Whether Joe Investor collects these dividends or reinvests in more fund shares (most investors choose the reinvestment option), he'll owe tax on those dividends.

Dividend pass-through, though, is a small part of the problem. In the late 1990s, dividends were at their lowest levels in decades, with average yields under 2%. Most mutual funds were paying only around 1% to investors in the form of these income dividends.

Suppose, for example, that Mary Russell invests $10,000 in ABC Mutual Fund. If she receives a 1% income dividend this year, that's $100 in taxable income. Assuming an effective 40% tax rate, she'll owe $40 in tax, an insignificant amount compared to her $10,000 investment—which may have grown to $11,000, $12,000 or more.

Capital Comebacks

A much larger problem stems from capital gains distributions. Over the years, ABC Mutual Fund has attracted millions (perhaps billions) of dollars from investors like Mary. Those dollars have been used to buy shares in dozens of companies.

At most stock funds, the portfolio manager trades the fund's holdings actively. One year, for example, energy stocks look good. Then bank stocks. Then pharmaceuticals. Similarly, even within industries, different companies have varying prospects. One month Microsoft may look like a good stock to buy; a few months later, Intel might seem more promising.

In brief, mutual fund managers are constantly selling shares. On average, U.S. stock funds have a *turnover rate* around 90%. (By definition, a fund with a 100% turnover rate holds each investment for an average of one year before selling it.) Therefore, from one year to the next, most mutual funds do a lot of buying and selling.

Unless the shares are sold for exactly the same price at which they were purchased, which is extremely unlikely, each sale will result in a gain or loss for the fund. Ever since 1982, when stock prices began to rise sharply, mutual funds have had far more gains than losses.

In 1992, ABC Mutual Fund invested $1 million in XYZ Technology Co. In 1999, ABC sold those shares, which were then valued at $4 million. On this trade, ABC posted a $3 million capital gain.

Over the course of a year, ABC will buy and sell shares regularly, registering gains as well as losses. At some point, generally at the end of the year, ABC will tally up all the gains and losses; if there is a net gain, those gains must be distributed to shareholders if ABC is to maintain its status as a mutual fund.

Suppose, for example, that ABC has $100 million worth of trading gains and $90 million worth of trading losses in 1999, for a net gain of $10 million. If ABC has 5 million shares outstanding, each investor will get a distribution of $2 per share.

These distributions have the effect of reducing a mutual fund's share price. If ABC trades at $20 per share in mid-December, then distributes $2 per share in capital gains distributions, its share price will fall to $18: Instead of a share worth $20, investors will have a share worth $18 and $2 in cash. Indeed, many of these investors will simply reinvest the $2-per-share distributions in more shares of ABC.

Phantom Income, Real Taxes

If that were all that happened, this would be no big deal. Instead of owning, say, 450 shares of ABC at $20, an investor might own 500 shares of ABC at $18. Either way, this investor's stake in ABC is $9,000.

There is a problem, though: taxes. When this investor receives that $2-per-share distribution, he incurs a tax obligation. What's more, some of that distribution may consist of highly taxed short-term gains as well as long-term gains at 20%.

Suppose, for example, that Jack Davis owned 450 shares of ABC, so he received a $900 distribution. If Jack owed tax on that distribution at an effective 25% blended rate, he'd owe the IRS $225: That's true even if he reinvested that distribution and never put a dime in his pocket.

Even worse, consider the fate of Ellen Perry, who buys 500 shares of ABC for $10,000 one week before the distribution. She receives her $1,000 distribution (500 shares times $2 per share) and reinvests that money in ABC. If she owes tax at 25%, she'll have to pay $250 in tax *even though she invested after the profits were made and enjoyed none of the benefit.* Ellen pays tax on the gains earned by other investors!

Gored by the Bull

These problems are hardly academic. In 1997, mutual funds paid out a total of $334 billion: $204 billion in capital gains and $130 billion in ordinary dividends. Nearly 50 mutual funds paid distributions that year that were at least 25% of their assets.

At that rate, a fund selling at $20 per share would distribute at least $5 per share to investors, who'd owe tax on that distribution whether or not they collected any cash.

After the long bull market, most mutual funds have large unrealized capital gains. Each year, they're likely to sell some of their appreciated stocks and incur gains that have to be passed through to investors.

Mutual funds must announce their potential capital gain exposure. In 1998, for example, T. Rowe Price Small-Cap Value Fund had potential capital gain exposure of 37%, while the number for Lindner Growth Fund was 39%. Assuming a 20% tax rate, buying a fund with a 39% capital gain exposure is like paying $100 for assets worth $92.20, after tax.

Fund's assets	$1,000,000
Capital gain exposure	39%
Potential capital gain (39% of $1 million)	$390,000
Potential capital gains tax @ 20%	$78,000
After-tax value of assets (minus tax)	$922,000

Less Taxing Solutions

With all the tax disadvantages of mutual funds, there are also sound reasons for investing there. For relatively little money investors get diversification and professional management. If your clients have other things to do with their lives besides tracking their investment portfolios, mutual funds may make a lot of sense.

Moreover, there are ways to invest in mutual funds yet still avoid a tax disaster:

■ *Invest after a capital gains distribution, not before.* Especially if clients are investing late in the year, they should wait until the fund makes its distribution and the share price drops, then buy at the lower price per share.

■ *Invest in a tax-deferred retirement account.* Indeed, for someone who's investing for an IRA, a Keogh plan, or a simplified employee plan (SEP), mutual funds may make good choices. It doesn't matter how much a fund distributes to shareholders; as long as the money stays inside a retirement plan no tax will be due.

- *Invest in a low-turnover fund.* As mentioned, the average stock fund has a 90% turnover rate. However, that average covers a wide range: Some funds have higher turnover rates while some have lower rates.

  Indeed, some mutual fund managers prefer to hold onto their stocks for years, trading rarely. These funds might have turnover rates of 10% to 20%. With such scant trading activity, capital gains generally aren't realized, so they don't have to be distributed to shareholders. All mutual funds post their historic turnover rates, so investors can get an idea of what to expect in the future.

- *Invest in an index fund.* Some mutual funds are designed to mirror the results of a particular index, such as the S&P 500. These funds won't beat the market, but they won't lag it, either. Because index fund portfolio managers aren't picking stocks (they're merely holding the stocks in the index), management fees generally are lower than the norm.

  In addition, index funds have low turnover rates. Rather than jump in and out of stocks, the managers stay with the stocks included in the index: An S&P 500 index fund, for example, will always hold GE, Coke, Microsoft, and so on. Again, low turnover means fewer realized gains and few taxable distributions to investors.

- *Invest in a tax-managed fund.* Some stock funds are especially managed to minimize taxes. Generally, they pursue a buy-and-hold strategy. If these funds take gains, for any reason, they also endeavor to take an offsetting loss so there will not be net gains to pass on to investors. Moreover, these funds can use certain accounting techniques to hold down investors' taxes.

  For an example of a tax-managed fund, consider Schwab 1000. This fund, created in 1991, invests in the 1,000 largest U.S. companies, not including investment companies. In the first seven years of the fund's existence, it distributed no capital gains to shareholders. Income dividends were passed through, but those were in the 1% to 2% range.

  As of this writing, Schwab 1000 had delivered 21.64% total returns per year to shareholders for the previous five years. In that time period, the after-tax return to a top-bracket investor was 20.99%. Thus, taxable investors wound up with 97% of the fund's pretax return.

A number of tax-managed funds exist, so if your clients are interested you can help them choose the ones that suit their needs.

Hot Spots

If you're looking for the top-performing mutual funds during the 1980s to 1990s bull market, you should look at *sector funds*. However, sector funds may pose tax challenges that need to be addressed.

Sector funds are mutual funds that specialize in a given industry, and some of those industries have posted great records. In 1998, for example, technology sector funds were up more than 51%, on average, while the average domestic stock fund's return was around 14%. Nor was 1998 a fluke: Through 1998, technology sector funds had returned 22% for preceding three years, 23% for the preceding five years, and 22% for the preceding 10 years.

Other sector funds have delivered excellent returns, too. Both health care and financial funds had 10-year average returns in excess of 21%, ahead of the 19% posted by the S&P 500 and the 16% annual returns of the average domestic stock fund. To put those numbers in perspective, $10,000 invested in 1988 in Vanguard Specialized Health Care, which gained 22% a year for the next 10 years, would have been worth over $75,000 in 1998.

Living on the Edge

Going forward, sector funds may be appropriate for aggressive investors. They increase risk within a portfolio, but they also provide the opportunity for higher returns. Generally, younger, growth-oriented investors are most suitable for sector funds.

If you're considering sector funds for your clients, here are the areas that have been the most profitable:

- *Financial services.* Although some financial sector funds focus on brokerage and insurance stocks, most of the entries are bank-stock funds holding BankAmerica, Chase Manhattan, Bank of New York, and so on. Falling interest rates and industry consolidation have driven these stocks higher; as of this writing, mergers are still exciting investors, along with higher fees and profitable credit card operations.

- *Technology funds.* While some technology funds are very special-ized, focusing on semiconductors or communications, others in-clude software, biotech, medical devices, and the like. The tech funds with the best 10-year returns are the ones with varied invest-ments in the technology sector.

- *Health care.* Some health care funds focus on big-cap drug compa-nies while others specialize in biotechnology, medical devices, hos-pitals, and HMOs. The top-ranked funds have emphasized large pharmaceutical companies.

A High-Octane Portfolio

Considering the performance of the 1980s and 1990s, one strategy might be for investors to put most of their stock market money into an S&P 500 index fund to get a broad stock market play, and then to fill out their portfolio with finance, health care, and technology sector funds to boost returns.

Harry S. Dent, author of *The Roaring 2000s,* recommends a portfo-lio that's 25% invested in a mutual fund that tracks the Dow Jones Industrials (30 extremely large companies) and 25% each invested in mutual funds specializing in technology, health care, and financial ser-vices.

If your clients are willing to take some investment risks they shouldn't be intimidated by sector funds. These funds have acquired a negative image among some people who equate investing in sector funds with market timing. In truth, sector funds are just a means of giving more weight to certain types of stocks. Investors might want to forecast the three or four greatest profit trends in the national or world economy, then decide if it makes sense to overweight these sectors in their portfolio.

Sector funds, though, may be tax-inefficient. That's especially true for technology funds, which often have high turnover rates.

Therefore, if your clients decide to hold sector funds, they probably should hold them in tax-deferred retirement plans to maximize long-term wealth building and minimize the annual tax bill. If clients don't have that option—perhaps their 401(k) plan doesn't have sector funds on the menu—so that they must invest in a taxable account, they should look for a fund that has a history of not making substantial capital gains distributions to its shareholders.

80 Cents on the Dollar

All investment funds aren't mutual funds: *Closed-end funds* also are available, and they may offer advantages to sophisticated individuals.

Closed-end funds are similar to mutual funds because they, too, contain an assortment of securities selected by professional managers. However, the funds are "closed-end" because their managers have a certain amount of money to invest from funds raised in an initial public offering (IPO). (Additional capital may be raised in secondary offerings.) By contrast, mutual funds are "open-end" because they continually take in new money and redeem existing shareholders' investments.

After their IPO, closed-end funds trade like stocks, often on the New York Stock Exchange. Thus, their trading prices are determined by supply and demand rather than by the value of the underlying securities they hold. As a result, closed-ends typically trade at a discount or a premium to net asset value (NAV).

In 1999, for example, the Templeton China closed-end fund held assets valued at $7.16 per share, yet the fund was trading at $5.6875. Thus, investors could buy $7.16 worth of Chinese stock for $5.6875—a discount of more than 17%. At the same time, investors in Templeton Emerging Markets were willing to pay $10.0625 for $18.57 worth of stocks—a premium of more than 17%. This disparity between market price and asset value offers investors an intriguing prospect of buying depressed international stocks at a discount—along with a heightened level of risk.

When your clients invest in closed-end funds, they need to be right about the underlying securities. Thus, a China closed-end fund will be a profitable investment only if the Chinese market advances. In addition, clients need to be right about discounts and premiums. It's possible to be right about the fundamentals and yet lose money if a discount widens, a premium shrinks, or a premium turns into a discount.

Pros advise investors to track a closed-end fund for at least six months, keeping a moving average of its premiums and discounts. The time to buy is when the discount is at least 5 points wider than the average. That is, if a fund's average discount to NAV is 10%, investors should try to buy it when the discount is at least 15%.

In addition, the time to buy a fund is when its discount is at least as wide as the discounts on similar funds. If all the closed-end funds specializing in German stocks have an average 20% discount from NAV, investors should not buy the one with a 15% discount, even if that's a wider-than-average discount for this particular fund.

The Case Is Closed

Closed-end funds have advantages over open-ends, according to their adherents. Closed-ends don't have to keep cash on hand to meet redemptions, so the extra money they can put into stocks or bonds will probably boost long-term returns. In addition, closed-ends aren't subject to the redemption-driven, buy-at-the-top-sell-at-the-bottom phenomenon that may afflict mutual funds.

That is, if the stock market falls sharply, closed-end funds won't be threatened by redemptions. When there are more sellers than buyers, trading prices will go down, but the funds' portfolios can stay intact. Open-end mutual funds, on the other hand, may be forced to sell illiquid securities into a falling market—some mutual funds may run into serious trouble if redemptions mount to dangerous levels.

As another advantage, closed-end funds have no minimum investment. Many mutual funds now require several thousand dollars to invest, in some cases even more. If a closed-end fund is trading at $8 a share, investors can buy a round lot (100 shares) for $800. Thus, for $5,000 or $10,000 your clients can buy a nice assortment of closed-ends. By exercising patience, moreover, those funds could be acquired when they're selling at discounts, so $10,000 might buy $11,000 or $12,000 worth of stock.

Although tracking these vehicles may not be easy, depressed closed-end funds may pay off for diligent investors. Increasingly, dissatisfied shareholders are pressuring discounted closed-end funds to convert to mutual funds and thus trade at NAV. If closed-end funds are "open-ended" in this manner, investors stand to pick up solid gains.

What about taxes? Closed-end funds, like open-ends, distribute realized capital gains to investors, who'll owe income tax. Again, investors may prefer to hold closed-ends inside a tax-deferred retirement plan. If that's not practical, before investing they should ask about a fund's record of distributing capital gains.

Recap

- Mutual funds pass through income dividends as well as realized net capital gains to shareholders.

- Thus, shareholders may receive large amounts of unwelcome taxable gains each year, even if those gains are reinvested.

- Investors should try to invest after, rather than before, a capital gains distribution.

- Other strategies for avoiding this tax trap include investing inside a retirement plan or investing in funds that don't realize large amounts of net gains each year.

- Sector funds have been extremely successful in the past and may continue to shine in the technology, health care, and financial areas.

- Closed-end funds offer investors the opportunity to buy stocks and bonds at a discount.

CHAPTER

8

Mutual Funds Now, Taxes Later

Variable Annuities Can Enrich Your Retirement

In Chapter 7 we described a scenario that's familiar to most mutual fund investors. Money is invested in a mutual fund and the distributions are reinvested. Nevertheless, sizable taxes are due each year. What's more, whenever funds are switched from one mutual fund to another, taxes are triggered: If there have been gains, a check goes to the IRS.

One way your clients can avoid this outcome is to invest in mutual funds inside a tax-deferred retirement plan, such as a 401(k) plan (see Chapter 3). In that case, distributions aren't taxed and neither are switches from one fund to another.

There's another way to invest in mutual funds without owing any tax: Buy a variable annuity. These annuities are similar in some ways to the fixed annuities described in Chapter 5. They can be bought from insurers, banks, and other financial institutions, either with a single premium or a series of premiums.

That's where the resemblance stops, though. With a variable annuity the buyer decides where the premium will be invested. The more successful the investments, the greater the buildup in the account. However, some of the investment choices may lead to an actual loss of investment value inside the annuity.

To see how a variable annuity might work, consider this simple example. George Parker buys a variable annuity from Worldwide Insurance Co., investing $30,000. The variable annuity offers three choices: Worldwide Stock Fund, Worldwide Bond Fund, and Worldwide Money Market Fund. George can direct his $30,000 among these three funds in any manner he chooses. (In a variable annuity, they're called *subaccounts.*)

He could put all $30,000 into the stock fund; he could divide his premium into three $10,000 chunks; he could decide to invest $22,000 in the stock fund, $5,000 in the bond fund, and $3,000 in the money market fund.

In short, George can do virtually whatever he wants with his premium. Moreover, he can switch the money among these subaccounts, subject to fairly generous limits.

From that point on, variable annuities again resemble fixed annuities. Any investment buildup inside the subaccounts is untaxed; switches among subaccounts don't produce taxable gains. Indeed, there is no tax due until the money comes out of the annuity.

In our example, suppose George puts all $30,000 into the stock fund. Over time, his stock fund may grow to $50,000, $100,000, or more—and no tax will be due until he withdraws money.

In essence, George has discovered how to invest in mutual funds without owing any tax.

Multiple Choice

In reality, investing in variable annuities is a bit more complex. Most variable annuities have far more than three subaccounts to choose among: Some offer dozens of investment choices.

Some subaccounts are clones of leading mutual funds, managed by the same portfolio managers. Just to cite one example, Nationwide Life Insurance offers a Best of America variable annuity with more than 40 subaccounts, including entries managed by American Century, Dreyfus, Morgan Stanley, Neuberger & Berman, Oppenheimer, Fidelity, and Warburg Pincus.

Even though the names are the same, you shouldn't assume variable annuity subaccounts are true clones with identical performance. Often, variable annuity subaccounts are much smaller than mutual funds, so managers can focus more on small-cap issues that get lost in a full-sized mutual fund. Also, managers may trade more inside a variable annuity because there will be no tax consequences for investors. This active trading may increase investment volatility. The bottom line is that your clients need to read the offering materials carefully before choosing among variable annuity subaccounts.

In addition to subaccounts that resemble mutual funds, some subaccounts are *total return* or *asset manager* funds, designed to provide investors with some help in putting together a diversified portfolio inside the variable. Such funds may be appropriate for investors who don't wish to actively manage their annuity contracts.

That's the good news. Variable annuities enable investors to build up large amounts inside the contract, assuming the subaccounts perform well. Income taxes won't be due, regardless of whether the fund manager takes gains or how often the investor switches subaccounts.

This can make a sizable difference. Take Neuberger & Berman's Guardian Fund, a popular (over $4 billion in assets as of this writing) mutual fund with a clone in some variable annuities. As of this writing (early 1999), the fund has produced a 15% average annual return for the previous 10 years. At that rate, a $10,000 investment would have grown to about $40,000.

However, an investor in the top tax bracket would have received only 12.75% per year, after tax. At that rate, $10,000 would have grown to only $33,000.

Thus, after 10 years, an investor holding this fund in a tax-deferred retirement plan or in a variable annuity would have been more than 20% ahead of a top-bracket investor in a taxable account. Over longer time periods, the advantages of tax deferral become even more pronounced.

Plus Factors

Variable annuities offer other advantages. Some states protect annuities from creditors. (The protection generally is greater if your client's spouse and children are named as beneficiaries.) If that's the case, investing through a variable annuity may be more attractive than buying mutual funds, which are exposed to creditors. In addition, annuity contracts don't go through probate at the owner's death: They pass directly to a named beneficiary.

Moreover, annuities offer a form of life insurance. As you might expect, investors who choose the wrong subaccounts can suffer losses. If that happens, George Parker's $30,000 investment might drop to $25,000, $20,000, or less.

However, if George dies while his subaccounts are in negative territory, his beneficiary will receive at least the amount invested in the variable annuity. Suppose, his original $30,000 had dwindled to $10,000 after a string of disastrous subaccount selections. At his death, his beneficiary would receive $30,000.

In fact, some variable annuities periodically raise the floor under this guaranteed death benefit. A contract might call for a review every five years: If the account value has grown, that value becomes the new guaranteed death benefit.

Minus Signs

Unfortunately, there also are drawbacks to investing through a variable annuity:

- *Extra costs.* Whenever you invest in mutual funds you pay the portfolio manager. For the average domestic stock fund, expenses run to about 1.4% of assets per year.

  Investing through a variable annuity adds an extra layer of cost for administration and for the aforementioned insurance benefit (not to mention sales commissions). Altogether, costs might run 2% or 2.25% of assets per year.

  In the example provided, a 15% annual return caused $10,000 to grow to $40,000 after 10 years. However, if the variable annuity's subaccount has to bear the added costs, it might actually net only 14.25% per year, dropping the 10-year buildup to $38,000.

- *Surrender charges.* The same rules that apply to fixed annuities apply here, too. There are limits to the amount that can be taken out of a variable annuity each year without paying a fee to the insurance company. Generally, surrender charges decline over a period of several years.

■ *Early withdrawal penalties.* As is the case with any deferred annuity, money that's withdrawn from a variable annuity is subject to income tax up to the amount of total earnings. There's also a 10% penalty before age 59½.

Suppose, for example, George Parker's $30,000 grows to $70,000 over the years. If he runs into a financial emergency and needs to take money from his variable annuity, the first $40,000 will be subject to income tax. (Subsequent withdrawals will be tax-free.) If George withdraws $40,000 before he reaches age 59½, he'll owe another $4,000.

■ *Loss of the capital gains tax break.* As mentioned in Chapter 1, long-term capital gains are taxed no higher than 20% (no higher than 10% for those in a low tax bracket). However, if those capital gains are realized inside a variable annuity, this tax break is not available. All taxable withdrawals are subject to ordinary income tax rates, up to 39.6%.

Continuing our example, suppose George Parker invested his $10,000 in a regular taxable account. After 10 years of paying tax each year, George accumulates $39,000.

Assume (1) George has reinvested $1,000 worth of dividends, bringing his basis up to $11,000, and (2) he is not in the lowest tax bracket. If he cashes in this fund, he'll have $28,000 in taxable gains ($39,000 minus his $11,000 basis), owe $5,600 to the IRS at 20%, and wind up with $33,400.

On the other hand, suppose George had put that $10,000 into a variable annuity subaccount that grew to $45,000 over 10 years. If he withdraws all the money at once, he'd owe tax on a $35,000 gain. In a top 39.6% federal tax bracket, he'd owe nearly $14,000 in tax and wind up with about $31,000—he'd actually be behind the taxable account by more than $2,000.

In a 28% tax bracket, he'd owe $9,800 in tax and pocket $35,200, so he'd be ahead by $1,800. In between, in the 31% and the 36% tax brackets, he'd be slightly ahead or slightly behind, respectively. (See Table 8.1.)

TABLE 8.1 Mutual Funds versus Variable Annuities

Mutual Funds

Amount invested	$10,000
Dividends reinvested	1,000
Basis	11,000
After-tax amount after 10 years	39,000
Taxable gain on sale ($39,000 – 11,000)	28,000
Capital gains tax @ 20%	(5,600)
Net proceeds ($39,000 – $5,600)	33,400

Variable Annuity

Amount invested	$10,000
Contract value after 10 years	45,000
Taxable gain ($45,000 – $10,000)	35,000
Income tax @ 39.6%	(13,860)
Net proceeds	31,140
Income tax @ 36%	(12,600)
Net proceeds	32,400
Income tax @ 31%	(10,850)
Net proceeds	34,150
Income tax @ 28%	(9,800)
Net proceeds	35,200

- *Estate tax troubles.* Anyone who dies with a balance in a variable annuity account—that is, dies before annuitizing the deferred annuity, as explained in Chapter 5—will bequeath an income tax liability. Someday, someone will have to pay all the deferred income tax.

  If George Parker dies with a $70,000 balance in his variable annuity, and he paid $30,000, his beneficiary will have to recognize $40,000 in income. (As explained in Chapter 5, there are several ways to defer the income tax, but it must be paid eventually.) What's more, the annuity will be included in George's taxable estate.

Between income and estate tax, George's beneficiary may not have much to show for all the years that George's money was in the annuity. In some cases, a beneficiary may lose as much as 75% of the value of an inherited variable annuity.

Finding a Fit

Now that we've examined the advantages and disadvantages of variable annuities, we can determine who should invest in them. The ideal investor is someone who:

1. *Pays substantial amounts of tax each year on mutual fund investments.* A client who buys and holds individual stocks, for example, wouldn't be suitable for variable annuities. The same is true for someone who has a few mutual fund investments that throw off a few hundred dollars a year in taxable income. Such an investor is better off paying $100 or so in tax each year rather than getting involved with a variable annuity.

    On the other hand, a client who pays hundreds or thousands of dollars in tax each year from mutual fund trades and distributions might wish to consider a variable annuity.

2. *Has a long time horizon.* At the very least, an investor should plan to hold onto a variable annuity until age 59½, when the 10% penalty no longer applies.

    For the best results, a variable annuity should be held for at least 10 years and probably 20 years for the investment to make sense. That's how long it usually takes for the benefits of tax deferral to outweigh the extra costs, compared with a direct investment in a mutual fund.

3. *Will invest in the stock fund subaccounts.* In addition to a long time frame, investors need to earn high returns inside a variable annuity to make the most of the tax deferral. Earning 6% or 7% in a fixed-income subaccount will not build the amount of wealth necessary to make a variable annuity pay off.

    To get the double-digit annual returns needed inside a variable annuity, your clients must direct their premiums to the equity subaccounts and others with the potential for high returns, such as real estate and junk bonds. Moreover, investors need the staying power to stick with subaccounts even during years when the financial markets suffer steep declines.

4. *Expects to use up the variable annuity in retirement.* Variable annuities are meant to provide supplementary retirement income. At some point, investors can annuitize their contracts or withdraw money from the contract, as explained in Chapter 5. By spending down an annuity, clients can hold onto appreciated stocks and mutual funds, bequeathing them to their heirs, who'll inherit with a basis step-up and owe no income tax on the accumulated profits.

However, some variable annuity buyers take little or no cash from the contract. They let the contract value keep growing, convinced they're building wealth on a tax-deferred basis. Then they die with all that money in the contract, whereupon the combination of income tax and estate tax strips out most of the value.

Any client who doesn't expect to use the money in the contract shouldn't buy a variable annuity. Investors who don't need the income from a deferred annuity can use that annuity to satisfy a charitable bequest, which will save income and estate taxes. Another option is to annuitize the contract, receive the payments, and give away the after-tax proceeds to an irrevocable trust. This strategy not only removes the value of the gift from the donor's taxable estate, it also provides trust beneficiaries with asset protection. If the gifts to the trust are used to buy life insurance, the tax-free death benefit may exceed the income taxes paid on the annuity distributions.

5. *Probably will not be in a top tax bracket in retirement.* Investors who will be in the 36% and 39.6% brackets will owe huge amounts when the money comes out of a variable annuity, especially if they take fully taxable withdrawals. Such clients may be better off investing directly in mutual funds and paying capital gains tax at a 20% rate.

On the other hand, moderate-income retirees (those in the 28% or 31% brackets) may be better off investing for tax deferral in a variable annuity. That's especially true for those who can defer the tax on investment income during their working years, then take money out of a variable annuity in a lower tax bracket during retirement.

Switch-Hits

Some sophisticated strategies can enhance the value of investing in a variable annuity. As mentioned, variable annuity investors are guaranteed that their beneficiaries will always receive at least the amount invested in the contract, no matter what happens in the subaccounts. This effectively puts a floor under the value of variable annuity investments.

Some variable annuities periodically raise this floor, but that's not always the case. Investors who buy a variable annuity without an automatic escalator can raise the floor themselves: They can switch annuities after the surrender fees lapse.

For example, Betty Jackson bought a variable annuity in 1992 with a $50,000 investment. The annuity imposes surrender charges for seven years.

Betty invests in equity subaccounts that perform well, so her contract value grows to $125,000 in 1999, when the surrender charges are no longer in force. At this point, Betty can exchange her variable annuity for another, tax-free, using a 1035 exchange (see page 117). Her new annuity will have a floor of $125,000, not $50,000, essentially locking in Betty's gains so far.

Better Than the Bank

Although variable annuities are meant to be long-term stock market vehicles, they can be used for short-term, low-risk investing under certain circumstances. What are those circumstances?

- Clients are in their late 50s or older.
- They are well-off financially, but their total assets don't exceed $1 million ($2 million if they're married).
- They have at least $25,000 sitting in bank CDs. This is money set aside not for current spending but for an emergency, such as a long nursing-home stay.

You can advise clients who fit this profile to consider moving money from bank CDs to a variable annuity and investing in the "stable income subaccount" within the contract. Most variable annuities have an account that will pay a bondlike return with no risk of principal. These accounts might include guaranteed investment contracts (GICs), which offer a set return for a certain number of years. After the guarantee period, the rate is reset. GIC rates often are higher than CD rates.

Thus, the account value will go up steadily and not suffer any loss of principal. Inside the annuity, no tax will be due.

You can help your clients to find a variable annuity that:

- Charges very low fees on money kept in these stable income subaccounts.

- Provides access to investors' money with low or no surrender charges, providing liquidity.

- Is issued by an insurer that's well rated for financial strength.

Once such a variable annuity is in place, investors can arrange for the interest earned on the stable income account to be swept into one or more equity subaccounts. Thus, the principal won't be at risk, but earnings will be invested in the stock market, where returns may be greater than those of bank CDs.

If this emergency money is needed, it's available at little or no cost. If it turns out that the money is never needed, it will go to named beneficiaries.

In any case, income taxes will be due. However, it's better to pay them later rather than sooner, as would have been the case if the money had been kept in CDs. As long as your clients are over age 59½, they won't owe a 10% penalty tax on early withdrawals; as long as they're under the $1 million ($2 million if married) threshold, no estate tax will be due on the annuity's value.

The preceding strategy can provide higher returns and tax deferral. As an added benefit, moving money from a CD to a variable annuity may reduce the tax owed on Social Security benefits each year. That's because CD income counts when determining taxes on a client's benefits, but buildup inside a deferred annuity isn't included.

Loan Arrangers

Not everyone who buys a variable annuity will be able to hold on for the long term. Taking money out of a variable annuity is expensive, especially for clients who are younger than 59½ (subject to a 10% tax penalty) and in the early years of their contract (subject to surrender fees). Those charges are in addition to the income tax that will be owed on withdrawals.

What can an annuity buyer do if he or she needs cash? One alternative is to use a home equity loan or a margin loan for the money that's needed. The interest likely will be deductible; when your clients are in their 40s or 50s they probably will be able to take the interest deductions during their peak earning years, when the deductions are most valuable. In the meantime, the money in the variable annuity can continue to grow, tax-free.

After age 59½, borrowers can tap their annuity to pay down the debt they've incurred. By that time the 10% penalty won't apply and the surrender charges likely will be lower or nonexistent. They may be in a lower tax bracket, too, especially if they've retired. If so, the tax consequences of withdrawing funds from a deferred annuity may be reduced.

Holding Patterns

Do annuities belong inside a tax-deferred retirement plan? Probably not. It's redundant to hold a tax-deferred annuity inside a tax-deferred retirement plan. You're paying extra fees without receiving any real benefit.

On the other hand, variable annuities may be a valuable investment vehicle for a trust. There's no current tax to pay; there are no worries about reinvestment; and long-term returns may beat "safe" fixed-income vehicles. Annuities often work well in a marital trust (known as the *A trust*) left to one spouse after the other spouse dies.

However, investing trust funds in annuities is not always the right approach. "A non-natural person cannot buy a deferred annuity and enjoy the tax deferral," says Bill George, partner in the law firm Helm, Purcell & Wakeman, Westlake Village, California. "If a corporation, a partnership, or a certain type of trust holds a deferred annuity, the income will be taxable each year." Therefore, investors need to work with a top tax attorney in this area. (See Appendix C.)

Recap

- Variable annuities permit investors to allocate their premiums among subaccounts that resemble mutual funds.

- No taxes will be due on activity within a variable annuity, including fund switches and capital gains distribution.

- Although income taxes will be due when money comes out of a variable annuity, tax deferral and possible tax-bracket reduction in retirement may make these investments pay off.

- The ideal variable annuity investor is someone who pays substantial taxes on mutual funds each year, who is able to hold onto the contract for many years before withdrawing funds, and who is willing to focus on the equity subaccounts.

- Because of a quirk in the tax code, variable annuities make more sense for moderate-income retirees than for top-bracket retirees.

- Spending down a variable annuity in retirement is often a better choice than holding on until death.

Mutual Funds Now, Taxes Never

Variable Life Insurance Makes Taxes Disappear

In Chapter 8 we examined the tax-deferral power of variable annuities. Investors can channel their money into mutual fund look-alikes, or *subaccounts,* and owe no tax on any investment buildup. Only when the money is paid out will tax be due. Therefore, variable annuities can be a powerful tool for those clients who want to increase their retirement income.

For all their benefits, though, variable annuities pose some disadvantages:

1. They offer tax deferral, not tax avoidance. At some point, all the deferred income must be paid, either by the initial investor or by a beneficiary.

2. When money comes out of a variable annuity it will be subject to tax at ordinary income rates: your clients' highest marginal tax rates. That's true even if most of the buildup has been in stock market appreciation. In other words, the favorable tax treatment of long-term capital gains is lost when your clients buy a variable annuity.

3. The contract value of a variable annuity will be subject to estate taxes. Most variable annuities are not used for retirement income; instead, they build up until the investor dies. Then estate tax as well as income tax may be due.

   For example, consider the case of John Burns, who invested $100,000 in a variable annuity at a broker's "suggestion." John had other sources of retirement income, so he held onto his variable annuity for nearly 30 years, until his death. At that point, the balance in the annuity was over $800,000.

   John's estate was large enough to put him into the 55% bracket, so $440,000 of the annuity was lost to estate taxes. Counting income tax, over 70% of his annuity balance went to the IRS. His children wound up with little more than $200,000 out of his "$800,000 annuity."

That's Life

Investors such as John would have been better off buying variable life insurance instead. In many ways, variable life is comparable to a variable annuity:

- Both vehicles offer a variety of subaccounts into which premiums can be directed.

- These subaccounts may be managed by top mutual fund portfolio managers.

- Investors' premiums can be allocated among these subaccounts as desired, and money can be switched among subaccounts with no tax consequences.

The difference, though, is that variable life is life insurance, entitled to all the tax benefits of permanent life insurance, as revealed in Chapter 6:

1. *Tax-free buildup of cash value.* This is comparable to the tax-free buildup inside a variable annuity.

2. *Tax-free loans and withdrawals.* Up to certain limits, investors are allowed to pull money out of a variable life insurance policy without paying income tax. That's not possible with a variable annuity.

3. *Income tax–free death benefits.* A variable life policy is designed to pay a death benefit that's larger than the cash value, free of income tax. By contrast, income tax will always be owed on variable annuity payouts, before or after the investor's death.

With variable life, if clients invest well, their cash value and their death benefit will increase. If they invest poorly, the cash value will shrink but they'll still have the minimum death benefit that was guaranteed—usually, the amount of premiums paid.

Some variable life policies are *variable universal,* which means investors can increase or decrease the premium that's paid each year. Besides flexibility, variable universal policies give your clients a full range of investment options along with fewer guarantees and lower premiums for a given amount of insurance coverage.

Death Benefit

In our example, we saw what happened to John Burns, who invested $100,000 in a variable annuity and saw it grow to $800,000 over the years—only to have it stripped by taxes at his death so that his children received only around $200,000.

If John had put that same $100,000 into a variable insurance policy and chosen the same subaccounts, his cash value might have grown to $700,000 or $750,000 over the years. The costs of a variable life insurance policy are greater than the costs of a variable annuity, so the investment accumulation will lag.

However, if John had died without tapping the policy, his beneficiary would have received a death benefit that might have been $900,000, $1 million, or even more, depending on John's age and health when he applied for the policy. His beneficiary would have received that amount free of income tax.

Had John's death benefit been $1 million and the proceeds subject to estate tax at 55%, his beneficiaries would have wound up with $450,000 after tax—over twice as much as the payoff from a variable annuity.

These results assume John held the policy until death. But what if an emergency had arisen and he needed cash 5 or 10 or 20 years into the life of the policy? John would have been able to tap the cash value via withdrawals (up to the amount of premiums he paid) and policy loans. As long as he tapped the cash value cautiously he could have pulled money out of his insurance policy without owing income tax.

Robert Condon, a principal at Foundation Investment Group in Berkeley, California, provides the following example: "We looked at the numbers for a 45-year-old nonsmoking male who invests $10,000 per year for 20 years in either a variable life policy or a variable annuity. We assumed investment returns at 10% per year, before expenses. Beginning at age 65, the man in our illustration is assumed to tap the variable life policy or the variable annuity for about $38,500 per year."

The results are eye-opening. Assuming the man dies at age 84, his $200,000 investment would generate $772,000, after tax, from the variable life insurance policy, while the variable annuity would pay out only $556,000. At every age of death, the net present value of the cash flow from the life insurance is far greater than that of the annuity. Those numbers assume a 28% tax bracket. If a higher bracket is assumed, variable life is even further ahead.

Balancing Act

For another perspective on how variable life insurance might work, take the example of Nick Richards, who buys a policy at age 50 and pays a $20,000 premium every year for 15 years. Assuming that his subaccounts earn 10% per year, which nets to around 8.5% to 9% after expenses, the $300,000 he puts in might grow to around $530,000 after 15 years.

If that is indeed the case, Nick could retire at age 65 and begin to withdraw and borrow around $53,000 per year (10%) from the policy. He might be able to do that for 16 years, pulling out a total of around $850,000, tax-free. At that point, there might be so little in the cash value that no more money could be pulled out. In this scenario, there would be a minimal death benefit, perhaps $150,000, at age 85 or 90. Further policy loans might cause the policy to terminate and generate a huge tax bill. (See Table 9.1.)

Another approach assumes that Nick makes the same $300,000 in premium payments and builds up the same $530,000 in cash value.

TABLE 9.1 Variable Life Insurance—Withdrawing $53,000 Annually at 10%	
Annual premiums	$ 20,000
Total premiums over 15 years	$300,000
Subaccounts' gross annual returns	10%
Subaccounts' net annual returns (after expenses)	8.5%
Cash value buildup after 15 years	$530,000
Annual withdrawals and loans @ 10%	$53,000
Withdrawals and loans over 16 years	$850,000
Further withdrawals and loans possible	No
Death benefit at age 85	$150,000

Instead of withdrawing and borrowing $53,000 per year, he might take out $40,000 (about 7.5%) per year. Nick might be able to take that much tax-free cash out of the policy indefinitely. What's more, the death benefit might be much greater, around $600,000 at age 85 or 90. (See Table 9.2.)

Note all the "might be" language in these examples. Many factors,

TABLE 9.2 Variable Life Insurance—Withdrawing $40,000 Annually at 7.5%	
Annual premiums	$ 20,000
Total premiums over 15 years	$300,000
Subaccounts' gross annual returns	10%
Subaccounts' net annual returns (after expenses)	8.5%
Cash value buildup after 15 years	$530,000
Annual withdrawals and loans @ 7.5%	$40,000
Withdrawals and loans over 16 years	$640,000
Further withdrawals and loans possible	Yes
Death benefit at age 85	$600,000

especially disappointing investment results, could change the picture. Nevertheless, it is possible to structure an insurance policy that provides tax-free cash to your clients as well as a substantial death benefit (again, free of income tax) to their loved ones.

Taking distributions from a variable life policy can be tricky. Clients may want to take out large amounts, but stripping the policy of too much cash value may cause it to lapse, triggering all the deferred income tax. Thus, a variable life policy must be administered and monitored with care.

Many insurers have systems that are set up to send out notices whenever the danger point is near. However, it's really the responsibility of the insurance agent or financial advisor to keep the client informed. Ideally, review of a variable life policy should be included in a planner's regular meetings with clients.

Needs-Based Policy

When does variable life insurance make sense? Primarily, when a client has loved ones who'll benefit from the life insurance proceeds. If a client merely wants to supplement his or her own retirement income, a variable annuity is a better deal. That's because all of the money that's accumulated in a variable annuity can be—should be— used up by the investor during his or her lifetime.

With life insurance, though, spending all the cash value is a disastrous strategy: The policy will lapse and all the deferred income tax will be due.

Instead, variable life insurance can be viewed as a hybrid. Some of the investment buildup will be available to your clients for tax-free retirement income, while the rest will be paid to your clients' survivors as an income tax–free death benefit.

What's more, buying variable life insurance makes sense only for clients who have a long time horizon. After the sales commissions are paid, it takes a while to build up a substantial amount of cash value and realize the benefits of tax-free accumulation.

With variable life, clients should emphasize the subaccounts resembling stock funds, because stocks likely will provide the greatest long-term payoff. Variable life tends to be more expensive than other types of cash value insurance, so clients will need the high returns that equities may provide to justify those costs over time.

To reduce the risks of the equity subaccounts, your clients can direct their premiums to stable-income subaccounts for "parking," then move the money into stocks on a periodic basis to achieve dollar cost averaging. With a time horizon of 15 years or longer, well-managed variable life equity subaccounts should ride out any market corrections and deliver significant returns to investors.

Assuming there's a time horizon of 15 years or longer and a commitment to equities, variable life insurance can be a good choice for several types of clients. For example, you might be working with business owners or professionals who don't want to sponsor a retirement plan for employees. Such clients might consider using variable life insurance as a retirement plan that's solely for themselves. Alternatively, some clients might participate in a retirement plan and want to go beyond the limits they can contribute. Here, variable life insurance can serve as a supplement.

College education funding may be another practical application of variable life. A policy that's bought for a newborn will have 18 years of buildup; over almost any 18-year time period, stocks are likely to do well. Clients can then start taking money from the cash value when college payments come due. If the insured should die in the meantime, the death benefits may be used for college costs.

In addition, some clients are very concerned about asset protection. In many states, life insurance policies can't be attached by a creditor. (Stocks, bonds, and mutual funds may be vulnerable to creditors.) Thus, there are clients who'll prefer to do their investing through variable life insurance.

Winning the Endgame

Although variable life insurance death benefits are income tax–free, they may not be "tax-free." If the policy is owned by your client, it will be included in his taxable estate and subject to estate tax.

Can't the policy be owned by another party or by a trust to remove it from the client's estate? Certainly, but that means your client will depend on that other party or the trustee to take policy loans or withdrawals and distribute the cash, if necessary. Your client will lose control over the policy. That's the trade-off: If a client wants absolute access to the cash value, the client will have to accept the inclusion of death benefits in his or her taxable estate.

Therefore, the use of variable life insurance as part retirement plan, part family protection may be best suited for clients of moderate means. Current law allows people to have $1 million in net worth ($2 million for married couples) and not owe any estate tax, provided they die after 2005. Clients who fall below those thresholds may be good candidates for this hybrid use of variable life insurance because the policy proceeds won't be halved by estate tax. Clients who have more than $1 million ($2 million if married) in net worth may not need to supplement retirement income by tapping their variable life insurance cash value.

The main appeal of variable life insurance may be its can-win, can't-lose outlook. Money invested in such policies may enjoy stock market appreciation without current taxation, and distributions also may escape income tax. Investors can't accomplish that with straight mutual fund investing, qualified retirement plans, or IRAs. Whether or not the cash value is needed, the policyholder's beneficiary will receive a death benefit at some point, also free of income tax.

Stocking Up

Although variable life insurance can serve as a hybrid, that's not necessarily the case. Some clients will want to use variable life mainly for protection purposes or for estate liquidity; estate tax can be avoided if the policy is held by a child or by a trust. Indeed, certain types of trusts are used primarily to hold life insurance out of the insured individual's taxable estate. For those types of trusts, variable life insurance may be an excellent holding.

Why would variable life be chosen over other types of permanent life insurance? In an era when clients are urged to use equities to meet long-term financial goals, using bond-type vehicles to fund life insurance policies may not be appropriate. Over the long term, the cost of any type of insurance likely will come down if the premiums are invested in equities.

In essence, clients who buy variable life and earn equity-level returns likely will get more insurance coverage for their dollar than clients who buy universal or whole life policies and earn bond-level returns. With the variable universal (flexible-premium) policies that have become popular, clients who enjoy strong subaccount performance can maintain premiums and see cash values as well as death benefits rise, or they can trim premium payments in the future yet still sustain insurance coverage.

Therefore, clients must understand and be comfortable with the stock market if they're to be suitable prospects for variable life. The market will go up and down; clients have to be prepared to live with that.

The younger the client, the more appropriate variable life may be. At relatively young ages, variable life isn't that much more expensive than other types of permanent life insurance. As clients get older, the difference tends to increase. In addition, younger clients will have more years to hold onto the policy and take advantage of stock market appreciation. The longer the holding period, the more likely that variable life will live up to its promise. Second-to-die variable life policies are gaining acceptance for estate planning. These policies usually are designed to pay off when both spouses die and estate taxes are due. Over time, estates may grow, and so will the estate tax obligation. Variable life may be able to grow as well, to keep up with the tax bill. Policies typically are held in trust to avoid estate taxes, so the policy's cash value would be available to the trust beneficiaries, not to the insured individual.

Shedding Light on Illustrations

Most variable life policies are sold with the aid of a policy illustration, a computer-generated printout showing cash values and death benefits in future years. However, when recommending variable life to clients, you need to be cautious about overemphasizing policy illustrations, which are merely estimates. Some insurers and advisors have run into liability problems by touting "vanishing premium" policies where the premiums never vanished or reappeared after a few years.

Securities and Exchange Commission (SEC) rules prohibit variable life illustrations from using projected returns over 12%. That's a gross return, before fees—net of fees, a 12% illustrated return is comparable to a 10.2% or 10.3% total return from a mutual fund, as reported by the leading services, so that may be a reasonable long-term projection. According to Morningstar, domestic stock funds posted an average 15.6% total return for the past 10 years, through 1998.

Even though a 12% gross return might be reasonable, you may be reluctant to rely on such numbers in a policy illustration. If that's the case, you can ask the insurer for an illustration showing potential annual returns at 8%, perhaps, or 10%. You might also ask for illustrations at 6% and even 0%, to show a full range of possible outcomes to your clients. Aggressive illustrations may expose advisors to liability if the subaccounts don't perform well and the consequences have not been adequately disclosed to clients.

If clients plan to keep funding a variable life policy, there should be no problem. However, if the plan is to build up and then tap cash value, you'd better keep a close eye on the cash value buildup. You might prefer a variable life policy that's overfunded (extra premiums paid), not minimum-funded, in order to provide some breathing room. Indeed, clients who want to know how little they can pay may not be suitable for variable life. Advisors who recommend variable life policies using minimum funding may be heading for trouble.

You should scrutinize fees and expenses, too. One approach is to write to a number of variable life insurers on a client's behalf, telling them what the client wants to spend and what assumptions you want to use. The illustrations you'll receive in return likely will show huge long-term variations in cash values and death benefits from one policy to another—going from an insurer with high expenses to one with low expenses can make a big difference.

Success in a variable life policy depends not only on the fee structure but also on the ability of the subaccounts' managers. Nevertheless, continued strength in stocks likely will benefit most policyholders. After a long bull market, some clients have become true stock market believers—and variable life prospects—while others fear the market as being too pricey. You might tell clients that paying variable life premiums over a period of years is a form of dollar cost averaging. Over time, regular investing in the equity subaccounts is likely to pay off.

Indeed, that's another difference between investing in variable life and investing in variable annuities. Many (perhaps most) variable annuities are bought with a single premium. However, if a client buys any life insurance policy—including variable life—with one premium, he or she has purchased not true life insurance but a *modified endowment contract* (see Chapter 10). In that case, tax-free loans and withdrawals are not permitted.

Therefore, to make the most of variable life, clients should make relatively equal premium payments over a period of at least five years. If they do so, not only will they enjoy full life insurance tax benefits, they'll reduce their risk of mistiming the stock market.

Hard Times

With all the benefits of variable life, why do these policies lag variable annuities in terms of total assets? Often, that's a function of what brokers and financial planners wish to sell.

Virtually anyone who can hold a pen can buy a variable annuity without having to clear an obstacle course of blood tests, urine samples, and so on. Selling a variable life insurance policy means more work, so some advisors don't bother. However, the extra bother may turn out to be well worth the effort in terms of increased wealth to clients and their families.

Recap

- With variable life insurance, clients can direct their premium payments among many investment options.

- No tax will be owed on the investment buildup.

- Clients may supplement their retirement income by taking policy loans and withdrawals, effectively tapping investment gains, tax-free.

- Eventually, variable life policies will pay a death benefit that's free of income tax.

- Therefore, variable life insurance offers a way for clients to invest and never pay any income tax.

- Although variable life can be a powerful investment tool, it's appropriate only for clients who have a loved one to receive the insurance proceeds.

Heads You Win, Tails You Don't Lose

Modified Endowment Contracts for You and Your Heirs

As we discussed in Chapter 8, variable annuities have become incredibly popular investment vehicles. In October 1998, *Financial Planning* magazine reported that, "The variable annuity juggernaut keeps on charging forward. Second-quarter sales are up 17% from the first quarter and 27% compared with the second quarter of last year." *Barron's* predicted that sales of variable annuities would top $100 billion in 1998.

What's more, variable annuities are just part of the deferred annuity marketplace. Conservative investors continue to pour billions more into fixed annuities. Between fixed and variable annuities, millions of Americans have invested sizable sums in search of tax shelter.

Many of those investors could have done better. Deferred annuities (fixed and variable) often are purchased with a single large up-front premium, anywhere from $25,000 to sums reaching well into six figures. If your clients are considering such an outlay, you might advise them to look into a little-known alternative, the *modified endowment contract* (MEC).

Life History

To understand the advantages of a MEC (rhymes with check), you need to know a little history. In the 1980s, single-premium life insurance emerged as a hot tax shelter, pitched heavily by brokerage firms and insurance companies. As the name indicates, consumers could buy life insurance with one premium.

These policies were structured so that relatively little life insurance was purchased with that one premium. Instead, most of the money went into the policy's cash value, where it could compound on a tax-deferred basis. Single-premium life insurance issuers often promised annual returns of 8% or 9%.

Thus, a $50,000 single premium would grow to $100,000 in 8 or 9 years, to $200,000 in 15 or 20 years. A 50-year-old investor could expect to have an impressive amount of cash value by retirement age.

At that point, he could start to take tax-free loans and withdrawals. With $200,000 in cash value, he might withdraw $15,000 per year (30% of his original investment) each year for the rest of his life and still provide $250,000 or so worth of life insurance benefits for his family.

In short, single-premium life was sold heavily as a "tax-free retirement plan" that did not have to comply with all the government regulations covering IRAs, 401(k)s, and so on. The life insurance benefits were sold as a *kicker,* an extra benefit for loved ones in the event of the investor's untimely death.

Slamming the Door

Sales of single-premium life grew so rapidly that the IRS complained to Congress, which ended this "abusive tax shelter" in 1988. Existing policies were grandfathered: They retained the aforementioned tax benefits as long as the policies weren't changed. New policies, however, are covered by the new rules.

Ever since the passage of that 1988 law, permanent life insurance has been subject to a *seven-pay test.* This test must be met in order for life insurance to qualify for a key tax benefit: tax-free loans and withdrawals. (Note that the other two major tax benefits of life insurance were not affected. All life insurance policies still qualify for tax-free investment buildup and income tax–free death benefits, regardless of whether they meet this test.)

The seven-pay test is meant to insure that life insurance is bought as insurance, with a series of premiums paid over a period of years. Despite the name, most insurers and their tax advisors feel that this test can be met if substantially equal amounts are paid for at least five years. Whether the minimum is five years or seven years, though, one point is clear: Single-premium life insurance no longer qualifies for all the tax advantages of life insurance.

The new law did not state that life insurance cannot be purchased with a single premium. Instead, insurance policies that do not meet the seven-pay test were called *modified endowment contracts,* or MECs.

Thus, the single-premium life insurance policies of the 1980s became the MECs of the 1990s.

Win without Losing

Under the 1988 law, when money is borrowed or withdrawn from a MEC, the investment income will be taxed immediately. Suppose a client invests $100,000 in a MEC and the cash value grows to $150,000 in five years. If the client wants to take money from the MEC, the first $50,000 will be subject to income tax. After that $50,000, further loans or withdrawals will be tax-free returns of the client's own money.

In addition, there's a 10% penalty tax for any taxable withdrawals or policy loans before the policy owner turns age 59½. (The MEC distribution rules are similar to those that apply to withdrawals from a deferred annuity, which is explained in Chapter 5.)

Naturally, MECs fell out of favor after this law was implemented. If clients are going to buy permanent life insurance, they might as well spread out the premiums and buy real life insurance, where money can be borrowed or withdrawn tax-free.

Thus, MECs do not compare well with permanent life insurance policies. However, when MECs are compared with deferred annuities, another picture emerges.

As mentioned, many deferred annuities are purchased with a single premium. What's more, most deferred annuities are not annuitized. (Reportedly, only 1% of annuity investors annuitize their contracts.) Thus, investors often buy an annuity with a single premium and let the money build up until they die. At that time, all the deferred income tax must be paid.

MECs can offer a better deal. A client can buy a MEC with a single premium and let the money build up until death. At that point, no deferred income tax will be due; in fact, under the laws covering life insurance, the client's beneficiary must receive a death benefit that's larger than the cash value.

What if the client needs money during his or her lifetime? In that situation, a MEC looks just like a deferred annuity. Income tax will be owed on loans and withdrawals up to the amount of earnings on the premium that was paid, with a 10% penalty tax before age 59½. The laws are the same for both a MEC and a deferred annuity.

MECs are known as "turbocharged annuities" for these reasons.

- They provide the same tax-deferred buildup as an investor would get with a single-premium deferred annuity.

- Loans and withdrawals from a MEC are taxed the same as loans and withdrawals from a deferred annuity.

- If the investor dies without ever needing the money, a MEC will pay a much larger death benefit than a deferred annuity.

Heads (the money is not needed) and the client's heirs win; tails (the money is needed) and the client doesn't lose. That's why MECs compare favorably with single-premium deferred annuities.

Ahead at the Finish

That's not to say that MECs are right for every client. Often, MECs are heavy on cash value and relatively light on life insurance. Therefore, clients who are mainly interested in buying the most insurance protection for the lowest possible premium are usually not good candidates for MECs.

The picture changes, though, when you're working with a client who's considering a single-premium deferred annuity (SPDA). Perhaps you're thinking about recommending that a client pull a five- or six-figure sum from a CD or a taxable mutual fund and buy an SPDA, fixed or variable.

The big selling point for SPDAs versus bank accounts and securities is the tax-deferred accumulation. At some point, though, the tax deferral will cease and the tax will become due. That may occur during the client's life or after death, but it will occur.

Suppose, for example, a client invests $100,000 in an SPDA that grows at a 9% rate. After 16 years, the SPDA will be worth some $400,000, of which $300,000 is taxable. If the client annuitizes the contract, the money will be paid out each month and most of each payment will be taxable.

If the client dies before annuitizing, the income tax bill will become due immediately at the spouse's death, within five years, or in monthly payments, depending on the contract and the beneficiary's decisions. In any event, that $300,000 gain will be subject to income tax. If it's taxed at the client's death at a 40% rate, only $280,000 will be left to distribute to the beneficiary.

A MEC may be a viable alternative. During the client's life, it looks like an SPDA. There are fixed and variable MECs; investment income is sheltered from income tax. Withdrawals from a MEC are taxed the same as withdrawals from a deferred annuity.

At death, though, the MEC delivers the tax advantage of a life insurance policy: no income tax on the death benefit. What's more, the death benefit must be larger than the cash value, so there will be a bonus, not an income tax haircut, for the client's beneficiaries. Depending on the client's age and health when he or she put $100,000 into a MEC, it might pay $450,000, $500,000 or more if the client dies 16 years later.

Different Strokes

On the downside, clients who are extremely old or ill may find MECs virtually impossible to obtain. Even for healthy clients, the life insurance in a MEC has a price. As the client grows older, mortality costs increase, eroding the returns in a MEC.

The extra mortality cost might shave a 9% return in an SPDA to 8% or 8.5% in a MEC, other factors being equal. Instead of growing to

$400,000 in an SPDA, that $100,000 outlay might become only $340,000 or $370,000 in a similar MEC. (See Table 10.1.)

The bottom line? An SPDA works better if your client is investing for greater retirement income. On the other hand, if the money won't be needed during the client's lifetime, a MEC will be the superior choice.

Indeed, clients can use MECs as a means to transfer wealth from one generation to another. As long as there are a lot of other dollars around for retirement income, money that would merely be warehoused can go into a MEC.

Moreover, a MEC may be an option for a client who wants a tax-deferred savings vehicle as well as some life insurance. When you sit down with a client who needs life insurance, you can recommend various payment options. Some clients will prefer to fund a policy with additional premium dollars up front to reduce the necessity of making future payments.

In addition to wealth transfer, a MEC may be useful for long-term care planning. Some MECs permit policyholders to accelerate the death benefit in case custodial care is needed, either at home or in a nursing home: Policyholders might have access to 2% of the death benefit per month.

Suppose a client buys a MEC for $100,000 and gets a $300,000 death benefit. If long-term care is needed, up to $6,000 per month may be paid out. This money may be income tax–free because it's an accel-

TABLE 10.1 Comparing SPDA and MEC Policies

	SPDA	MEC
Amount invested	$100,000	$100,000
Buildup after 16 years	400,000	340,000
Investment earnings	300,000	240,000
Tax on investment earnings	120,000	0
Net to heirs at death	280,000	450,000

Note: Figures are examples of possible outcomes.

eration of the death benefit. If the client had invested $100,000 in an SPDA, withdrawals for long-term care would be taxable.

Money that a client holds in a MEC account should generally be the last funds spent—after using up IRAs, deferred annuities, mutual funds, and individual securities. That's because there are exceptional tax benefits for the beneficiaries of those who hold onto their MECs until death.

With an inherited MEC, all the investment buildup that's been enjoyed stays in the family: No capital gains tax is ever paid!

Tops for Trusts

For some clients, there may be another advantage to MECs as compared to SPDAs. We mentioned in Chapter 8 that a nonnatural person cannot buy a deferred annuity and enjoy the tax deferral. If a corporation, a partnership, or a certain type of trust holds a deferred annuity, the income will be taxable each year.

A MEC, on the other hand, may be held by such entities. For example, take the typical estate plan for a client with $2 million, where $1 million goes to the widow and the other $1 million to the client's children (assuming a death after 2005). Because of the unified gift and estate tax credit, the $1 million left to the children will escape estate tax, while the $1 million left to the widow will also be untaxed because it's a marital bequest.

In most cases, the $1 million left to the children will go into an irrevocable trust, which might be called a *B trust,* a *credit shelter trust,* or a *family trust.* The trustee likely will have the ability to distribute cash to the widow in case the $1 million she inherits proves inadequate. At her death, the trust assets pass to the children.

How should the trustee invest the trust fund? Some of the money might go into a MEC covering the life of the widow or be split between a fixed and a variable MEC. The money invested in MECs can build up, free of income taxes. If the widow needs funds, the trustee can tap the MECs and make taxable distributions. At the widow's death, the MECs will pay a death benefit to the children, named as beneficiaries. No income or estate tax will be due, and all the investment income will be passed on tax-free.

Indeed, a MEC may be purchased by and held in any irrevocable trust. If a client's main goal is wealth transfer, and tapping the cash value is not expected, holding a MEC in an irrevocable trust may reduce estate tax as well as income tax. This strategy means the client has no access to the MEC's cash value, although the trustee may borrow from the MEC and distribute funds to the trust beneficiaries.

The decision on whether or not to use a trust for holding a MEC is no different than the decision on using a trust for holding a standard life insurance policy: If a trust is the appropriate owner for the insurance, that's where it should go. In trust, the policy proceeds will be sheltered from estate tax as well as from creditors. Writing one big check for the policy or a stream of different checks is another decision—one that determines whether your client buys a MEC or traditional life insurance.

Flex Plans

Beyond the preceding tax benefits, MECs enjoy all the other advantages of permanent life insurance: tax-free exchange privileges, creditor protection, privacy, probate avoidance. As long as no money is withdrawn, MEC buildup isn't counted as income for the purpose of calculating taxes on Social Security benefits.

Clients who buy MECs are not locked in. They have considerable leeway to switch among them without owing any taxes. Suppose, for example, a client buys a fixed MEC paying 7%. A few years later, when it's time to reset the rate, the issuer puts it at 5%. At the same time, another top-ranked company is offering 8% on its fixed MECs. Your client can switch from one to the other and earn the higher rate. (As a practical matter, this ability of investors to exchange MECs keeps issuers from lowballing rates. To protect your clients, look for a bailout clause that allows a buyer to switch MECs, free of surrender charges, if the fixed interest rate drops by a certain amount.)

Investors can switch from one variable MEC to another if investment performance lags the market. Again, they should look for MECs that permit switches without surrender charges or at least curtail the surrender charges. Often, a surrender charge will dwindle each year until disappearing altogether, perhaps after six or seven years.

Clients can switch freely among MECs, regardless of whether they're fixed or variable. The account balance won't be reduced as long as surrender charges are avoided. Under Section 1035 of the Internal Revenue Code, no income tax or penalty tax is due when one MEC is exchanged for another. (Section 1035 also permits tax-free switches among annuities and life insurance policies.)

Mastering MECs

How can you help clients choose among MECs? For fixed MECs, look for a financially strong issuer, rated AA or higher by Standard & Poor's, Moody's, or Duff & Phelps, or rated as A+ by A.M. Best. You should also ask about a company's history of setting investment yields: Avoid issuers with a practice of starting out with attractive rates and then dropping them sharply.

For variable MECs, look for a wide range of investment accounts managed by respected professionals. Often, portfolio managers of top-performing mutual funds are responsible for MEC accounts. Pay particular attention to the stock funds; if clients invest in a variable MEC, they'll likely want most of their money invested in stocks.

For both types of MECs, investigate the surrender charges. Clients should not have to pay a 10% fee forever to move money into another MEC.

Finding MECs may not be easy, particularly the variable MECs that are likely to appeal to investment-oriented clients. While there are literally hundreds of variable annuities on the market, only a few dozen companies offer variable MECs. Thus, advisors need to do some work to find one that meets the needs of a particular client.

The Near-MEC Solution

A client doesn't have to buy a MEC. If he or she has $100,000 to invest, for example, it can go into a side fund that will gradually pay premiums on a life insurance policy that's eligible for tax-free policy loans. With careful planning, your client can have all the advantages of a MEC without the downside. Here's a simple strategy:

1. Your client can put the cash intended for the investment into a money market fund or some other liquid account.

2. Then the client can buy life insurance—a variable universal life (VUL) insurance policy offers investment options and flexible premium payments.

3. Premiums can be paid from the liquid account for the next five years, so the client winds up with a policy that's projected to be paid up, without need of future premiums.

4. By working with a savvy insurance professional, your client can maximize the life insurance premiums paid each year (and the tax-deferred buildup inside the cash value) without running into the MEC rules.

The more money front-loaded into the policy, the greater the amount earning tax-free buildup. By putting in just enough but not too much, clients will avoid the MEC restrictions on lifetime distributions. As a result, by carefully monitoring such a "near-MEC," your client can wind up with the opportunity to take tax-free loans and withdrawals if he or she needs the money. The client can pay additional premiums, if desired, for a greater cash value and death benefit.

Nevertheless, some clients may prefer to put their money into MECs right away to maximize the tax-deferred buildup. As with annuities and permanent life insurance, clients who buy MECs will incur fees and charges that may be substantial. They should insist on full disclosure before investing. Generally, if they're in for the long term (at least 15 years), the tax advantages will outweigh the added costs. (See Appendix D.)

Recap

- A life insurance policy bought with a single large payment is a modified endowment contract (MEC).

- MECs receive most of the tax benefits of life insurance, but they do not offer the chance for tax-free policy loans and withdrawals.

- Clients who are considering buying a single-premium deferred annuity may be better off buying a MEC, which can be fixed or variable.

- While clients are alive, they can tap a MEC in the same way they can tap an annuity.

- When clients die, their beneficiaries will receive much more from a MEC than from a deferred annuity.

- By spreading their premiums over a few years, clients can enjoy most of the investment advantages of a MEC along with all the tax advantages of life insurance.

Real Shelters

The Payoff in Property Ownership

The bull market in stocks during the 1980s and 1990s changed a lot of minds. Just before this surge began, in mid-1982, so-called experts were saying that "equities are dead." After all, the Dow Jones Industrials first grazed the 1,000 mark in early 1966, reaching 995, and were mired at 777 in August 1982, more than 16 years later. Who wanted to buy stocks?

During this time period, investors turned their eyes toward real estate. Property prices shot up and fortunes were made. This success, in turn, led to widespread failure. Real estate was so popular that too many properties were built, tenants could not be found, and real estate went through its own turmoil in the late 1980s and early 1990s.

Boom or bust, you likely will have some clients who own investment property. If the real estate recovery that began in the mid-1990s continues, more clients will want to participate; that's especially true if the stock market hits another long period of stagnation. Therefore, you probably should be familiar with the risks as well as the rewards of real estate investing.

Double-Edged Sword

From an investment perspective, the key advantage of investing in real estate is the potential use of leverage. A $1 million property often can be purchased with $200,000, or even $100,000, in cash. When the market is strong, this leverage leads to enormous profits.

Suppose, for example, a client buys a $1 million property with a $200,000 (20%) down payment, borrowing (getting a mortgage for) the other $800,000. A year later, the building sells for $1.2 million. Your client can repay the $800,000 loan and pocket $400,000. On a 20% gain in property value (from $1 million to $1.2 million), your client has a 100% profit.

Of course, leverage cuts the other way, too. Suppose the building drops 20% in value, to $800,000. With an $800,000 loan outstanding, your client has no equity in the building and loses 100% of his or her money.

There are other disadvantages to owning real estate directly. Such investments take time and effort; clients who don't want to handle matters directly will have to hire a property manager, which will reduce their returns. What's more, real estate is an illiquid asset. If your client decides to sell, it might take months to find a buyer at an acceptable price.

Offsetting these negatives, though, is yet another factor: the tax code. Real estate investments enjoy many tax advantages that can turn a good deal into a great one.

Appreciating Depreciation

Investment real estate can be depreciated over 39 years, or 27.5 years for residential property. Depreciation deductions are limited to the structures and not the land. Thus, you might think depreciation deductions would be about 2.5% to 4% per year. However, investment properties also include components (furnishings, partitions) that qualify for seven-year depreciation. Some savvy accounting may lead to as much as 75% of a building's cost qualifying for 7-year rather than 39-year depreciation.

For some investors, then, the annual depreciation likely will be much more than 2.5% of the property's cost. What's more, depreciation will be taken on the entire cost, not just on the cash down payment.

Suppose, for example, that Ed Barnes buys an investment property for $1 million and that depreciation deductions come to 6% of that amount, or $60,000. If Ed has paid $200,000 in cash, his depreciation deduction will be 30% of the total.

Why are depreciation deductions so important? Because they're a noncash expense. They reduce the amount of gain (or increase the loss) that's reported to the IRS, but they don't come out of an investor's pocket. What's more, depreciation deductions may be taken even though the property is actually appreciating in value. Because of this seeming paradox, depreciation deductions can provide some further tax advantages for investors.

Phantom Losses

Suppose, in the preceding example, that Ed Barnes receives $100,000 per year in rent from his $1 million property and that his cash expenses (including his payments on a $800,000 loan) come to $100,000. From Ed's point of view, he has broken even.

To the IRS, though, Ed reports a $60,000 loss, thanks to his $60,000 noncash depreciation deduction. Can Ed deduct this $60,000 from other income? Probably not. Under the tax code, a loss from an investment in rental real estate is considered a *passive loss*. Such passive losses generally can be deducted only if Ed is in the real estate business or if Ed has a like amount of *passive income,* perhaps from another real estate investment.

However, another provision of the tax code may permit Ed to deduct some of those passive losses. Taxpayers with adjusted gross income (AGI) of $100,000 or less can deduct $25,000 worth of passive losses per year. As AGI increases by $2, the allowable loss shrinks by $1, so that no deduction is permitted by the time AGI reaches $150,000.

Suppose, for example, Ed's AGI this year is $138,000. He loses $19,000 worth of his allowable passive loss, bringing the deduction down to $6,000.

Ed's AGI	$138,000
Amount over $100,000 threshold	38,000
Penalty for excess AGI ($38,000 × ½)	19,000
Basic passive loss deduction	25,000
Net passive loss deduction ($25,000 − $19,000)	6,000

Still, this isn't a bad deal for Ed. While his real estate breaks even, he gets to deduct $6,000. Assuming a 35% effective tax rate, he saves $2,100 per year in tax.

There are a few conditions for Ed to meet in order to get the passive loss deduction as described. Most important, he must take an active role in managing the property. He can hire a property manager if he wishes, but he must play some part in setting rents, approving capital expenditures, setting standards for tenants, and so forth.

Ed does not have to own the building by himself to qualify for this tax break. He can be one of a group of investors and deduct his pro rata share of any loss as long as his ownership interest is at least 10%. However, if he is a limited partner he can't deduct any passive losses.

In the preceding example, when Ed deducts $6,000 of his $60,000 loss, what happens to the other $54,000? That amount is carried forward, along with carryforwards from other years. When Ed finally sells the property, those built-up passive losses can be used to reduce the tax he'll owe then.

Free Cash

Suppose, after a few years, Ed's cash flow from rents increases to $120,000 but his expenses move up to only $110,000. (Debt service, his largest expense, is fixed.) Now Ed actually is putting $10,000 in cash into his pocket. However, if depreciation deductions remain at $60,000, he'll show a $50,000 loss to the IRS.

Thus, his $10,000 in positive cash flow will be tax-free. (In truth, his basis will be reduced, so his future taxable gain will be greater.) What's more, Ed can deduct up to $25,000 of that passive loss as long as his AGI is below $150,000 for the year.

Another tactic can provide Ed with even more tax-free cash. Suppose, over the years, Ed's cash flow keeps increasing faster than his expenses increase. Not only will Ed have more cash to put into his pocket—sheltered from income tax by depreciation deductions—but his property's value may increase as well.

At some point, the building he purchased for $1 million may be worth $1.5 million. If that's the case, he might be able to refinance the property. Assuming the same 80% loan-to-value ratio, he'd be able to borrow $1.2 million. Then he could pay off his old $800,000 loan and pocket the extra $400,000. Not only would this amount be twice his original outlay, it would be tax-free, because loan proceeds aren't included in taxable income.

As long as his property keeps appreciating and rents keep growing, Ed may be able to keep refinancing, pulling tax-free cash from the property.

Happy Endings

How will Ed wind up his real estate investment? He has several options.

1. *He can sell the property.* In this case, the tax bill may be steep. Suppose, for example, Ed has taken $600,000 worth of depreciation deductions over 10 years. Now his basis in the $1 million property has been reduced to $400,000. If he sells the property for $1.5 million, his taxable gain will be $1.1 million, not $500,000.

Original basis in property	$1,000,000
Depreciation deductions (10 years × $60,000/yr.)	(600,000)
Depreciated basis in property	400,000
Selling price	1,500,000
Taxable gain (selling price minus depreciated basis)	1,100,000

   Of that $1.1 million, the $600,000 in depreciation deductions already taken would be "recaptured" at a 25% rate while the $500,000 in price appreciation would be taxed at the 20% rate on long-term capital gains. Altogether, Ed would owe $250,000 in tax.

Depreciation recapture ($600,000 @ 25%)	$150,000
Long-term gain ($500,000 @20%)	100,000
Total tax	$250,000

Moreover, that $250,000 would be only the *federal* income tax. State and possibly local taxes would be due as well. Still, that's not a terrible outcome, considering that Ed has sold the property for $1.5 million.

Sales proceeds	$1,500,000
Minus debt repayment	(800,000)
Minus taxes payable	(250,000)
Net proceeds	$450,000

On his $200,000 outlay, Ed would have an after-tax return of 125% after 10 years. That's in addition to the tax savings and cash flow he has enjoyed over the years. What's more, it's likely that his tax bill won't be as high as indicated: Any unused passive losses can be deducted at this point, offsetting the taxable gain on sale.

2. *He can hold the property.* Nevertheless, Ed may not want to pay $250,000, $150,000, or even $50,000 in tax after selling his property. Another option, as noted, would be for Ed to hold onto his property and keep borrowing against its value, tax-free. If he holds onto it, he'll never owe any capital gains tax.

Ed may hold onto the property until he dies. If that's the case, Ed's heirs will inherit with a basis that's stepped up to market value. Even if Ed has depreciated the property down to zero and the heirs sell it soon after Ed's death for $2 million, no capital gains tax will be due.

Trading Places

Ed may not want to own this particular property until he dies, however. Suppose he owns a professional office building near his home in Illinois. He has always devoted a great deal of time and effort to this property, but now he wants to move to California and slow down a bit. Will he have to (1) sell his office building or (2) become an absentee landlord?

Fortunately, there's another solution. Ed can sell his old property without owing tax by reinvesting the proceeds in new investment property. As long as he pays close attention to the rules, the entire transaction will qualify as a tax-deferred exchange. What's more, he can defer the capital gains tax indefinitely, until it disappears altogether at his death.

Tax-deferred exchanges, also called *like-kind exchanges,* are specifically permitted by Section 1031 of the tax code. Investors must exchange investment property rather than personal residences, but the properties can be dissimilar. For example, Ed can exchange his office building for an apartment house or a shopping center or even a marina on the California coastline.

In practice, property exchanges are seldom a one-for-one value. It's unlikely that Ed would find a marina owner in California who's willing to do a straight exchange for his office building in Illinois. Most exchanges are multiparty deferred exchanges, often involving the services of a third party known as an *accommodator.* (You may be able to find such an intermediary through a local real estate agent.)

To see how a tax-deferred exchange might work, assume that Ed sells his Illinois office building for $1.5 million. The proceeds from this sale go not into Ed's bank account but to the intermediary, who puts the money into an escrow account. (Relatives and people involved in a business relationship with Ed can't act as intermediaries.) Thus, the money is never under Ed's control.

To protect all the parties involved, a formal contract should be in place between Ed and the intermediary stating that an exchange is planned. Ed can secure the sale proceeds from his property by insisting that the intermediary provide a third-party guarantee, such as a bank letter of credit.

Watching the Clock

After Ed sells his property, a clock starts. He has 45 days to identify potential replacement properties, in writing, to the intermediary. Several properties may be identified (in case an intended acquisition falls through): up to three properties of any value or any number of properties with an aggregate value no more than 200% of the price Ed received for his property.

Simultaneous to the 45-day clock, another time period is under way. Ed has 180 days from the time he sells his property to actually close a deal for replacement property.

When that purchase is made, the intermediary takes the money out of escrow and uses the funds to buy the replacement property. Ed thus has shifted ownership from one property to another without ever touching cash from a sale. He has entered into an exchange, so capital gains taxes are deferred.

There are other forms of exchanges. Suppose, for example, Ed finds a buyer for his office building in Illinois. If that buyer is willing, he can buy the marina in California, then trade it for Ed's building.

Tax-deferred exchanges may be more complex, involving multiple parties. No matter what form of exchange is used, though, there are certain criteria that must be met for taxes to be deferred:

- The amount paid for the replacement property must be at least as much as the amount received for the property that was sold.

- All the cash received must be reinvested in the new property.

- Any debt relief must be replaced by a combination of new debt and additional cash put into the new property.

If the first two requirements are met, the third will fall into place. A seller who winds up with net cash or net debt relief will have taxable income known as *boot*.

To illustrate, suppose that Ed sells his property for $1.5 million and that he had $800,000 worth of debt outstanding. After paying off the mortgage, he nets $700,000. To get the tax deferral, he'd have to make a cash down payment of at least $700,000 in the new property.

What's his basis in the new property? The purchase price minus the deferred gain. If the marina costs $1.5 million, and a $1.1 million taxable gain is deferred, Ed's new basis is $400,000.

Sunnier Climes

Intermediaries receive either a flat fee or a percentage of the amount they hold. Thus, investors need to weigh the fee versus the value of the tax deferral. On highly mortgaged properties, where a large portion of any sale goes to debt repayment, property exchanges may be particularly valuable.

Many exchanges involve relocation, where a seller does not want to keep a long-distance watch on investment property. Another common reason for an exchange is the desire to own property in a vacation area. In such cases, there may be some controversy about how long replacement property must remain investment property.

Suppose, for example, a client swaps a rental property close to home for a rental condo in Boca Raton. To qualify for a tax-deferred exchange, the Florida condo must be held out for rental, and personal use is limited to 14 days or 10% of the days the condo is rented, whichever is greater.

What if your client eventually decides to stop renting the condo and uses it for a residence or a vacation home? There are no regulations or case law on this subject, but the property should be held as investment property for at least a year. After that, conversion to personal use has smaller tax risk.

Going the other way, a client might be able to implement a tax-deferred exchange on a personal residence. Suppose Ron Harris is selling a highly appreciated residence and the usual $250,000 tax exclusion rule doesn't provide total shelter. Ron might first convert his old residence to investment property, renting it out for at least a year. Once it has been established as investment property, it can be swapped for another investment property, and the capital gains can be deferred, perhaps indefinitely.

Remember, though, when you discuss capital gains deferral with your clients that any property held until death may be subject to estate tax. What's more, it may not be easy for heirs to sell the property quickly in order to raise the funds for estate tax payments. To make things easier for those heirs, liquid assets should be available to cover estate tax obligations; life insurance may be a practical means of providing that liquidity.

Go Now, Deduct Later

Sizable gains can be made from investment property and tax benefits can enhance those gains. On the other hand, don't think that there's easy money to be made in real estate. Successful investors tend to spend a great deal of time finding good properties, buying them at the right price, and then monitoring operations. For that reason, you're probably better off investing in property near your home, where you can spot a good location and keep an eye on your property.

That may be the rule, but there are still plenty of people who buy investment property in a remote location. Wall Streeters buy ski chalets in Colorado; Main Streeters buy apartments in college towns so their children will have a place to live while they're students.

In such situations, real estate investors naturally take trips to visit those properties. Are those trips deductible? That depends. If clients keep good records and the expenses involved are in line with the potential profits the properties may produce, you may discover yet another tax advantage of investment real estate.

Recap

- Real estate investors can take deductions for depreciation, a non-cash expense.

- Depreciation deductions may enable investors to deduct paper losses, to receive untaxed cash flow, or both.

- Successful real estate investments permit property owners to tap their profits, tax-free, by borrowing.

- Instead of selling investment property and paying tax, many investors prefer to enter into tax-deferred exchanges for other properties.

- When real estate is held until death, the heirs get a basis step-up allowing them to sell the property without owing capital gains tax.

- Investors with out-of-town properties may deduct the costs of visits to inspect and maintain their properties.

Blasts from the Past
Partnerships That Still Provide Shelter

After thriving during the late 1970s and early 1980s, the days of the syndicated limited partnership are now largely gone and, for many financial advisors, best forgotten. Nevertheless, a few widely sold offerings have survived, including low-income housing (LIH) partnerships. These programs have delivered the tax savings they promised, to a considerable degree, and they continue to be one of the few real tax shelters left, complete with Washington's seal of approval.

The LIH tax credit contained in the tax code offers 10 years' worth of tax breaks with a single investment. Tax credits are prefunded, or attached to a property for the full time period. Congress can't change the rules in the middle of the game and rescind the tax benefits.

Your clients can get the LIH credit on their own if they build, buy, or improve residential real estate and then rent to low- and moderate-income tenants. However, the rules are complicated enough that your clients probably will prefer investing in a syndicated limited partnership, relying on the general partner to deal with all the requirements.

Such partnerships buy apartment properties in several areas, handle the paperwork necessary to qualify for government subsidies, and make sure the apartments are occupied by suitable tenants. "Low-income" housing is not "no-income housing" rented to welfare recipients; apartments owned by these partnerships usually are occupied by retirees or by workers earning below the local median. Properties tend to be garden apartments in suburbs or small towns.

Coming Out Ahead

Although the credits run for 10 years, the period will often stretch to 11 or 12 years because it may take some time for a partnership to invest all of its capital. That is, clients may get partial tax credits in the early and later years as they phase in and phase out of the deal.

Once the partnerships are up and running, investors are expected to receive around 12% per year in tax credits. For example, suppose Lou Baker invests $10,000 in an LIH partnership. Lou is projected to receive annual tax credits of around $1,200 a year for 10 years, saving about $12,000 in taxes. That would put him ahead by $2,000 after tax.

During this period, Lou is not likely to receive much cash flow from the venture, because rents are held down for low-income tenants. A retiree living on Social Security might be paying $400 a month to rent an apartment that otherwise would be renting for $500 a month. The rental income goes almost entirely to debt service, operating expenses, and property maintenance, so there won't be much left over to distribute to investors. On the positive side, the below-market rents likely will boost occupancy rates.

What happens after the tax breaks have run their course? Some LIH partnerships may be able to refinance their properties, pulling out tax-free cash for distribution to investors. Nonprofit housing groups may purchase some properties to continue serving these tenants. Another alternative might be a sale to a new group of investors who'll be able to start the tax credit cycle all over again.

The end results may be uncertain, as is the case with any equity investment, but the bottom line is that your clients practically lock in a profit from the tax credits alone. If the real estate maintains or increases its value over the years, your clients will enjoy substantial returns.

Real Returns

At first glance, tax credit returns don't appear magnificent. A client who invests $10,000 will receive $12,000 over 10 years—a paltry 20%

profit. But that's an after-tax return (your clients won't owe income tax on tax credits), and that return is continuous, not a deferred payment from the sale of a long-term stockholding.

If the partnership's real estate has no value at the end of the holding period—an unlikely result—clients will wind up with a positive return. The tax savings alone are equivalent to a 7% annual after-tax return, considering the time value of the added cash flow. If clients receive no more than their money back from the real estate in addition to the tax credits, their effective annual return (probably 15 years after the investment) will be about 12%, after tax.

LIH tax credit investments may be especially worthwhile for clients who own C corporations. These partnerships generate passive losses that clients probably cannot use personally. However, C corporations can use passive losses to offset operating income, in addition to the LIH tax credits, so they may enjoy even greater returns from these partnerships.

Bumping the Ceiling

LIH tax credit partnerships offer upside with little downside, as well as diversification from the stock market, so they have become extremely popular. So popular, in fact, that there are limits to how many credits investors can use. For most clients, the upper limit is a *deduction equivalent* of $25,000 per year.

Suppose Lou Baker is in a 39.6% federal income tax bracket. Multiply 39.6% by $25,000 to get $9,900. That's the maximum amount of tax credits Lou can use in one year. In a lower bracket, he can use fewer credits: $7,000 worth of LIH credits in a 28% bracket, for example. (Tax credits, of course, are a dollar-for-dollar reduction in a taxpayer's obligation.) There are no income-based phaseouts, so LIH partnerships may be suitable even for your highest-income clients.

Additional LIH credits can offset any tax Lou owes on passive income, but not on investment income such as interest or dividends. Thus, if Lou owns investment property, generating taxable income from this passive activity, he can use excess LIH credits to offset that tax.

On the other hand, if Lou is deducting passive losses from actively managed property (see Chapter 11), that deduction will directly reduce his $25,000 deduction equivalent. Suppose that Lou deducts

$6,000 each year from a hands-on real estate investment. His deduction equivalent for LIH credits would be reduced to $19,000, so he can use only $7,524 in LIH tax credits (not $9,900) in a 39.6% tax bracket.

The math may be even more complicated, because the preceding scenario assumes Lou has a full $25,000 worth of income in the 39.6% bracket. Suppose, though, that he winds up the year with $10,000 in the 39.6% bracket and $15,000 in the 36% bracket. Now he'll be entitled to only $9,360 worth of tax credits for the year (not $9,900). Here's how it's calculated: With $10,000 of income in the 39.6% tax bracket, his partial deduction equivalent is $3,960 ($10,000 × 39.6%). The remainder of his $25,000 deduction equivalent will be $5,400 ($15,000 × 36%). Therefore, Lou's total deduction equivalent is $9,360 ($3,960 + $5,400).

Suppose Lou has claimed a $6,000 loss from his investment property. In this case, his maximum use of LIH credits drops to $7,200, as follows: Deduct the $6,000 investment-property loss from the $25,000 deduction equivalent, which equals $19,000. With $10,000 of income in the 39.6% tax bracket, his partial deduction equivalent is $3,960 ($10,000 × 39.6%). The remainder of his $19,000 deduction equivalent will be $3,240 ($9,000 × 36%), for a total deduction equivalent of $7,200.

It may be impossible to forecast exactly how many LIH tax credits a client will use over the next 10 to 12 years, but you should have a reasonable estimate. If you think a client will be able to use $7,000 worth of credits per year, for example, you might recommend an investment of up to $58,000. With a 12% tax credit, your client will receive about $7,000 worth of credits per year.

LIH tax credits that can't be used in a given year can be carried back three years or forward up to 15 years. Nevertheless, it doesn't pay to overinvest and receive excess credits.

Besides the risk of investing too much and receiving suspended credits, what are the other hazards of LIH partnerships? For one, the LIH credit can't be used to offset taxes below the alternative minimum tax (AMT) liability. For example, if a client's regular tax obligation is $35,000 and his AMT obligation is $33,000, he can use only $2,000 worth of tax credits.

You may need to perform some complex calculations so that a client invests enough to maximize tax credits without plunging into the AMT, now or in the future. As a rule of thumb, anyone investing over $30,000 in a tax credit partnership should check closely into his or her AMT exposure.

As another risk, participating in an LIH deal is a long-term, illiquid investment. For example, to satisfy a cash need five years from now, your client can probably sell his or her partnership shares, but new investors will expect a discount for such a bailout. Realistically, investors should plan on holding for at least 12 years.

A River of Cash Flow

A successful LIH investment may open financial planning opportunities. The tax savings can increase a client's cash flow each year by a fairly regular amount, and those savings might be invested in equity mutual funds. After 10 or 12 years of such dollar cost averaging, a substantial sum may be added to a client's portfolio.

Retirees can invest in these programs without exposing their Social Security to income tax because tax credits aren't counted in that calculation. Indeed, moderate-income retirees may wipe out all or most of their tax bills with LIH credits. The credits are not considered earned income, so benefits won't be reduced.

What's more, you may be pleasantly surprised by clients' reactions to these investments. Each year, when they file their income tax returns, they'll see the results in actual tax savings—a welcome outcome for virtually every client.

If you are interested in LIH partnerships for your clients, look for a sponsor with a successful track record. You'll want a general partner who can verify tenant eligibility, handle all the paperwork, and provide investors with clear reports.

Check on a sponsor carefully before investing; ask to speak with other investors who have at least five years of positive experiences to relate. Ask to see the sponsor's reports to investors in past programs. These reports should show tax credits throughout the program and indicate how they match the original projections. You also should ask the sponsor what help is provided to clients' accountants when it's time to prepare the necessary tax return schedules.

There are many technical requirements to comply with and many things that can go wrong; violation of the 15-year property occupancy requirements, for example, will lead to recapture of some tax credits previously taken. An experienced general partner will know how to avoid these pitfalls.

LIH partnerships can offer tax reduction, real estate participation, and something more—the opportunity to provide affordable housing for those of modest means. Some clients will appreciate the feeling of "giving something back" while they take out a significant return for themselves.

Foundation for the Future

Some tax breaks become more powerful when used in combination with other tax breaks. That's often the case with LIH tax credits.

After clients reach age 70½, for example, they have to begin taking minimum withdrawals from their IRAs. What will they do with that money? Assuming they don't need the money for retirement living, they can invest in an LIH partnership and receive tax credits that will offset the income tax due on up to $25,000 worth of plan withdrawals each year.

Some or all of the tax savings can be transferred to an irrevocable trust. Once the money is in trust, the trustee can invest in permanent life insurance, in growth stocks, in municipal bonds, or in a combination of these. The trust fund will grow, untaxed or lightly taxed.

As long as the trustee is cooperative, your client (and a spouse, if the client is married) can enjoy access to the trust funds. If your clients never need those funds, they can be used by the heirs to pay estate tax. In many cases, funds held in trust will exceed the estate tax obligation and the trust will retain substantial assets, providing benefits for future generations.

Net Profits

Other types of partnerships can also provide tax breaks along with portfolio diversification. For example, net lease deals offer some of the property ownership tax breaks described in Chapter 11. These are truly passive investments, about as low-risk as real estate can be. Yet yields are fairly high (around 7% to 8% as of this writing) and there is some upside potential.

A *net lease* or a *triple-net lease,* in real estate parlance, is a deal in which the tenant assumes full responsibility for all real estate–related expenses, such as taxes, insurance, and property maintenance. In addition, the tenant pays rent to the property owner.

Net leases are sometimes known as "hell or high water" leases, because the tenant puts its full faith and credit on the line. It's obliged to pay all the expenses, plus the rent, no matter what. Therefore, net leases have low risks for investors.

Naturally, the stronger the tenant's credit rating, the lower the risk to investors. There's less risk in net-leasing a storefront to Burger King, for example, than in net-leasing to a new restaurant chain.

Low risks usually mean low rewards, so clients can't expect to make a fortune in net lease deals. However, there's usually some provision to increase the initial rental income received from the tenant.

In many cases, particularly deals involving restaurants and retail stores, the tenant agrees to pay an *overage.* That is, if sales volume for the tenant exceeds certain levels, a fraction is added to the monthly rent. Or there may be an escalator based on the consumer price index (CPI) that kicks in every few years. (Net lease deals typically have lengthy initial terms, plus renewal rights for tenants.) Either way, investors have some protection against inflation.

Besides the initial cash flow and the prospect of future increases, investors generally receive tax advantages, too. They share in the property's depreciation; these deductions can raise the after-tax return.

Suppose, for example, Ken Jackson invests $10,000 in a net lease partnership and receives $800 (8%) in distributions in 1999. Thanks to depreciation deductions, though, Ken's share of taxable income might be only $600. Assuming a 40% tax rate, Ken would pay $240 and net $560, or 5.6% after tax. If Ken had received an 8% yield on a fully taxable investment, his net yield would be only 4.8%.

Net lease deals are generally structured as limited partnerships or real estate investment trusts. Sponsors raise money from investors, usually with a $5,000 minimum, and buy several properties, which they net-lease to tenants after checking on creditworthiness. Several sponsors in this industry have long histories of providing cash flow to investors.

Well-Equipped Partnerships

Another way to diversify a portfolio is by investing in an equipment-leasing partnership. *Equipment* might refer to a broad range of items used in business, from trucks and trailers to marine cargo containers and forklifts. The idea is to buy the equipment and lease it to users. Leases may be renewed. At some point, the partnership sells its equipment and distributes whatever is left to investors.

Computers and peripherals are now seldom used in leasing partnerships. They tend to lose value quickly because of obsolescence. Several partnerships formed in the 1970s and 1980s performed poorly because their computers could not be sold or re-leased profitably.

Investing in a leasing deal can be tricky. Investors are likely to get fairly high distributions up front (say, 9% to 10%), and the tax benefits may be generous because equipment depreciates faster than real estate. It's likely that most of each distribution will be tax-sheltered, providing tax-free income. However, the equipment that's purchased is probably going to lose value. Thus, investors' income may decline over time. Different partnerships handle this in different ways. Some reinvest part of their rental stream so the partnership has some new equipment to lease each year, swelling the revenue stream.

Some partnerships focus on short-term leases, even day-to-day rentals, which generally pay higher rates as a percentage of purchase price. Equipment on short-term leases may be re-leased at higher rates if the market tightens, but also may sit unused during slow periods, producing no income whatsoever.

Again, there are leasing sponsors with strong track records. Many sponsors or real estate and leasing partnerships are eager to work with financial planners and other independent advisors.

These investments provide a steady stream of substantial cash flow. Because they're meant to be diversifiers, clients should not overconcentrate them. Instead of advising clients to invest $25,000 in one deal, you should encourage them to put $5,000 in each of several deals, or spread the investments around several years. The latter strategy gives clients the benefit of dollar cost averaging: They'll buy some real estate or equipment when it's cheap and some when it's dear.

Recap

- Investors in low-income housing partnerships can get 10 years' worth of tax credits.

- Altogether, each $10,000 invested in an LIH partnership might lead to $12,000 in tax savings.

- If the real estate is eventually sold or refinanced, LIH partnership investors may wind up with a double-digit annual return, after tax.

- Investors are limited in how much they can invest in LIH deals by the passive loss rules and the alternative minimum tax.

- The key to investing in a successful LIH venture is to work with an experienced sponsor.

- Net lease real estate and equipment-leasing partnerships offer high distributions, partially sheltered from income tax.

Inside or Out?

Dividing a Portfolio between Taxable and Tax-Deferred Accounts

Most clients are best served if they hold a diversified investment portfolio: They should have some stocks, some bonds, and some cash reserves. What's more, investors probably should vary their stock market holdings among different-size companies in various industries and throw some foreign stocks into the mix. Combining these *asset classes,* as they're known, can enhance long-term returns while reducing an investor's exposure to a fall in one stock or one market sector.

However, there may be one more piece to this asset allocation puzzle. If clients have substantial funds to invest inside a tax-deferred retirement account as well as money invested outside such a plan, what goes where?

The preferred strategy is to put the vehicles with the least tax protection inside the retirement plan to utilize the tax deferral. For example, corporate bonds, mortgage-backed securities such as Ginnie Maes, and dividend-paying stocks are fully taxable. They should be held inside a plan, where the income will be sheltered.

Investors with managed accounts (where a money manager makes the decisions) should hold that money inside a retirement plan. Frequent trading and portfolio rebalancing can trigger taxes; inside a plan, any gains will be sheltered.

At the same time, tax-exempt and tax-deferred vehicles belong outside the plan because they're already sheltered. Thus, tax-advantaged investments such as annuities, permanent life insurance policies, and municipal bonds should be held outside qualified plans. The same is true for growth stocks that pay low dividends; clients who are buy-and-hold investors will owe little or no current income taxes from their growth stocks, so the retirement plan tax shelter isn't necessary.

In addition, cash equivalents (bank accounts, money market funds, Treasury bills) should be held outside a plan. Such assets generally are meant to provide liquidity in case there's a sudden need for cash, so clients will want their liquid assets outside of a plan, where they have access without paying taxes or penalties.

Spreading the Wealth

To see how this approach might work, consider the case of Paul Peters. Aside from his cash reserves (sitting in a taxable money market fund), Paul wants a portfolio that's 75% stocks and 25% bonds. Of his 75% in stocks, he wants to hold 60% in the United States, 32% in stocks of developed foreign countries, and 8% in emerging markets. Thus, 45% of his total portfolio is in domestic stocks, 24% in mainstream international stocks, and 6% in emerging markets stocks, with the remaining 25% in bonds. (See Table 13.1.)

Suppose Paul has to put half of these holdings inside a tax-deferred retirement plan and half in a taxable account. What goes where?

TABLE 13.1 **Portfolio Allocation**

Domestic stocks	45%
Mainstream international stocks	24%
Emerging markets stocks	6%
Equity subtotal	75%
Bonds	25%

To start with, Paul may well decide to hold his 30% international allocation (24% plus 6%) outside of the plan. This will keep him from losing a tax break. Whether Paul invests through individual foreign stocks or foreign mutual funds, any dividends he receives may be reduced by withholding of foreign taxes.

For example, suppose Paul receives $600 in foreign dividends in 1999 but $90 (15%) is withheld by the host countries. He'll receive one or more Form(s) 1099-DIV, showing the foreign taxes withheld. Then, Paul will have the option of either deducting that $90 on Schedule A as an itemized tax paid or claiming a credit for foreign taxes on Form 1116. (Claiming the credit usually works out better. Beginning with 1998 returns, the credit may be claimed on Form 1040 if foreign taxes paid were no more than $300, or $600 on a joint return.)

However, if Paul invests through a tax-deferred retirement plan, he won't receive a Form 1099 and won't be able to deduct foreign taxes or claim a credit. Therefore, the foreign taxes he pays, inside a retirement plan, are a dead loss.

For that reason, Paul decides to hold his foreign stocks, which make up 30% of his total portfolio, in a taxable account.

Stretching the Shelter

What about the other 70% of his portfolio? Where should Paul hold his 45% in domestic stocks and 25% in bonds?

One approach is to fill out his taxable account with tax-exempt bonds. In our example, Paul holds $500,000 outside of his plan, including $300,000 in foreign stocks. The other $200,000 (20% of his portfolio) could be in munis.

Then, $450,000 (45%) could be held in domestic stocks inside the plan. The remaining $50,000 (5%) could be allocated to the rest of his bonds. Inside the plan, Pete would not want to hold tax-exempt municipal bonds, because the interest would be taxed when it comes out. Instead, he should hold taxable bonds to make the most of the retirement plan tax shelter.

That's the standard strategy, but that may not be a good plan, taxwise, for two reasons:

1. *The retirement plan tax shelter may be wasted on domestic stocks.* Paul is a buy-and-hold investor, not a trader. He emphasizes low-dividend stocks, aiming for growth rather than current income. Therefore, his stock market portfolio doesn't generate much in the way of income tax each year.

   Suppose his $450,000 in domestic stocks generates $9,000 (2%) in investment income each year. Holding the stocks inside a plan saves him only $3,600 per year, assuming a 40% tax bracket. Even if the $50,000 worth of bonds pays $3,000 per year, and he saves another $1,200, the total tax savings in his $500,000 retirement plan portfolio is only $4,800 per year. (See Table 13.2.)

2. *He may lose the advantage of long-term gains by holding stocks inside a plan.* In the future, Paul plans to sell the (hopefully appreciated) stocks to help provide retirement income. Because he has emphasized growth rather than dividends, he expects to be rewarded with substantial gains over a 10-year holding period or longer.

   If those stocks are held outside of a retirement plan, those gains would largely be long term, eligible for favorable tax treatment (depending on the tax laws in effect at the time the gains are realized). Under present law, the federal income tax on long-term gains is capped at 20%.

   However, when long-term gains are realized inside a retirement plan, the proceeds are taxed as ordinary income when they're withdrawn. The tax rates will depend on the tax laws then in effect and on Paul's retirement income. Assuming today's

TABLE 13.2 Holding Stocks Inside a Plan

Domestic stocks	$450,000	
Yield @ 2%		$9,000
Taxable bonds	50,000	
Yield @ 6%		3,000
Total investment income		12,000
Tax savings @ 40%		$4,800

laws are still in effect, Paul could be converting a 20% tax bill into a 31%, a 36%, or even a 39.6% tax bill by holding stocks inside a retirement plan.

The same two reasons strengthen the case for holding foreign stocks outside of a retirement plan, in addition to the foreign-tax offset issue. So how might Paul structure a taxwise portfolio? Perhaps like this:

Inside Plan		Outside Plan	
Bonds	25%	Foreign Stocks	30%
Domestic Stocks	25%	Domestic Stocks	20%

As mentioned, the bonds held inside the plan should be taxable, perhaps a mix of Treasuries, corporates, and mortgage-backed securities (e.g., Ginnie Maes). Also, the domestic stocks held inside the plan could be those that generate the highest dividends. If Paul wants to include utility stocks, oils, banks, real estate investment trusts, and other high-yielding stocks in his portfolio, this is the place they should go. Generally, larger companies are more likely to pay substantial dividends.

Altogether, the stocks and bonds inside the plan might pay an average of 4% from interest and dividends. That's $20,000 per year on $500,000: At a 40% tax rate, the shelter is worth $8,000 per year.

Domestic stocks	$250,000	
Yield @ 2%		$ 5,000
Taxable bonds	250,000	
Yield @ 6%		15,000
Total investment income		20,000
Tax savings @ 40%		$ 8,000

That's much more shelter than the $4,800 annual tax savings he'd enjoy by holding all his domestic stocks inside the plan.

Outside the plan, along with foreign stocks can go the domestic stocks and stock funds that pay low or no dividends. Therefore, the annual tax bill likely will be meager. (The foreign tax credit will reduce the tax bill, too.) When the time comes to sell holdings and use the proceeds for retirement income, any profits will probably be favorably taxed as long-term capital gains.

What's more, there may be no need to sell the securities in the taxable account until Paul's death. If he's still holding on, he can leave them to his spouse and, eventually, to their children. The survivors will inherit with a step-up in basis to market value. Thus they can sell the shares after Paul's death (perhaps to raise money for estate tax) and owe no tax at all on the prior appreciation.

By contrast, anything that comes out of the retirement plan will be fully subject to income tax—*after* Paul's death as well as prior to it. That's yet another reason to hold assets that are likely to appreciate outside of a tax-deferred plan.

Focusing on Funds

The preceding analysis assumes that Paul invests in individual securities, at least for domestic stocks and bonds. Many people, though, invest mainly through mutual funds. As explained in Chapter 7, it's difficult to be a pure buy-and-hold investor with mutual funds, because the funds are constantly selling securities and passing capital gains on to investors.

Therefore, the inside-out strategy is different for mutual fund investors. If you're investing for the long term, you may be better off by keeping all your stocks in the tax-deferred plan.

T. Rowe Price, the mutual fund company, came to these conclusions after studying 20 years' worth of mutual fund data. Rather than looking at individual funds, the study used broad categories such as growth stock funds, growth and income stock funds, foreign stock funds, and so forth, as well as taxable bond funds.

In the study, T. Rowe Price assumed a portfolio that's evenly split between a taxable and a tax-deferred account. A hypothetical $10,000 investment was made into each account. For the following 10 or 20 years, these accounts earned the average for each fund category. With each comparison, a portfolio with stock funds inside the plan and bond funds outside the plan beat a portfolio of bond funds held inside and stock funds on the outside.

Why did stocks inside beat bonds inside, despite the extra tax bill such a strategy would incur by exposing bond fund distributions to income tax each year? Because all stock fund categories significantly outperformed the taxable bond fund category in these time periods. Investors were better off sheltering lightly taxed small-company stock funds, which returned 15.2% for the 20 years in question, than they were sheltering highly taxed bond funds, which returned only 9.2% per year.

Because stocks have performed so well over the long term, your clients might want to hold 75%, 80%, or more of their overall portfolios in equities. In such cases, they might hold four or five different categories of stock funds. Now the question is: Which stock funds go where?

T. Rowe Price found that it generally paid to hold the best-performing equity funds in the tax-deferred retirement plan, but it's difficult to know in advance which equity funds will have the best long-term performance. Therefore, clients might want high-turnover funds inside the plan, because such funds tend to generate large capital gains distributions. Inside the plan, those distributions can be sheltered.

Index funds and other tax-efficient mutual funds might be held outside of a plan, because those funds don't usually generate much tax obligation. Municipal bond funds, too, never belong inside a tax-deferred account. Investors will convert tax-exempt interest to taxable interest when they pull money out of the plan. Similarly, foreign funds may be held on the outside so the foreign tax credit can be used.

What if clients mix individual securities and mutual funds in their portfolios? They should hold the mutual funds inside the retirement plan, where capital gains distributions can be sheltered.

Weighing all of these factors, the inside-out question may not be answered easily. However, it's a question that clients need to ask in order to maximize wealth buildup for themselves and their families.

Recap

- Many clients will have to divide their investment portfolios between taxable and tax-deferred accounts.

- Assuming your clients are long-term buy-and-hold investors, they're better off holding low-dividend growth stocks in taxable accounts, because such holdings won't generate much taxable income.

- Holding bonds in a retirement plan makes better use of the tax deferral.

- A stocks-outside, bonds-inside strategy also keeps clients from converting long-term capital gains to highly taxed ordinary income.

- Clients who invest largely in mutual funds may be better off with the opposite strategy, loading up retirement plans with stock funds, especially those funds that generate sizable capital gains distributions each year.

- If clients hold a mix of assets, their individual stocks can be held outside a retirement plan and mutual funds on the inside.

Truly Tax-Free

Avoiding Estate Tax As Well As Income Tax

First, the good news. During most of the 1980s and 1990s, the stock market soared. People who invested in stocks throughout that period have seen their portfolios expand.

At the same time, the real estate market went from boom to bust and then back to boom in many areas of the United States. Again, many real estate investors have prospered.

There are many tactics your clients can use to defer, reduce, or even avoid the tax on these investments. To be more precise, the tactics described in earlier chapters can shelter clients from paying *income* tax. While you and your clients are planning to reduce the income tax on their investments, don't neglect to plan for *estate* taxes, too. After all, federal income taxes range from 10% to 39.6%, while federal estate tax rates start at 37% and go as high as 60%.

That's the bad news. The bull stampede of the 1980s and 1990s has the potential to gore some participants. Clients who have built seven- and eight-figure fortunes largely as a result of the surging stock market stand to owe huge amounts of estate tax when that wealth passes to the next generation. Even if clients live beyond 2005, when the estate tax shelter rises to $1 million per person, continuing stock market gains may swell portfolio values—and estate tax obligations.

Sky's the Limit

For example, Greg Matthews has built a net worth of $26 million, mainly held in an investment portfolio. Now that Greg is in his 70s, what's he doing? He's continuing to build his portfolio. If $26 million is good, surely $46 million is better.

Better, certainly, for the IRS. Taxable estates over $3 million are subject to a 55% estate tax, which bulges to 60% for estates in the $10 to $21 million range. State taxes may be assessed as well. Thus, for some clients, after a certain point, most of the money they accumulate will wind up in the tax collectors' pockets.

Of course, there are many reasons for continuing to focus on wealth accumulation. Some clients enjoy comfortable or even extravagant lifestyles; some want to provide for younger spouses. In truth, it may be hard to know how much is enough.

Financial projections may assume that both spouses will live into their 90s, with spending increasing each year. A cushion for long-term care may be thrown in, too. Depending on the assumptions used, clients may decide they'll need many millions of dollars to guarantee a long, affluent lifestyle.

All of those points certainly are valid. Nevertheless, not every client lives to be 99, takes an annual cruise around the world, or spends 10 years in a nursing home. Some will die in their 80s, 70s, or even younger. Without savvy planning, millions will disappear into the grasp of the IRS.

Generally, once clients amass several million dollars in assets, it's unlikely they're going to run out of money or face serious hardship as long as they have good professional advice. At that stage, serious thought should be given to a substantial gifting program. That is, assets should be given away in order to reduce future estate tax obligations.

Even if clients are reluctant to part with hundreds of thousands of dollars to pare their estates, modest gifts can be made each year, tax free, under the annual gift tax exclusion. (Each person can give up to $10,000 per recipient per year without tax consequences.) A couple who gives away $20,000 per year from ages 60 to 75 not only gives away $300,000, they give away assets that otherwise may have grown to $500,000 or even $1 million if retained until death.

Turning Point

With the stakes this high, how can planners help clients find the right inflection point? How can you encourage the creation of enough wealth so that clients (and surviving spouses) live comfortably, yet not so much wealth that huge amounts are lost in estate tax?

The answer generally lies in careful planning. Clients' individual situations must be monitored and reviewed at least once a year to help them wind up in the "Goldilocks position": not too much but not too little. Moreover, planners often have to follow up on the number crunching with some persuasion to convince clients to play the give-away game.

One basic approach is to start with current cash flow and net worth, and then project future scenarios. You might, for example, inflate current spending by 4% a year while assuming investment rates of return of 8% pretax and 5% after tax. Project these assumptions out 10 years—about as far as you may feel comfortable with such assumptions. If this analysis shows net worth to be increasing, estate tax planning may be in order.

Take the example of Len and Pat Clark. They're both in their mid-60s; Len is planning to retire. Both are very concerned that they won't have enough money to live on.

Using the projection analysis described, they estimated that over 10 years their expenses would increase from $80,000 per year to nearly $120,000, while their net worth (chiefly an investment portfolio and Len's retirement plan) would perhaps grow from $3.5 million to nearly $5 million. Now that they can see where they're going, they feel much more secure about their own future. To reduce future estate tax, they're starting a gifting plan. In case of an emergency, they can always cut back on their gifts.

The challenge of getting clients to focus on estate taxes may go beyond spreadsheets. A 70-year-old client may have accumulated $4 or $5 million through a lifetime of hard work. When you suggest that this client should change from a consumption mentality to a gifting mentality, he or she may not be able to shift gears. Some clients are very hard to persuade.

Nevertheless, it's important that you have such discussions with clients and repeat them regularly. Each year, you should go over the numbers with your clients. After a certain amount of time, clients may come to accept the schedules and believe in what they see there. Eventually, they may start to give away some of their assets.

Younger people may not be as inclined to start transferring their wealth. A client who's 50 or 55 may not be ready to give away assets, even though he or she knows the estate tax consequences. In general, people become more receptive to the idea of giving away their assets after they become grandparents and want to help provide for their grandchildren's education.

Even when clients are a bit older, in the early stages of retirement they may be reluctant to give away sizable amounts. Their expenses may be high, and they may be afraid they'll run out of money—even if they're worth $5 million. Once they reach 75 or 80, though, they have a good idea of how much they'll spend during the rest of their lives, so they may be willing to trim their estates.

Option Plays

Once the decision is made to transfer wealth, further choices must be made:

- *What should clients give away?* Generally, clients with sufficient cash flow will give away cash. If there isn't enough cash, they'll give appreciated assets. This relieves them of the tax burden when those assets are sold, and it may defer the tax far into the future, to the time when the recipients sell the assets.

- *How should gifts be made?* Some clients will make outright gifts as long as the recipients are responsible adults. Other clients prefer that gifts be made in trust. Again, appreciated assets may be given away to a trust.

An even better approach, for either outright gifts or gifts in trust, is to give away stock options, removing potential future appreciation at a modest gift tax cost. Increasingly, clients who are employed by publicly held companies are likely to have a large portion of their present and future wealth in stock options. According to the accounting firm Deloitte & Touche, 10% of 8,000 publicly traded firms currently offer stock options to a majority of their full-time employees.

Gifting stock options was a rare maneuver up until 1996. Since then, the SEC has permitted stock options to be given away to family members or to trusts set up to benefit relatives. Subsequently, many companies have amended their plans to permit transfers.

Initially, the ideal strategy was to give away options soon after they were granted and before those options were allowed to be exercised. Such options could be assigned extremely low values for gift tax purposes because their future worth was unknowable. If Mike Mason has options on ABC stock, exercisable at $20 per share from 2001 through 2011, how much are those options worth in 1999, with ABC trading at $21? Some executives gave away options that were not yet vested, put a meager value on the transfer, and removed any future growth from their taxable estate.

They did, that is, until the IRS issued a ruling in 1998 saying that a gift of an unvested stock option is not a completed gift. Mike really doesn't own those options until they're vested; until he owns them, he can't give them away.

Suppose Mike's stock options were awarded by ABC as an inducement to leave XYZ Company in 1998. He needs to work at ABC five years in order for those options to vest. Therefore, he can give away some or all of those options in 1999, but the gift won't be complete until 2003, when he reaches the five-year mark. The value of the gift, for tax purposes, will be the value as of the vesting date in 2003. Thus, when Mike gives away his options in 1998, he has no way of knowing what those options will be worth in 2003. If the stock shoots up between now and then, the options will become very valuable, and Mike could incur substantial amounts of gift tax.

The IRS addressed the valuation issue in another ruling issued the same day. Taxpayers can use the Black-Scholes option pricing model or "similar" models to value the options. No discounts will be permitted if the safe harbor principle is to apply.

Spurning Safety

Taken as a package, the IRS stance on giving away unvested options has met with some skepticism among professionals. Some experts believe that a taxpayer can, in fact, make a completed gift of an unvested option;

in addition, some professionals think that it is valid to discount gifts on unvested options for lack of marketability.

However, not every client will be eager to do battle with the IRS. The IRS position is that vested options can be given away using the Black-Scholes method to determine their value. A client who wants to give away options can follow these rules, save the cost of an appraisal, and avoid the risk of an IRS challenge.

For relatively small gifts, it's probably simpler just to use this approach. Giving away vested options is likely to be more tax-efficient than giving away actual holdings of the underlying stock: The Black-Scholes formula often puts the value of an option at about one-third the value of the common stock.

Giving away options—vested or unvested—has another tax benefit. When the options are exercised, income tax will be due at ordinary rates. This tax is owed by the executive who was awarded the options, even though the options may have been given away. The executive is effectively making a larger gift to the recipient, but no gift tax is owed on the income tax payment.

Moreover, the IRS has ruled that an executive giving away stock options is not subject to income tax until the recipient exercises them. After that, the recipient's basis in the stock is the exercise price plus the amount included in the executive's taxable income.

With these advantages, gifts of vested options likely will continue to some extent. In those cases, it's likely that the IRS ruling on valuation will be widely disregarded. This is a worst-case result, so why start there? Clients who give away stock options can hire an appraiser and claim substantial discounts. Even if the valuation is challenged, some negotiation is possible. Clients may wind up better off, and probably no worse off, than they would by adopting the safe harbor to begin with.

The Family Way

Clients who are hesitant about parting with assets may prefer to use some strings-attached strategies. A family limited partnership (FLP) may be an effective vehicle for transferring taxable wealth without giving up control—as long as clients aren't too aggressive with valuation discounts.

Typically, in an FLP the creator (or a corporation owned by the creator) acts as general partner, responsible for managing the partnership's assets, while limited partnership interests are given to younger relatives. Valuation discounts can reduce the gift tax consequences.

Suppose, for example, that Len and Pat Clark have a $2 million portfolio of stocks and bonds. If they hold onto those securities, by the time both spouses die and their assets pass to their children, the portfolio might be worth $3 million. The estate tax bill might be $1.65 million (at 55%).

Instead, Len and Pat set up an FLP and transfer their $2 million portfolio into it. They're essentially moving assets from one pocket to another, so no tax is due.

Then, Len and Pat give away a 99% limited partnership interest to their children. By retaining a 1% general partnership interest, they continue to manage the FLP's assets: the securities portfolio.

If they give away a 99% interest in a $2 million portfolio, is that a $1.98 million gift? Perhaps not. The Clarks are actually giving their children a limited partnership interest rather than the stocks and bonds. It's unlikely that a third party would buy this interest from the children for $1.98 million, because the buyer would have no control over the underlying shares.

An independent appraiser might put the value of the transfer at $1.3 million. If that's the case, the transfer can be made in 1999 without triggering a gift tax obligation, because both spouses are entitled to shelter up to $650,000 from gift tax that year. (The valuation might be placed at $1.5 million or $1.7 million, depending on the circumstances.) Yet they'll still control the stocks and bonds.

Thus, Len and Pat will have removed their investment portfolio (along with its future appreciation) from their taxable estates without paying gift tax on the full value of the transferred assets. As might be expected, the IRS is not enthusiastic about such maneuvers. Your clients may be better off if they also transfer other assets, such as investment property or shares in a closely held business, into their FLP.

What's more, the partnership documents should spell out reasons (other than tax avoidance) to hold investments inside an FLP. Such reasons might include centralized management, lower fees for professional management, and protection of family members who are not capable of holding investments outright.

Sweet Charity

Another way to dispose of securities is to donate them—especially if they've appreciated—to a charitable remainder trust (CRT). If clients donate appreciated assets, the assets and all future appreciation are out of the client's estate, while prior appreciation avoids capital gains tax. The client also receives an income stream as well as an immediate charitable deduction.

Suppose, for example, that Jack and Phyllis Martin own a portfolio of securities worth $3 million with a cost basis of $500,000. If they held those assets until both died, the $2.5 million capital gains obligation would disappear, because their heirs would inherit with a step-up in basis.

However, the $3 million portfolio would be subject to estate tax at a potential cost of $1.65 million. To avoid this tax, Jack and Phyllis could donate their portfolio to a CRT. This trust could promise to pay income to Jack and Phyllis for the rest of their lives. They might elect to receive 8% of trust assets each year, which would mean a first-year payout of $240,000. If the CRT earns more than 8% per year, their distributions would increase.

Thus, Jack and Phyllis guarantee themselves a sizable income they won't outlive. At the second death, the income payments will cease and the balance of the CRT will go to a charity or charities they've named. The entire portfolio will escape estate tax.

The catch, of course, is that their children won't receive $3 million worth of securities. They won't receive even the $1.35 million that would be left after estate tax. Everything will go to charity.

This may be acceptable to Jack and Phyllis if their children are otherwise provided for. However, they can replace the trust's assets through life insurance if they wish. In particular, they can buy a *second-to-die policy* that will pay off after both spouses die. Such a policy, held in an irrevocable trust, likely will escape estate and income tax.

Jack and Phyllis might buy a $1.35 million policy, providing the children with the amount they would have received after tax. They could buy a $3 million policy, restoring the full amount of the securities. Or they could buy a policy for some amount in between.

Such insurance policies are not inexpensive. Depending on their ages and their health, Jack and Phyllis might spend anywhere from $200,000 to $600,000, over a period of years, to buy a $2 million policy.

However, the CRT strategy can help to alleviate the costs. When making the initial contribution to the CRT, Jack and Phyllis will receive a large tax deduction, perhaps saving hundreds of thousands in taxes. Those savings, combined with some of the cash flow from the CRT, can provide money to buy the desired life insurance.

Keep the Cash Flowing

The strategies just described (FLPs and CRTs) work well for clients who hold appreciated securities outright or in a taxable brokerage account. However, many clients hold most of their investments inside tax-sheltered retirement plans, including IRAs. As explained in Chapter 3, an IRA can be passed down to children or grandchildren, producing enormous amounts of tax-deferred wealth.

Before such an IRA stretch-out can be implemented, though, it has to pass to a succeeding generation—at which time the account will be subject to estate tax. A $2 million IRA can generate over $1 million in federal estate tax.

Where will that $1 million come from? If it has to come out of the IRA, income tax will be due. An IRA that might have paid out millions will be stripped down by this double tax bite.

The answer, then, is to make some provision for future estate tax. Your client's family should have a pool of cash on hand to pay the estate tax bill. If so, the IRA can remain intact and the tax deferral can continue. Again, life insurance held in an irrevocable trust may be an effective vehicle for providing that liquidity.

Recap

- Clients who build up a large investment portfolio may wind up owing huge amounts of estate tax.

- The best way to avoid this tax is to give away assets that won't be needed during the lifetime of an investor or spouse.

- Among the best assets to give away may be stock options, which likely will have a low cost, thus minimizing gift taxes.

- More assets can be given away, with a smaller gift tax cost, if those assets are held inside a family limited partnership.

- Appreciated securities can be given to a charitable remainder trust, removing them from an investor's taxable estate, while life insurance replaces the inheritance that was given away.

- When large amounts of investments are held inside an IRA, using a pool of liquidity to pay estate tax can extend tax-deferred growth inside the IRA.

Trust Me on This

Sophisticated Asset Protection Strategies

Estate planning commonly calls for clients to transfer part of their wealth into an irrevocable trust. Once assets are in such a trust, they're out of the trust creator's (*grantor's*) taxable estate. In addition, those assets will be out of reach of the grantor's creditors, as long as no dishonesty was intended.

Chances are, clients will do their loved ones a favor by giving or leaving them money in trust, with a reliable trustee in place. If money is held in trust for youngsters, for example, the trust fund can build up until it's needed for college, a down payment on a house, or any other purpose.

However, money that's transferred to a trust must be invested, and trust tax rates are punishing. The top 39.6% rate kicks in at only $8,450 in taxable income in 1999. If that's the case, what can trustees do?

One approach is to distribute trust income to the beneficiaries as it comes in. The trust gets a tax deduction, while the beneficiaries recognize taxable income. As long as the beneficiaries are in a lower income tax bracket than the trust, such a move will save taxes. However, distributing income from the trust may nullify some of the reasons for creating the trust in the first place.

A second strategy is for the trustee to invest in tax-exempt municipal bonds or bond funds. This not only will hold down trust income tax
but also trust income as well: As of this writing, most municipal bonds
were yielding 5% or less. Thus, although munis are an appropriate
investment vehicle for trusts, a trustee should not put too much money
there.

Instead, money can be invested in low-dividend growth stocks.
There the trust will incur little or no current income; any profits likely
will be taxed at the low 20% long-term capital gains rate. Another
approach is to invest the money that comes into the trust in life insurance, which will provide tax-free buildup of cash value and a tax-free
death benefit.

Growing by Shrinking

When clients are married, they likely will have a *two-trust* estate plan.
That is, the first spouse to die will leave a bequest to a *family trust,*
also known as a *credit shelter trust* or a *B trust.* The amount left to this
trust will equal the amount that can be sheltered by the gift and estate
tax unified credit: $650,000 in 1999, gradually increasing to $1 million by 2006.

Excess assets will be left to the *marital,* or *A, trust* for the benefit of
the surviving spouse. An unlimited marital deduction protects this
bequest from estate tax, which generally will be due at the death of the
surviving spouse.

If the marital trust remains relatively small and the surviving spouse
has few assets of his or her own, little or no estate tax will ever be due.
However, this may not always be the case. If the surviving spouse has
substantial assets and the marital trust grows, an enormous amount of
estate tax may be owed, at rates of up to 55%.

Suppose Howard Palmer dies at age 77, leaving Kate Palmer a 74-
year-old widow. At Howard's death in 2006, $1 million goes into a B
trust, of which Kate and their children are beneficiaries. The remainder of Howard's estate goes into an A trust for Kate. Combined with
Kate's own assets, the A trust gives her a total of $1 million.

During the remainder of Kate's lifetime, she takes out $100,000
a year: $50,000 from the children's B trust and $50,000 from her

own A trust. After income taxes, she may have $60,000 per year to spend.

Kate dies at age 84. In the intervening 10 years, after withdrawals, the assets post a net gain of 50%. Now the B trust contains $1.5 million, while Kate's estate (including the A trust) is worth $1.5 million.

At Kate's death, the children receive the $1.5 million in the B trust, free of estate taxes, because that trust was subject to tax at Howard's death. However, Kate's $1.5 million estate now is over the $1 million limitation. When her estate (including the A trust) passes to her children, they'll owe over $200,000 in estate tax.

This tax could have been avoided by using a strategy known as the *shrinking trust tactic.* Instead of taking $50,000 per year from both sides, Kate could have taken $100,000 from her own A trust. If her $1 million trust fund grows by $80,000 the first year and she takes out $100,000, her trust fund will shrink to $980,000. The next year, if her A trust generates $75,000 in income, she'll have to invade the principal for $25,000. And so on. She might even sell stock or real estate to the children's B trust to raise cash, as long as she receives a fair price on all transactions.

She can do this for as long as her A trust holds out. Suppose she dies with $400,000 in her A trust and few other assets. That's well below the $1 million limit, so no estate tax will be due.

At the same time, the children's B trust will be growing because Kate won't be withdrawing any money. If she dies with only $400,000 in her A trust, the B trust may hold over $2.6 million in assets. Those B trust assets, though, are outside of her estate. At her death, they will pass to the children free of estate tax, no matter how large this B trust has grown. (See Table 15.1.)

What if Kate lives so long that she spends down virtually all of the assets in the A trust? That's no problem. By then, the children's B trust may have grown to $3 million or more. Kate, as one of the beneficiaries, is entitled to all the income from this trust, so she should be able to live comfortably. (In most cases, the widow or widower will be able to invade the principal of the children's B trust if an emergency arises.)

There are many variations on this strategy, but the concept is the same. After the first spouse's death, the widower or the widow should

TABLE 15.1 **Estate Taxes with Shrinking Trust and without Shrinking Trust**

	Family B Trust	Kate's Estate (including A trust)
Without shrinking trust		
Original principal	$1,000,000	$1,000,000
Annual withdrawals	50,000	50,000
Principal 10 years later	1,500,000	1,500,000
Estate tax at Kate's death	0	210,000
With shrinking trust		
Original principal	$1,000,000	$1,000,000
Annual withdrawals	0	100,000
Principal 8 years later	2,600,000	400,000
Estate tax at Kate's death	0	0

spend his or her assets first, thus reducing the eventual estate tax bill. Assets in the children's trust should be allowed to grow, because they're outside of the estate of the surviving spouse.

Creating a Dynasty

With some careful planning, irrevocable trusts can become *dynasty trusts*. As the name suggests, these trusts are meant to provide for a client's descendants as well as for the client and possibly a spouse. A dynasty trust not only offers all the advantages of irrevocable trusts—estate tax reduction, privacy, probate avoidance, incapacity planning, asset protection—it can provide these benefits for children, grandchildren, great-grandchildren, and perhaps even further generations.

Generally, a client's children and grandchildren will be the beneficiaries of a dynasty trust. (A savvy attorney may be able to get yet-unborn descendants added to the list.) The trustee will be able to distribute trust income and principal among those beneficiaries as needed. However, the assets won't actually belong to the beneficiaries, so their creditors (including spouses in divorce proceedings) won't have any claims to the trust assets. Similarly, those assets won't be included in the beneficiaries' taxable estates at their deaths.

Certain steps can enhance a dynasty trust and create a unique Wealth Trust. For example, a client might include a provision enabling the trustee to buy and hold residential real estate. The trustee may be given the discretionary power—but not the obligation—to let the beneficiaries use the trust property or properties. If the trust owns a beach house on Cape Cod, for example, all of the beneficiaries can use it as a vacation home. When not being used by family members, the property can be rented out for income. The trust also can own homes that beneficiaries live in as their principal residences.

In addition, a Wealth Trust can contain a provision enabling the trustee, with the consent of the beneficiaries, to make distributions to pay the premiums for life insurance covering the grantor's grandchildren, which might come in handy if those grandchildren leave taxable estates. Assuming the grandchildren are very young when the policies are purchased, such insurance will be relatively inexpensive.

The trustee of a dynasty trust is generally given wide-ranging discretionary powers, so the selection of the trustee is vital. Generally, a grantor should *not* be the trustee of a dynasty trust, because the IRS and creditors may assert that trust assets really belong to the grantor. Instead, the client can name a child or children as trustees, while grandchildren may be designated as successor trustees. If desired, other parties can be named as cotrustees.

Another approach is to name a close family friend, a personal advisor, or a relative (a cousin, perhaps) as trustee. Such trustees probably will need to be paid, but they may be able to arbitrate family disputes. Your client's first concern should be to name a friendly trustee who'll be sympathetic to the needs of the trust beneficiaries, perhaps in combination with someone or some institution that can handle financial matters.

Imperfect by Intent

If properly handled, a dynasty trust can be a *defective grantor trust.* That is, even though the assets in the trust are out of your client's taxable estate, the trust income is still your client's responsibility. Thus, your client can pay the trust's income tax without having that payment considered a taxable gift. This maneuver allows your client to get more assets out of his or her taxable estate and allows more growth inside the trust.

After the trust creator's death (or the death of a surviving spouse), some cash in the trust may be used to buy assets from the estate or to loan money to the estate, providing liquidity for paying estate tax. The assets thus purchased (or the notes payable from the loans) can stay in trust for succeeding generations, not subject to estate tax at anyone's death.

The trustee can sprinkle trust assets as necessary to help the beneficiaries with medical bills, school expenses, housing costs, business start-ups, and so forth. If a creditor gains a judgment against one of the beneficiaries in the future, or if there's a nasty divorce, the trust assets won't be exposed.

A dynasty trust may prove to be especially valuable for any client who has a large retirement plan that he or she intends to leave to the next generation, because the retirement plan can be left intact. If the plan needs to be tapped for cash to pay estate tax, income tax will be triggered and the plan will shrink.

In most states, trusts can be set up to last until 21 years after the death of the last family member who was alive when the trust was created. Thus, if a client names a 5-year-old grandson as beneficiary and the client lives another 79 years, the trust can stay intact for 100 years, providing a century of estate tax–free wealth building. Moreover, Alaska, Delaware, Idaho, Illinois, South Dakota, and Wisconsin all permit perpetual trusts.

However, your clients may not want a single trust to stay in effect for 100 years or longer. By the second or third generation, there may be too many beneficiaries with competing demands for the trustees to serve well. Thus, a dynasty trust might be structured to divide into smaller trusts after the grantor's death. If your client dies with three children and $3 million in a dynasty trust, for example, three new trusts can be created, each with $1 million in assets. This process can be repeated, keeping the trusts manageable, while each new *subtrust* will continue to provide sheltered wealth for the beneficiaries.

Because money will stay in trust and under the management of a trustee with fiduciary responsibility, life will be easier—but not too easy—for grandchildren and their children. Some people don't like the idea of leaving a grandchild a large sum of money, or even a regular income, fearing their incentive will be stunted. But that won't be a problem if a trust is structured to provide grandchildren with a pool of capital and perhaps a rent-free home. In fact, these trusts can be structured to *provide* an incentive to grandchildren: They might receive trust distributions equal to 10% of the income they earn, for example. Such a plan will relieve grandchildren of some financial burdens, but they'll still have to work to earn money for food, clothing, and other living expenses. What better legacy could your clients desire?

Worst-Case Scenario

In some cases, a dynasty trust can serve as a backup retirement plan for the trust grantor. This type of dynasty trust is funded by gifts from one spouse of a married couple. Indeed, each spouse can have his or her own dynasty trust. If one spouse creates the trust, the other spouse may serve as trustee and make distributions to the trust beneficiaries, including him- or herself.

Consider the example of Ken Lane, who transferred some of his wealth to his wife Peggy. Peggy then used $650,000 to fund a dynasty trust, naming Ken as trustee. Their children and grandchildren are named as beneficiaries, along with Ken.

Ken, as trustee, can distribute trust assets to any of the beneficiaries, including himself. If such distributions are required by the trust documents to be for "health, education, maintenance, and support," the trust assets will not be included in Ken's taxable estate. In practice, virtually any important need can be covered by those four words, so Ken can distribute funds to himself in case of an emergency.

Therefore, one of your clients can serve as the trustee of a spouse's dynasty trust. However, a dynasty trust grantor should not be the trustee, too, because the IRS and creditors may assert that trust assets really belong to the grantor.

Warming Up to a Superfreeze

Sometimes, large wealth accumulations can lead to large tax problems. In turn, such problems can be solved by innovative planning.

For example, Steve and Barbara Williams are in their mid-70s, with four children and five grandchildren. They have a $17 million estate, and they want to minimize estate taxes. Moreover, they are extremely interested in privacy and wish to keep their holdings confidential.

By 1999, Steve and Barbara had used their $1.3 million-per-couple unified credit exemption allowance by giving assets to their children. In addition, they had been giving $20,000 per year to each of their children and grandchildren in order to have the pleasure of seeing their loved ones enjoy a comfortable lifestyle.

With their $17 million estate, family situation, and goals, Steve and Barbara were the perfect candidates for the *superfreeze strategy.* Here's how it worked:

1. They established a family limited partnership (FLP) and placed $1 million of securities on the general partnership side. Steve was the general partner, in control of the FLP. They placed $10 million of securities on the limited partnership side, with Steve and Barbara as the limited partners. Up to this point, no taxes were due.

2. Next, they established a dynasty trust as a defective grantor trust, where the grantor is responsible for the income taxes but the trust assets are out of the grantor's taxable estate.

3. The dynasty trust purchased the limited partnership side of the partnership, which held $10 million of securities. This purchase was structured using an interest-bearing balloon payment note. In order for such a sale to be recognized, the dynasty trust must be a *trust of substance.*

4. To make the dynasty trust a trust of substance, Steve and Barbara gave $500,000 in cash to the trust, incurring a $200,000 gift tax. With the $500,000, the dynasty trust purchased $7 million worth of second-to-die life insurance on Steve and Barbara.

Now the dynasty trust had substance, so it was able to purchase the $10 million limited partnership interest. Because a limited partnership is controlled by the general partner, the assets were discounted by 30%, resulting in a $7 million purchase price. Thus, for a $7 million note, the dynasty trust was able to purchase the limited partnership interest that held $10 million (face value) worth of securities. What's more, the $7 million note effectively held by Steve and Barbara is frozen: It will never increase in value even if the $10 million worth of securities in the dynasty trust appreciates.

As a result, Steve and Barbara have removed $3 million worth of assets from their estate. Should Steve or Barbara live long enough for the $10 million worth of securities to double to $20 million, they will have removed $13 million from their estate in exchange for a $200,000 gift tax payment.

What's more, the dynasty trust now holds $7 million worth of insurance on Steve and Barbara's lives. After both spouses die, the $7 million of life insurance will pay off the $7 million note.

In the meanwhile, Steve, as the general partner, will sell off enough securities each year to pay the interest on the note after paying capital gains tax. Because the trust is a grantor trust, the income will be taxable to Steve and Barbara as a long-term capital gain, taxed at 20% (perhaps 18% in the future). If the income had been taxable to the trust, the tax rate would be 39.6%.

The dynasty trust that holds this growing portfolio can stay in existence for three generations in the state where Steve and Barbara live. Later, it can be transferred to a state that permits perpetual trusts, so it can last as long as future beneficiaries wish. Thus, the millions of dollars in the dynasty trust can stay in the family for at least 100 years and maybe up to 1,000 years. The dynasty trust can subdivide in the future, for easier management. The net result is that Steve and Barbara have cut millions of dollars from their estate tax bill and arranged their affairs so that those millions benefit their descendants for generations to come.

Recap

- Many estate planning strategies involve the use of irrevocable trusts, because trust assets aren't subject to estate tax.

- Estate tax rates are extremely steep, so trustees must invest trust funds with care.

- Although some trust funds may be invested in tax-exempt bonds, the main vehicles for trust investments are generally growth stocks and life insurance.

- After one spouse dies, the surviving spouse is better off spending down his or her assets, which will be subject to estate tax, and allowing assets already passed to the children to compound.

- Dynasty trusts may serve not only the trust creator but future generations as well.

- A dynasty trust may include incentive provisions to motivate grandchildren to become successful in their own careers.

Appendix A Tax Schedules

Caution: *Use **only** if your taxable income (Form 1040, line 39) is $100,000 or more. If less, use the **Tax Table**. Even though you cannot use the Tax Schedules below if your taxable income is less than $100,000, all levels of taxable income are shown so taxpayers can see the tax rate that applies at each level.*

Schedule X—Use if your filing status is **Single**

If taxable income is: Over—	But not over—	Enter on Form 1040, line 40		of the amount over—
$0	$25,750	. . .	15%	$0
25,750	62,450	$3,862.50 +	28%	25,750
62,450	130,250	14,138.00 +	31%	62,450
130,250	283,150	35,156.50 +	36%	130,250
283,150	. . .	90,200.50 +	39.6%	283,150

Schedule Y-1—Use if your filing status is **Married filing jointly** or **Qualifying widow(er)**

If taxable income is: Over—	But not over—	Enter on Form 1040, line 40		of the amount over—
$0	$43,050	. . .	15%	$0
43,050	104,050	$6,457.50 +	28%	43,050
104,050	158,550	23,537.50 +	31%	104,050
158,550	283,150	40,432.50 +	36%	158,550
283,150	. . .	85,288.50 +	39.6%	283,150

Schedule Y-2—Use if your filing status is **Married filing separately**

If taxable income is: Over—	But not over—	Enter on Form 1040, line 40		of the amount over—
0	$21,525	...	15%	$0
21,525	52,025	$3,228.75 +	28%	21,525
52,025	79,275	11,768.75 +	31%	52,025
79,275	141,575	20,216.25 +	36%	79,275
141,575	...	42,644.25 + 39.6%		141,575

Schedule Z—Use if your filing status is **Head of household**

If taxable income is: Over—	But not over—	Enter on Form 1040, line 40		of the amount over—
$0	$34,550	...	15%	$0
34,550	89,150	$5,182.50 +	28%	34,550
89,150	144,400	20,470.50 +	31%	89,150
144,400	283,150	37,598.00 +	36%	144,400
283,150	...	87,548.00 + 39.6%		283,150

Itemized Deductions
    1999   1998

Itemized deduction phaseout begins:
Most taxpayers
    $126,600 $124,500

Married taxpayers
    $63,300 $62,250

Personal Exemptions
Personal exemption amount
    1999   1998
    $2,750 $2,700

Exemption phaseout begins:
Married filing jointly
   $189,950 $186,800

Single
   $126,000 $124,500

Head of Household
   $158,300 $155,650

Married Filing separately
   $94,975 $93,400

Appendix B IRA Stretch-Out

Assumptions:

Initial plan balance	$1,000,000	
10% growth		
40% tax bracket		
Owner	Age 65	(Death assumed age 83)
Spouse	Age 63	(Death assumed age 87)
Child #1	Age 38	
Child #2	Age 37	
Grandchild #1	Age 5	
Grandchild #2	Age 2	

Total Net After-Tax Income

Owner and spouse	(24 years' distribution)	$1,834,906*
Child #1	(20 years' distribution)	$1,097,797
Child #2	(21 years' distribution)	$1,161,854
Subtotal		**$2,259,651**
Grandchild #1	(51 years' distribution)	$9,884,694
Grandchild #2	(54 years' distribution)	$12,369,429
Subtotal		**$22,254,123**
Total IRA potential income		**$26,348,680**

*Please keep in mind that these figures are based on minimum distributions. You may increase your distributions at any time during your lifetime.

173

Mr. and Mrs. Client
Initial plan balance $1,000,000
Current ages 65 and 63

1. Minimum distributions based on husband's and wife's joint life expectancies.

2. Assume upon husband's death at age 83 in year 2016, wife takes a spousal rollover. She also names the children and/or grandchildren as her joint beneficiaries and takes minimum distributions during her lifetime based on their joint life expectancies. (Regardless of age, children and grandchildren are deemed to be 10 years younger than the wife.)

3. Assume wife dies at age 87 in year 2022, the IRA balance splits into inherited IRAs for each of the children and/or grandchildren. Children and/or grandchildren will then take minimum distributions based on their own individual life expectancies.

Minimum Distributions—Alternative #1

Year	Client L/E	Spouse L/E	Joint L/E	2nd Benef. L/E	2nd Joint L/E	Pension Fund Begin Value	Life Exp.	Minimum Distributions
1998	20.0	21.6	26.0	44.4	45.1	$1,000,000	26.0	$0
1999	19.2	20.8	25.1	43.5	44.1	$1,100,000	25.1	$0
2000	18.4	20.0	24.2	42.5	43.1	$1,210,000	24.2	$0
2001	17.6	19.2	23.3	41.5	42.2	$1,331,000	23.3	$0
2002	16.8	18.4	22.4	40.6	41.2	$1,464,100	22.4	$0
2003	16.0	17.6	21.5	39.6	40.2	$1,610,510	21.5	$74,907
2004	15.3	16.6	20.2	38.7	39.3	$1,689,163	20.2	$83,622
2005	14.6	15.6	19.4	37.7	38.3	$1,766,095	19.4	$91,036
2006	13.9	14.6	18.5	36.8	37.3	$1,842,565	18.5	$99,598
2007	13.2	13.6	17.3	35.9	36.4	$1,917,264	17.3	$110,825
2008	12.5	12.6	16.5	34.9	35.4	$1,987,083	16.5	$120,429
2009	11.9	11.6	15.4	34.0	34.5	$2,053,319	15.4	$133,332
2010	11.2	10.6	14.6	33.1	33.6	$2,111,986	14.6	$144,657
2011	10.6	9.6	13.5	32.2	32.6	$2,164,062	13.5	$160,301
2012	10.0	8.6	12.5	31.3	31.7	$2,204,137	12.5	$176,331
2013	9.5	7.6	11.6	30.4	30.8	$2,230,587	11.6	$192,292
2014	8.9	6.6	10.8	29.5	29.9	$2,242,125	10.8	$207,604
2015	8.4	5.6	9.8	28.6	29.0	$2,237,973	9.8	$228,365
*2016	7.9	4.6	8.9	27.7	28.1	$2,210,569	8.9	$248,379
2017	0.0	8.4	3.6	26.8	27.2	$2,158,409	16.0	$134,901
2018	0.0	7.9	2.6	25.8	25.4	$2,225,859	15.3	$145,481
2019	0.0	7.4	1.6	24.8	24.5	$2,288,416	14.5	$157,822
2020	0.0	6.9	0.6	23.8	23.7	$2,343,653	13.8	$169,830
2021	0.0	6.5	0.0	22.8	22.8	$2,391,205	13.1	$182,535
*2022	0.0	6.1	0.0	21.8	21.9	$2,429,537	12.4	$195,930

Minimum Distributions—Alternative #1 (*continued*)

Year	Client L/E	Spouse L/E	Joint L/E	2nd Benef. L/E	2nd Joint L/E	Pension Fund Begin Value	Life Exp.	Minimum Distributions
2023	0.0	0.0	0.0	20.8	20.8	$2,456,968	20.8	$118,123
2024	0.0	0.0	0.0	19.8	19.8	$2,572,730	19.8	$129,936
2025	0.0	0.0	0.0	18.8	18.8	$2,687,073	18.8	$142,929
2026	0.0	0.0	0.0	17.8	17.8	$2,798,558	17.8	$157,222
2027	0.0	0.0	0.0	16.8	16.8	$2,905,470	16.8	$172,945
2028	0.0	0.0	0.0	15.8	15.8	$3,005,778	15.8	$190,239
2029	0.0	0.0	0.0	14.8	14.8	$3,097,093	14.8	$209,263
2030	0.0	0.0	0.0	13.8	13.8	$3,176,613	13.8	$230,189
2031	0.0	0.0	0.0	12.8	12.8	$3,241,066	12.8	$253,208
2032	0.0	0.0	0.0	11.8	11.8	$3,286,644	11.8	$278,529
2033	0.0	0.0	0.0	10.8	10.8	$3,308,927	10.8	$306,382
2034	0.0	0.0	0.0	9.8	9.8	$3,302,800	9.8	$337,020

Mr. and Mrs. Client
Initial plan balance $1,000,000
Current ages 65 and 63

1. Minimum distributions based on husband's and wife's joint life expectancies.

2. Assume upon husband's death at age 83 in year 2016, wife takes a spousal rollover. She also names the children and/or grandchildren as her joint beneficiaries and takes minimum distributions during her lifetime based on their joint life expectancies. (Regardless of age, children and grandchildren are deemed to be 10 years younger than the wife.)

3. Assume wife dies at age 87 in year 2022, the IRA balance splits into inherited IRAs for each of the children and/or grandchildren. Children and/or grandchildren will then take minimum distributions based on their own individual life expectancies.

Total Distributions—Alternative #1

Year	Pension Fund Distributions	Inc. Tax on Distributions	Yearly After-Tax Distributions	Cumulative After-Tax Distributions
1998	$0	$0	$0	$0
1999	$0	$0	$0	$0
2000	$0	$0	$0	$0

(*continues*)

Total Distributions—Alternative #1 (*continued*)

Year	Pension Fund Distributions	Inc. Tax on Distributions	Yearly After-Tax Distributions	Cumulative After-Tax Distributions
2001	$0	$0	$0	$0
2002	$0	$0	$0	$0
2003	$74,907	$29,963	$44,944	$44,944
2004	$83,622	$33,449	$50,173	$95,117
2005	$91,036	$36,414	$54,622	$149,739
2006	$99,598	$39,839	$59,759	$209,498
2007	$110,825	$44,330	$66,495	$275,993
2008	$120,429	$48,172	$72,257	$348,250
2009	$133,332	$53,333	$79,999	$428,249
2010	$144,657	$57,863	$86,794	$515,043
2011	$160,301	$64,120	$96,181	$611,224
2012	$176,331	$70,532	$105,799	$717,023
2013	$192,292	$76,917	$115,375	$832,398
2014	$207,604	$83,042	$124,562	$956,960
2015	$228,365	$91,346	$137,019	$1,093,979
2016	$248,379	$99,352	$149,027	$1,243,006
2017	$134,901	$53,960	$80,941	$1,323,947
2018	$145,481	$58,192	$87,289	$1,411,236
2019	$157,822	$63,129	$94,693	$1,505,929
2020	$169,830	$67,932	$101,898	$1,607,827
2021	$182,535	$73,014	$109,521	$1,717,348
*2022	$195,930	$78,372	$117,558	$1,834,906
2023	$118,123	$26,368	$91,755	$1,926,661
2024	$129,936	$29,005	$100,931	$2,027,592
2025	$142,929	$31,905	$111,024	$2,138,616
2026	$157,222	$35,096	$122,126	$2,260,742
2027	$172,945	$38,605	$134,340	$2,395,082
2028	$190,239	$42,466	$147,773	$2,542,855
2029	$209,263	$46,712	$162,551	$2,705,406
2030	$230,189	$51,384	$178,805	$2,884,211
2031	$253,208	$56,522	$196,686	$3,080,897
2032	$278,529	$62,174	$216,355	$3,297,252

Child #1
Born 5/6/60
Inherited IRA $607,384

(Assuming upon wife's death at age 87 in year 2022, the balance of $2,429,537 splits into four inherited IRAs of $607,384 for each child and grandchild.)

Minimum Distributions—Alternative #1

Year	2nd Benef. L/E	2nd Joint L/E	Pension Fund Begin Value	Life Exp.	Minimum Distributions
2023	20.8	20.8	$607,384	20.8	$29,201
2024	19.8	19.8	$636,001	19.8	$32,121
2025	18.8	18.8	$664,268	18.8	$35,333
2026	17.8	17.8	$691,829	17.8	$38,867
2027	16.8	16.8	$718,258	16.8	$42,753
2028	15.8	15.8	$743,056	15.8	$47,029
2029	14.8	14.8	$765,630	14.8	$51,732
2030	13.8	13.8	$785,288	13.8	$56,905
2031	12.8	12.8	$801,221	12.8	$62,595
2032	11.8	11.8	$812,489	11.8	$68,855
2033	10.8	10.8	$817,997	10.8	$75,740
2034	9.8	9.8	$816,483	9.8	$83,315
2035	8.8	8.8	$806,485	8.8	$91,646
2036	7.8	7.8	$786,323	7.8	$100,811
2037	6.8	6.8	$754,063	6.8	$110,892
2038	5.8	5.8	$707,488	5.8	$121,981
2039	4.8	4.8	$644,058	4.8	$134,179
2040	3.8	3.8	$560,867	3.8	$147,597
2041	2.8	2.8	$454,597	2.8	$162,356
2042	1.8	1.8	$321,465	1.8	$178,592
2043	0.8	0.8	$157,160	0.8	$157,160
2044	0.0	0.0	$0	0.0	$0
2045	0.0	0.0	$0	0.0	$0
2046	0.0	0.0	$0	0.0	$0
2047	0.0	0.0	$0	0.0	$0
2048	0.0	0.0	$0	0.0	$0
2049	0.0	0.0	$0	0.0	$0
2050	0.0	0.0	$0	0.0	$0
2051	0.0	0.0	$0	0.0	$0
2052	0.0	0.0	$0	0.0	$0
2053	0.0	0.0	$0	0.0	$0
2054	0.0	0.0	$0	0.0	$0
2055	0.0	0.0	$0	0.0	$0
2056	0.0	0.0	$0	0.0	$0
2057	0.0	0.0	$0	0.0	$0
2058	0.0	0.0	$0	0.0	$0
2059	0.0	0.0	$0	0.0	$0
2060	0.0	0.0	$0	0.0	$0
2061	0.0	0.0	$0	0.0	$0

(*continues*)

Minimum Distributions—Alternative #1 (*continued*)

Year	2nd Benef. L/E	2nd Joint L/E	Pension Fund Begin Value	Life Exp.	Minimum Distributions
2062	0.0	0.0	$0	0.0	$0
2063	0.0	0.0	$0	0.0	$0
2064	0.0	0.0	$0	0.0	$0
2065	0.0	0.0	$0	0.0	$0
2066	0.0	0.0	$0	0.0	$0
2067	0.0	0.0	$0	0.0	$0
2068	0.0	0.0	$0	0.0	$0
2069	0.0	0.0	$0	0.0	$0

Child #1
Born 5/6/60
Inherited IRA $607,384

(Assuming upon wife's death at age 87 in year 2022, the balance of $2,429,537 splits into four inherited IRAs of $607,384 for each child and grandchild.)

Total Distributions—Alternative #1

Year	Pension Fund Distributions	Inc. Tax on Distributions	Yearly After-Tax Distributions	Cumulative After-Tax Distributions
2023	$29,201	$11,680	$17,521	$17,521
2024	$32,121	$12,848	$19,273	$36,794
2025	$35,333	$14,133	$21,200	$57,994
2026	$38,867	$15,547	$23,320	$81,314
2027	$42,753	$17,101	$25,652	$106,966
2028	$47,029	$18,812	$28,217	$135,183
2029	$51,732	$20,693	$31,039	$166,222
2030	$56,905	$22,762	$34,143	$200,365
2031	$62,595	$25,038	$37,557	$237,922
2032	$68,855	$27,542	$41,313	$279,235
2033	$75,740	$30,296	$45,444	$324,679
2034	$83,315	$33,326	$49,989	$374,668
2035	$91,646	$36,658	$54,988	$429,656
2036	$100,811	$40,324	$60,487	$490,143
2037	$110,892	$44,357	$66,535	$556,678
2038	$121,981	$48,792	$73,189	$629,867
2039	$134,179	$53,672	$80,507	$710,374
2040	$147,597	$59,039	$88,558	$798,932
2041	$162,356	$64,942	$97,414	$896,346
2042	$178,592	$71,437	$107,155	$1,003,501
2043	$157,160	$62,864	$94,296	$1,097,797
2044	$0	$0	$0	$1,097,797

Year	Pension Fund Distributions	Inc. Tax on Distributions	Yearly After-Tax Distributions	Cumulative After-Tax Distributions
2045	$0	$0	$0	$1,097,797
2046	$0	$0	$0	$1,097,797
2047	$0	$0	$0	$1,097,797
2048	$0	$0	$0	$1,097,797
2049	$0	$0	$0	$1,097,797
2050	$0	$0	$0	$1,097,797
2051	$0	$0	$0	$1,097,797
2052	$0	$0	$0	$1,097,797
2053	$0	$0	$0	$1,097,797
2054	$0	$0	$0	$1,097,797
2055	$0	$0	$0	$1,097,797
2056	$0	$0	$0	$1,097,797
2057	$0	$0	$0	$1,097,797
2058	$0	$0	$0	$1,097,797
2059	$0	$0	$0	$1,097,797
2060	$0	$0	$0	$1,097,797
2061	$0	$0	$0	$1,097,797
2062	$0	$0	$0	$1,097,797
2063	$0	$0	$0	$1,097,797
2064	$0	$0	$0	$1,097,797
2065	$0	$0	$0	$1,097,797
2066	$0	$0	$0	$1,097,797
2067	$0	$0	$0	$1,097,797

Child #2
Born 12/29/61
Inherited IRA $607,384

(Assuming upon wife's death at age 87 in year 2022, the balance of $2,429,537 splits into four inherited IRAs of $607,384 for each child and grandchild.)

Minimum Distributions—Alternative #1

Year	2nd Benef. L/E	2nd Joint L/E	Pension Fund Begin Value	Life Exp.	Minimum Distributions
2023	21.7	21.7	$607,384	21.7	$27,990
2024	20.7	20.7	$637,333	20.7	$30,789
2025	19.7	19.7	$667,198	19.7	$33,868
2026	18.7	18.7	$696,663	18.7	$37,255
2027	17.7	17.7	$725,349	17.7	$40,980
2028	16.7	16.7	$752,806	16.7	$45,078

(continues)

Minimum Distributions—Alternative #1 (*continued*)

Year	2nd Benef. L/E	2nd Joint L/E	Pension Fund Begin Value	Life Exp.	Minimum Distributions
2029	15.7	15.7	$778,501	15.7	$49,586
2030	14.7	14.7	$801,807	14.7	$54,545
2031	13.7	13.7	$821,988	13.7	$59,999
2032	12.7	12.7	$838,188	12.7	$65,999
2033	11.7	11.7	$849,408	11.7	$72,599
2034	10.7	10.7	$854,490	10.7	$79,859
2035	9.7	9.7	$852,094	9.7	$87,845
2036	8.7	8.7	$840,674	8.7	$96,629
2037	7.7	7.7	$818,450	7.7	$106,292
2038	6.7	6.7	$783,374	6.7	$116,921
2039	5.7	5.7	$733,098	5.7	$128,614
2040	4.7	4.7	$664,932	4.7	$141,475
2041	3.7	3.7	$575,803	3.7	$155,622
2042	2.7	2.7	$462,199	2.7	$171,185
2043	1.7	1.7	$320,115	1.7	$188,303
2044	0.7	0.7	$144,993	0.7	$144,993
2045	0.0	0.0	$0	0.0	$0
2046	0.0	0.0	$0	0.0	$0
2047	0.0	0.0	$0	0.0	$0
2048	0.0	0.0	$0	0.0	$0
2049	0.0	0.0	$0	0.0	$0
2050	0.0	0.0	$0	0.0	$0
2051	0.0	0.0	$0	0.0	$0
2052	0.0	0.0	$0	0.0	$0
2053	0.0	0.0	$0	0.0	$0
2054	0.0	0.0	$0	0.0	$0
2055	0.0	0.0	$0	0.0	$0
2056	0.0	0.0	$0	0.0	$0
2057	0.0	0.0	$0	0.0	$0
2058	0.0	0.0	$0	0.0	$0
2059	0.0	0.0	$0	0.0	$0
2060	0.0	0.0	$0	0.0	$0
2061	0.0	0.0	$0	0.0	$0
2062	0.0	0.0	$0	0.0	$0
2063	0.0	0.0	$0	0.0	$0
2064	0.0	0.0	$0	0.0	$0
2065	0.0	0.0	$0	0.0	$0
2066	0.0	0.0	$0	0.0	$0
2067	0.0	0.0	$0	0.0	$0
2068	0.0	0.0	$0	0.0	$0
2069	0.0	0.0	$0	0.0	$0

Child #2
Born 12/29/61
Inherited IRA $607,384

(Assuming upon wife's death at age 87 in year 2022, the balance of $2,429,537 splits into four inherited IRAs of $607,384 for each child and grandchild.)

Total Distributions—Alternative #1

Year	Pension Fund Distributions	Inc. Tax on Distributions	Yearly After-Tax Distributions	Cumulative After-Tax Distributions
2023	$27,990	$11,196	$16,794	$16,794
2024	$30,789	$12,316	$18,473	$35,267
2025	$33,868	$13,547	$20,321	$55,588
2026	$37,255	$14,902	$22,353	$77,941
2027	$40,980	$16,392	$24,588	$102,529
2028	$45,078	$18,031	$27,047	$129,576
2029	$49,586	$19,834	$29,752	$159,328
2030	$54,545	$21,818	$32,727	$192,055
2031	$59,999	$24,000	$35,999	$228,054
2032	$65,999	$26,400	$39,599	$267,653
2033	$72,599	$29,040	$43,559	$311,212
2034	$79,859	$31,944	$47,915	$359,127
2035	$87,845	$35,138	$52,707	$411,834
2036	$96,629	$38,652	$57,977	$469,811
2037	$106,292	$42,517	$63,775	$533,586
2038	$116,921	$46,768	$70,153	$603,739
2039	$128,614	$51,446	$77,168	$680,907
2040	$141,475	$56,590	$84,885	$765,792
2041	$155,622	$62,249	$93,373	$859,165
2042	$171,185	$68,474	$102,711	$961,876
2043	$188,303	$75,321	$112,982	$1,074,858
2044	$144,993	$57,997	$86,996	$1,161,854
2045	$0	$0	$0	$1,161,854
2046	$0	$0	$0	$1,161,854
2047	$0	$0	$0	$1,161,854
2048	$0	$0	$0	$1,161,854
2049	$0	$0	$0	$1,161,854
2050	$0	$0	$0	$1,161,854
2051	$0	$0	$0	$1,161,854
2052	$0	$0	$0	$1,161,854
2053	$0	$0	$0	$1,161,854
2054	$0	$0	$0	$1,161,854
2055	$0	$0	$0	$1,161,854
2056	$0	$0	$0	$1,161,854
2057	$0	$0	$0	$1,161,854
2058	$0	$0	$0	$1,161,854
2059	$0	$0	$0	$1,161,854
2060	$0	$0	$0	$1,161,854

(continues)

Total Distributions—Alternative #1 (*continued*)

Year	Pension Fund Distributions	Inc. Tax on Distributions	Yearly After-Tax Distributions	Cumulative After-Tax Distributions
2061	$0	$0	$0	$1,161,854
2062	$0	$0	$0	$1,161,854
2063	$0	$0	$0	$1,161,854
2064	$0	$0	$0	$1,161,854
2065	$0	$0	$0	$1,161,854
2066	$0	$0	$0	$1,161,854
2067	$0	$0	$0	$1,161,854

Grandchild #1
Born 10/18/93
Inherited IRA $607,384

(Assuming upon wife's death at age 87 in year 2022, the balance of $2,429,537 splits into four inherited IRAs of $607,384 for each child and grandchild.)

Minimum Distributions—Alternative #1

Year	2nd Benef. L/E	2nd Joint L/E	Pension Fund Begin Value	Life Exp.	Minimum Distributions
2023	52.0	52.0	$607,384	52.0	$11,680
2024	51.0	51.0	$655,274	51.0	$12,849
2025	50.0	50.0	$706,668	50.0	$14,133
2026	49.0	49.0	$761,789	49.0	$15,547
2027	48.0	48.0	$820,866	48.0	$17,101
2028	47.0	47.0	$884,142	47.0	$18,812
2029	46.0	46.0	$951,863	46.0	$20,693
2030	45.0	45.0	$1,024,287	45.0	$22,762
2031	44.0	44.0	$1,101,678	44.0	$25,038
2032	43.0	43.0	$1,184,304	43.0	$27,542
2033	42.0	42.0	$1,272,438	42.0	$30,296
2034	41.0	41.0	$1,366,356	41.0	$33,326
2035	40.0	40.0	$1,466,333	40.0	$36,658
2036	39.0	39.0	$1,572,643	39.0	$40,324
2037	38.0	38.0	$1,685,551	38.0	$44,357
2038	37.0	37.0	$1,805,313	37.0	$48,792
2039	36.0	36.0	$1,932,173	36.0	$53,671
2040	35.0	35.0	$2,066,352	35.0	$59,039
2041	34.0	34.0	$2,208,044	34.0	$64,942
2042	33.0	33.0	$2,357,412	33.0	$71,437
2043	32.0	32.0	$2,514,573	32.0	$78,580
2044	31.0	31.0	$2,679,592	31.0	$86,438
2045	30.0	30.0	$2,852,469	30.0	$95,082
2046	29.0	29.0	$3,033,126	29.0	$104,591

Minimum Distributions—Alternative #1 (*continued*)

Year	2nd Benef. L/E	2nd Joint L/E	Pension Fund Begin Value	Life Exp.	Minimum Distributions
2047	28.0	28.0	$3,221,389	28.0	$115,050
2048	27.0	27.0	$3,416,973	27.0	$126,555
2049	26.0	26.0	$3,619,460	26.0	$139,210
2050	25.0	25.0	$3,828,275	25.0	$153,131
2051	24.0	24.0	$4,042,658	24.0	$168,444
2052	23.0	23.0	$4,261,635	23.0	$185,288
2053	22.0	22.0	$4,483,982	22.0	$203,817
2054	21.0	21.0	$4,708,182	21.0	$224,199
2055	20.0	20.0	$4,932,381	20.0	$246,619
2056	19.0	19.0	$5,154,338	19.0	$271,281
2057	18.0	18.0	$5,371,363	18.0	$298,409
2058	17.0	17.0	$5,580,249	17.0	$328,250
2059	16.0	16.0	$5,777,199	16.0	$361,075
2060	15.0	15.0	$5,957,736	15.0	$397,182
2061	14.0	14.0	$6,116,609	14.0	$436,901
2062	13.0	13.0	$6,247,679	13.0	$480,591
2063	12.0	12.0	$6,343,797	12.0	$528,650
2064	11.0	11.0	$6,396,662	11.0	$581,515
2065	10.0	10.0	$6,396,662	10.0	$639,666
2066	9.0	9.0	$6,332,696	9.0	$703,633
2067	8.0	8.0	$6,191,969	8.0	$773,996
2068	7.0	7.0	$5,959,770	7.0	$851,396
2069	6.0	6.0	$5,619,211	6.0	$936,535

Grandchild #1
Born 10/18/93
Inherited IRA $607,384

(Assuming upon wife's death at age 87 in year 2022, the balance of $2,429,537 splits into four inherited IRAs of $607,384 for each child and grandchild.)

Minimum Distributions—Alternative #1

Year	2nd Benef. L/E	2nd Joint L/E	Pension Fund Begin Value	Life Exp.	Minimum Distributions
2070	5.0	5.0	$5,150,944	5.0	$1,030,189
2071	4.0	4.0	$4,532,831	4.0	$1,133,208
2072	3.0	3.0	$3,739,585	3.0	$1,246,528
2073	2.0	2.0	$2,742,363	2.0	$1,371,182
2074	1.0	1.0	$1,508,299	1.0	$1,508,299
2075	0.0	0.0	$0	0.0	$0
2076	0.0	0.0	$0	0.0	$0
2077	0.0	0.0	$0	0.0	$0
2078	0.0	0.0	$0	0.0	$0
2079	0.0	0.0	$0	0.0	$0
2080	0.0	0.0	$0	0.0	$0
2081	0.0	0.0	$0	0.0	$0
2082	0.0	0.0	$0	0.0	$0

Grandchild #1
Born 10/18/93
Inherited IRA $607,384

(Assuming upon wife's death at age 87 in year 2022, the balance of $2,429,537 splits into four inherited IRAs of $607,384 for each child and grandchild.)

Total Distributions—Alternative #1

Year	Pension Fund Distributions	Inc. Tax on Distributions	Yearly After-Tax Distributions	Cumulative After-Tax Distributions
2023	$11,680	$4,672	$7,008	$7,008
2024	$12,849	$5,140	$7,709	$14,717
2025	$14,133	$5,653	$8,480	$23,197
2026	$15,547	$6,219	$9,328	$32,525
2027	$17,101	$6,840	$10,261	$42,786
2028	$18,812	$7,525	$11,287	$54,073

Year	Pension Fund Distributions	Inc. Tax on Distributions	Yearly After-Tax Distributions	Cumulative After-Tax Distributions
2029	$20,693	$8,277	$12,416	$66,489
2030	$22,762	$9,105	$13,657	$80,146
2031	$25,038	$10,015	$15,023	$95,169
2032	$27,542	$11,017	$16,525	$111,694
2033	$30,296	$12,118	$18,178	$129,872
2034	$33,326	$13,330	$19,996	$149,868
2035	$36,658	$14,663	$21,995	$171,863
2036	$40,324	$16,130	$24,194	$196,057
2037	$44,357	$17,743	$26,614	$222,671
2038	$48,792	$19,517	$29,275	$251,946
2039	$53,671	$21,468	$32,203	$284,149
2040	$59,039	$23,616	$35,423	$319,572
2041	$64,942	$25,977	$38,965	$358,537
2042	$71,437	$28,575	$42,862	$401,399
2043	$78,580	$31,432	$47,148	$448,547
2044	$86,438	$34,575	$51,863	$500,410
2045	$95,082	$38,033	$57,049	$557,459
2046	$104,591	$41,836	$62,755	$620,214
2047	$115,050	$46,020	$69,030	$689,244
2048	$126,555	$50,622	$75,933	$765,177
2049	$139,210	$55,684	$83,526	$848,703
2050	$153,131	$61,252	$91,879	$940,582
2051	$168,444	$67,378	$101,066	$1,041,648
2052	$185,288	$74,115	$111,173	$1,152,821
2053	$203,817	$81,527	$122,290	$1,275,111
2054	$224,199	$89,680	$134,519	$1,409,630
2055	$246,619	$98,648	$147,971	$1,557,601
2056	$271,281	$108,512	$162,769	$1,720,370
2057	$298,409	$119,364	$179,045	$1,899,415
2058	$328,250	$131,300	$196,950	$2,096,365
2059	$361,075	$144,430	$216,645	$2,313,010
2060	$397,182	$158,873	$238,309	$2,551,319
2061	$436,901	$174,760	$262,141	$2,813,460
2062	$480,591	$192,236	$288,355	$3,101,815
2063	$528,650	$211,460	$317,190	$3,419,005
2064	$581,515	$232,606	$348,909	$3,767,914
2065	$639,666	$255,866	$383,800	$4,151,714
2066	$703,633	$281,453	$422,180	$4,573,894
2067	$773,996	$309,598	$464,398	$5,038,292

Grandchild #1
Born 10/18/93
Inherited IRA $607,384

(Assuming upon wife's death at age 87 in year 2022, the balance of $2,429,537 splits into four inherited IRAs of $607,384 for each child and grandchild.)

Total Distributions—Alternative #1

Year	Pension Fund Distributions	Inc. Tax on Distributions	Yearly After-Tax Distributions	Cumulative After-Tax Distributions
2068	$851,396	$340,558	$510,838	$5,549,130
2069	$936,535	$374,614	$561,921	$6,111,051
2070	$1,030,189	$412,076	$618,113	$6,729,164
2071	$1,133,208	$453,283	$679,925	$7,409,089
2072	$1,246,528	$498,611	$747,917	$8,157,006
2073	$1,371,182	$548,473	$822,709	$8,979,715
2074	$1,508,299	$603,320	$904,979	$9,884,694
2075	$0	$0	$0	$9,884,694
2076	$0	$0	$0	$9,884,694
2077	$0	$0	$0	$9,884,694
2078	$0	$0	$0	$9,884,694
2079	$0	$0	$0	$9,884,694
2080	$0	$0	$0	$9,884,694
2081	$0	$0	$0	$9,884,694
2082	$0	$0	$0	$9,884,694

Grandchild #2
Born 3/15/96
Inherited IRA $607,384

(Assuming upon wife's death at age 87 in year 2022, the balance of $2,429,537 splits into four inherited IRAs of $607,384 for each child and grandchild.)

Minimum Distributions—Alternative #1

Year	2nd Benef. L/E	2nd Joint L/E	Pension Fund Begin Value	Life Exp.	Minimum Distributions
2023	54.9	54.9	$607,384	54.9	$11,063
2024	53.9	53.9	$655,953	53.9	$12,170
2025	52.9	52.9	$708,161	52.9	$13,387
2026	51.9	51.9	$764,251	51.9	$14,725
2027	50.9	50.9	$824,479	50.9	$16,198

Year	2nd Benef. L/E	2nd Joint L/E	Pension Fund Begin Value	Life Exp.	Minimum Distributions
2028	49.9	49.9	$889,109	49.9	$17,818
2029	48.9	48.9	$958,420	48.9	$19,600
2030	47.9	47.9	$1,032,702	47.9	$21,560
2031	46.9	46.9	$1,112,256	46.9	$23,715
2032	45.9	45.9	$1,197,395	45.9	$26,087
2033	44.9	44.9	$1,288,439	44.9	$28,696
2034	43.9	43.9	$1,385,717	43.9	$31,565
2035	42.9	42.9	$1,489,567	42.9	$34,722
2036	41.9	41.9	$1,600,330	41.9	$38,194
2037	40.9	40.9	$1,718,350	40.9	$42,013
2038	39.9	39.9	$1,843,971	39.9	$46,215
2039	38.9	38.9	$1,977,532	38.9	$50,836
2040	37.9	37.9	$2,119,366	37.9	$55,920
2041	36.9	36.9	$2,269,791	36.9	$61,512
2042	35.9	35.9	$2,429,107	35.9	$67,663
2043	34.9	34.9	$2,597,588	34.9	$74,429
2044	33.9	33.9	$2,775,475	33.9	$81,872
2045	32.9	32.9	$2,962,963	32.9	$90,060
2046	31.9	31.9	$3,160,193	31.9	$99,066
2047	30.9	30.9	$3,367,240	30.9	$108,972
2048	29.9	29.9	$3,584,095	29.9	$119,869
2049	28.9	28.9	$3,810,649	28.9	$131,856
2050	27.9	27.9	$4,046,672	27.9	$145,042
2051	26.9	26.9	$4,291,793	26.9	$159,546
2052	25.9	25.9	$4,545,472	25.9	$175,501
2053	24.9	24.9	$4,806,968	24.9	$193,051
2054	23.9	23.9	$5,075,309	23.9	$212,356
2055	22.9	22.9	$5,349,248	22.9	$233,592
2056	21.9	21.9	$5,627,222	21.9	$256,951
2057	20.9	20.9	$5,907,298	20.9	$282,646
2058	19.9	19.9	$6,187,117	19.9	$310,910
2059	18.9	18.9	$6,463,828	18.9	$342,001
2060	17.9	17.9	$6,734,010	17.9	$376,202
2061	16.9	16.9	$6,993,589	16.9	$413,822
2062	15.9	15.9	$7,237,744	15.9	$455,204
2063	14.9	14.9	$7,460,794	14.9	$500,724
2064	13.9	13.9	$7,656,077	13.9	$550,797
2065	12.9	12.9	$7,815,808	12.9	$605,877
2066	11.9	11.9	$7,930,924	11.9	$666,464
2067	10.9	10.9	$7,990,906	10.9	$733,111
2068	9.9	9.9	$7,983,575	9.9	$806,422
2069	8.9	8.9	$7,894,868	8.9	$887,064

Grandchild #2
Born 3/15/96
Inherited IRA $607,384

(Assuming upon wife's death at age 87 in year 2022, the balance of $2,429,537 splits into four inherited IRAs of $607,384 for each child and grandchild.)

Minimum Distributions—Alternative #1

Year	2nd Benef. L/E	2nd Joint L/E	Pension Fund Begin Value	Life Exp.	Minimum Distributions
2070	7.9	7.9	$7,708,584	7.9	$975,770
2071	6.9	6.9	$7,406,095	6.9	$1,073,347
2072	5.9	5.9	$6,966,023	5.9	$1,180,682
2073	4.9	4.9	$6,363,875	4.9	$1,298,750
2074	3.9	3.9	$5,571,638	3.9	$1,428,625
2075	2.9	2.9	$4,557,314	2.9	$1,571,488
2076	1.9	1.9	$3,284,409	1.9	$1,728,636
2077	0.9	0.9	$1,711,350	0.9	$1,711,350
2078	0.0	0.0	$0	0.0	$0
2079	0.0	0.0	$0	0.0	$0
2080	0.0	0.0	$0	0.0	$0
2081	0.0	0.0	$0	0.0	$0
2082	0.0	0.0	$0	0.0	$0

Grandchild #2
Born 3/15/96
Inherited IRA $607,384

(Assuming upon wife's death at age 87 in year 2022, the balance of $2,429,537 splits into four inherited IRAs of $607,384 for each child and grandchild.)

Total Distributions—Alternative #1

Year	Pension Fund Distributions	Inc. Tax on Distributions	Yearly After-Tax Distributions	Cumulative After-Tax Distributions
2023	$11,063	$4,425	$6,638	$6,638
2024	$12,170	$4,868	$7,302	$13,940
2025	$13,387	$5,355	$8,032	$21,972
2026	$14,725	$5,890	$8,835	$30,807
2027	$16,198	$6,479	$9,719	$40,526
2028	$17,818	$7,127	$10,691	$51,217
2029	$19,600	$7,840	$11,760	$62,977

Year	Pension Fund Distributions	Inc. Tax on Distributions	Yearly After-Tax Distributions	Cumulative After-Tax Distributions
2030	$21,560	$8,624	$12,936	$75,913
2031	$23,715	$9,486	$14,229	$90,142
2032	$26,087	$10,435	$15,652	$105,794
2033	$28,696	$11,478	$17,218	$123,012
2034	$31,565	$12,626	$18,939	$141,951
2035	$34,722	$13,889	$20,833	$162,784
2036	$38,194	$15,278	$22,916	$185,700
2037	$42,013	$16,805	$25,208	$210,908
2038	$46,215	$18,486	$27,729	$238,637
2039	$50,836	$20,334	$30,502	$269,139
2040	$55,920	$22,368	$33,552	$302,691
2041	$61,512	$24,605	$36,907	$339,598
2042	$67,663	$27,065	$40,598	$380,196
2043	$74,429	$29,772	$44,657	$424,853
2044	$81,872	$32,749	$49,123	$473,976
2045	$90,060	$36,024	$54,036	$528,012
2046	$99,066	$39,626	$59,440	$587,452
2047	$108,972	$43,589	$65,383	$652,835
2048	$119,869	$47,948	$71,921	$724,756
2049	$131,856	$52,742	$79,114	$803,870
2050	$145,042	$58,017	$87,025	$890,895
2051	$159,546	$63,818	$95,728	$986,623
2052	$175,501	$70,200	$105,301	$1,091,924
2053	$193,051	$77,220	$115,831	$1,207,755
2054	$212,356	$84,942	$127,414	$1,335,169
2055	$233,592	$93,437	$140,155	$1,475,324
2056	$256,951	$102,780	$154,171	$1,629,495
2057	$282,646	$113,058	$169,588	$1,799,083
2058	$310,910	$124,364	$186,546	$1,985,629
2059	$342,001	$136,800	$205,201	$2,190,830
2060	$376,202	$150,481	$225,721	$2,416,551
2061	$413,822	$165,529	$248,293	$2,664,844
2062	$455,204	$182,082	$273,122	$2,937,966
2063	$500,724	$200,290	$300,434	$3,238,400
2064	$550,797	$220,319	$330,478	$3,568,878
2065	$605,877	$242,351	$363,526	$3,932,404
2066	$666,464	$266,586	$399,878	$4,332,282
2067	$733,111	$293,244	$439,867	$4,772,149

Grandchild #2
Born 3/15/96
Inherited IRA $607,384

(Assuming upon wife's death at age 87 in year 2022, the balance of $2,429,537 splits into four inherited IRAs of $607,384 for each child and grandchild.)

Total Distributions—Alternative #1

Year	Pension Fund Distributions	Inc. Tax on Distributions	Yearly After-Tax Distributions	Cumulative After-Tax Distributions
2068	$806,422	$322,569	$483,853	$5,256,002
2069	$887,064	$354,826	$532,238	$5,788,240
2070	$975,770	$390,308	$585,462	$6,373,702
2071	$1,073,347	$429,339	$644,008	$7,017,710
2072	$1,180,682	$472,273	$708,409	$7,726,119
2073	$1,298,750	$519,500	$779,250	$8,505,369
2074	$1,428,625	$571,450	$857,175	$9,362,544
2075	$1,571,488	$628,595	$942,893	$10,305,437
2076	$1,728,636	$691,454	$1,037,182	$11,342,619
2077	$1,711,350	$684,540	$1,026,810	$12,369,429
2078	$0	$0	$0	$12,369,429
2079	$0	$0	$0	$12,369,429
2080	$0	$0	$0	$12,369,429
2081	$0	$0	$0	$12,369,429
2082	$0	$0	$0	$12,369,429

How to Stretch Out Your IRA

Maximize the total income stream over your lifetime, your spouse's lifetime, and your children's lifetimes.

1. Elect the most beneficial payout method. We recommend recalculating life expectancy on the owner and term-certain on the wife. Minimum distributions will be based upon their joint life expectancy.

2. Upon the IRA owner's death, the wife will take a spousal rollover. At this point, there is no estate tax or income tax due between spouses.

3. The wife will take over the IRA. At this time she must elect the beneficiary designation and payout method. The wife should name the children and/or grandchildren as her own beneficiaries and elect a joint payout. Each beneficiary would have his or her own individual inherited IRAs. The children would be deemed 10 years younger than the wife, and the minimum distribution will be based on their joint life expectancies, thus stretching out the payout period.

    Keep in mind with this plan, you and your wife may increase your withdrawals at any time during your lifetimes if you need more income.

4. Upon the wife's death, the IRA balance would split into individual inherited IRAs for each beneficiary. The payouts would now be based on their individual term-certain life expectancy. At this point, the estate taxes would be due on the IRA balance going to the children. You should not withdraw monies from the IRA, because this would diminish the IRA balance after taxes are paid.

    We recommend utilizing assets other than the IRA to pay the estate tax. By preserving and allowing the IRA to grow, it could stretch out and slow down the distributions over the lifetimes of the children.

Appendix C   Excerpts from Sample Variable Annuity Contract

Summary

Your Variable Annuity Contract

You can invest for retirement by purchasing a contract if you properly complete a Customer Profile form (an application or enrollment form may be required in some states) and make a minimum initial contribution. In this prospectus, *you* and *your* mean the Annuitant, the person upon whose life the Annuity Benefit and the Death Benefit are based, usually the Owner of the contract. If the Annuitant does not own the contract, all of the rights under the contract belong to the Owner until annuity payments begin. If a Joint Owner is named, the contract rights are shared with the Owner. Contract changes or any transactions allowed under the contract require both signatures. The rules governing distribution at death apply when the first Owner dies. Your retirement or endowment date (*Retirement Date*) will be no later than your 98th birthday, or earlier if required by law, unless you notify us of a different date.

Your Benefits

Your contract provides an Account Value, an annuity benefit, and a death benefit. Your benefits may be received under a contract subject to the usual rules for taxation of annuities, including the tax deferral of earnings until withdrawal. The contract also can provide your benefits under certain tax-favored retirement programs, which are subject to special rules covering such matters as eligibility and contribution amounts.

How Your Contract Is Taxed

Under current law, any increases in the value of your contributions to your contract are tax deferred and will not be included in your taxable income until withdrawn.

Your Contributions

The minimum initial contribution in most states is currently $1,000. Subsequent contributions of at least $100 can be made. Special rules for lower minimum initial and subsequent contributions apply for certain tax-favored retirement plans.

Your Investment Options

You may allocate contributions to the Variable Account Options, to the Fixed Accounts, or both. The Variable Account Options and the Fixed Accounts are together referred to as the *Investment Options. Contributions may be allocated to up to nine Investment Options at any one time.*

Variable Account Options

The Variable Account Options, except the Divisions, invest in shares of corresponding investment portfolios of the Funds, each a "series" type of mutual fund. Each investment portfolio is referred to as a *Portfolio.* The investment objective of each Variable Account Option and its corresponding Portfolio is the same. Your value in a Variable Account Option will vary depending on the performance of the corresponding Portfolio. For a full description of a Fund, see each Fund's prospectus and the Fund's Statement of Additional Information. The Divisions invest directly in securities.

Account Value, Adjusted Account Value and Cash Value

The sum of your values under the Fixed Accounts plus your values in the Variable Account Options is referred to as the *Account Value.* Your *Adjusted Account Value* is your Account Value as increased or decreased (but not below the Minimum Value) by any Market Value Adjustments. Your *Cash Value* is equal to your adjusted Account Value reduced by any applicable contingent withdrawal charge and will be reduced by the pro rata portion of the annual administrative charge, if applicable. See "Charges and Fees" below.

Transfers

You may transfer all or portions of your Account Value among the Investment Options, subject to the conditions described under "Transfers." Transfers from any Investment Option must be for at least $250. Transfers may be arranged through our telephone transfer service. Transfers may also be made among certain investment Options under our following special services (1) Dollar Cost Averaging, (2) Customized Asset Rebalancing, (3) Asset Allocation and Rebalancing, or (4) to transfer your STO contributions.

Charges and Fees

If your Account Value is less than $50,000 as of the last day of any contract year prior to your Retirement Date, an annual administrative expense charge of $30 is deducted from your contract.

A charge at an effective annual rate of 1.35% of the Account Value of the assets in each Variable Account Option is made daily. We make this charge to cover mortality and expense risks (1.20%) and certain administrative expenses (0.15%). The charge will never be greater than an effective annual rate of 1.35% of the Account Value of the assets in each Variable Account Option.

Investment management fees and other expenses are deducted from amounts invested by the Separate Account in the Funds.

The advisory fees of a Fund or Division cannot be increased without the consent of its shareholders.

If you frequently transfer funds from one Investment Option to another, certain transfers may become subject to a charge. We will not, however, charge more than $20 per transfer.

When you make withdrawals from your contract, a contingent withdrawal charge may be deducted from your Account Value. This sales charge will be in addition to the Market Value Adjustment applicable to early withdrawals from GRO Accounts. Under certain circumstances, the contingent withdrawal charge and market value adjustment may be waived.

Withdrawals

You may make an unlimited number of withdrawals from your contract as frequently as you wish. Each withdrawal must be for at least $300. Unless specifically instructed otherwise, we will make withdrawals (including any applicable charges) from the Investment Options in the same ratio the Annuitant's Account Value in each Investment Option bears to the Annuitant's total Account Value. A sales charge of up to 8% of the contribution amount withdrawn, in excess of any free withdrawal amount (defined below), will be deducted from your Account Value, unless one of the exceptions applies. This charge defrays marketing expenses. Most withdrawals made by you prior to age 59½ are also subject to a 10% federal tax penalty. In addition, some tax-favored retirement programs limit withdrawals. For partial withdrawals, the total amount deducted from your Account Value will include the withdrawal amount requested, any applicable Market Value Adjustment, and any applicable withdrawal charge, so that the net amount you receive will be the amount requested.

The free withdrawal amount is a noncumulative amount which you may take as a partial withdrawal each contract year without being subject to the contingent withdrawal charge or any Market Value Adjustment. It is equal to 10% of the Account Value minus cumulative prior withdrawals in the current contract year. However, as explained above, a tax penalty still applies if you are under age 59½.

Your Initial Right to Revoke

Within 10 days after you receive your contract, you may cancel it by returning it to our Administrative Office. The 10-day period may be extended if required by state law. We will refund all your contributions with an adjustment for any investment gain or loss on the contributions put into each Variable Account Option from the date units were purchased until the date your contract is received by us, including any charges deducted. If state law instead requires a refund of your contributions without any adjustment, we will return that amount to you. For allocations to any of the GROs, we will refund to you the amount of your contributions.

Table of Annual Fees and Expenses

Contract Owner Transaction Expenses

Sales load on purchases	$0
Deferred sales load (1)	8% maximum
Exchange fee (2)	$0
Annual administrative charge (3)	$30

Annual Expenses of the Separate Accounts
(as a percentage of average account value)(4)

Mortality and expense risk charge	1.20%
Administrative expenses	.15%
Total separate account annual expenses	1.35%

Division Annual Expenses After Reimbursement
(as a percentage of average net assets)

Management Fees(13)	Other Expenses (14)	Total Annual Expenses (14)
0.50%	0.35%	0.85%

Deductions and Charges

Separate Account Charges

We deduct from the unit value every calendar day an amount equal to an effective annual rate of 1.35% of the Account Value in the Variable Account Options. This daily expense rate cannot be increased without your consent. Various portions of this total charge, as described below, pay for certain services to the Separate Account and the contracts. A daily charge equal to an effective annual rate of 0.15% of the value of each Variable Account Option is deducted for administrative expenses not covered by the annual administrative charge described below. The daily administrative charge, like the annual administrative charge, is designed to reimbuse Integrity for expenses actually incurred. A daily charge equal to an effective annual rate of 1.20% of the value of each Variable Account Option is deducted for the expense risk (0.85%) and the mortality risk (0.35%) under the contract. The expense risk is the risk that our actual expenses of administering the contracts will exceed the annual administrative expense charge. In this context, *mortality risk* refers to the cost of insuring the risk that annuitants, as a class of persons, will live longer than estimated and will therefore require us to pay out more annuity benefits than anticipated. The relative proportion of the mortality and expense risk charges may be modified, but the total effective annual risk charge of 1.20% of the value of the Variable Account Options may not be increased on your Contract.

We may realize a gain from these daily charges to the extent they are not needed to meet the actual expenses incurred.

Annual Administrative Charge

If your Account Value is less than $50,000 on the last day of any contract year prior to your Retirement Date, we charge an annual administrative charge of $30. This charge is deducted from your Account Value in each Investment Option on a pro rata basis. The portion of the charge applicable to the Variable Account Options will reduce the number of units credited to you. The portion of the charge applicable to the Fixed Accounts is withdrawn in dollars. The annual administrative charge will be prorated based on the number of days that have elapsed in the contract year in the event of the Annuitant's retirement, death, or termination of a contract during a contract year.

Reduction or Elimination of Separate Account or Administrative Charges

The separate account or administrative charges may be reduced or eliminated when contract sales are made to individuals or to a group of individuals in such a manner that results in savings of expenses. The entitlement to such a reduction will be based on either or both of the following:

1. The size and type of the group of individuals to whom the contract is offered.

2. The amount of expected contribution.

Any reduction or elimination of the separate account or administrative charges will not unlawfully discriminate against any person.

Fund and Division Charges

Separate Account II purchases shares of the Funds at net asset value. That price reflects investment management fees and other direct expenses that have already been deducted from the assets of the Funds. The amount charged for investment management may not be increased without the prior approval of a Fund's shareholders. The Divisions invest directly in securities, and certain investment management fees and other expenses are deducted directly from the Divisions.

State Premium Tax Deduction

We will not deduct state premium taxes from your contributions before applying the contributions to the Investment Options, unless required to pay such taxes under applicable state law. If the Annuitant elects an annuity benefit, we will deduct any applicable state premium taxes from the amount otherwise available for an annuity benefit. State premium taxes, if applicable, currently range up to 4%.

Deductions and Charges

Separate Account Charges

We deduct from the unit value every calendar day an amount equal to an effective annual rate of 1.35% of the Account Value in the Variable Account Options. This daily expense rate cannot be increased without your consent. Various portions of this total charge, as described below, pay for certain services to the Separate Account and the contracts.

Contingent Withdrawal Charge

No sales charges are applied when you make a contribution to the contract. Contributions withdrawn will be subject to a withdrawal charge of up to 8%. As shown below, the percentage charged varies, depending upon the "age" of the contributions included in the withdrawal—that is, the number of years that have elapsed since each contribution was made. The maximum percentage of 8% would apply if the entire amount of the withdrawal consisted of contributions made during your current contribution year. No withdrawal charge applies when you withdraw contributions made earlier than your sixth prior contribution year. For purposes of calculating the withdrawal charge, (1) the oldest contributions will be treated as the first withdrawn and more recent contributions next, and (2) partial withdrawals up to the free withdrawal amount will not be considered a withdrawal of any contributions. For partial withdrawals, the total amount deducted from your Account Value will include the withdrawal amount requested, any applicable Market Value Adjustment, and any applicable withdrawal charge and administrative expense charge, so that the net amount you receive will be the amount requested. During any contract year, no charge will be applied to your partial withdrawals that do not exceed the free withdrawal amount. On any Business Day, the free withdrawal amount is 10% of your Account Value less withdrawals during the current contract year. If any partial withdrawal exceeds the free withdrawal amount, we will deduct the applicable contingent withdrawal charge with respect to such excess amount. The contingent withdrawal charge is a sales charge to defray our costs of selling and promoting the contracts. We do not expect that revenues from contingent withdrawal charges will cover all of such costs. Any shortfall will be made up from our General Account assets, including any profits from other charges under the contracts.

Contribution Year in Which Withdrawn Contribution Was Made	Charge as a % of the Contribution Withdrawn
Current	8%
First prior	7%
Second prior	6%
Third prior	5%
Fourth prior	4%
Fifth prior	3%
Sixth prior	2%
Seventh prior and earlier	0%

No contingent withdrawal charge will be applied to any amount withdrawn if the Annuitant uses the withdrawal to purchase from

Integrity either an immediate annuity benefit with life contingencies or an immediate annuity without life contingencies that provides for level payments over five or more years with a restricted prepayment option. Similarly, no charge will be applied if the Annuitant dies and the withdrawal is made by the Annuitant's beneficiary.

Unless specifically instructed otherwise, we will make withdrawals (including any applicable charges) from the Investment Options in the same ratio the Annuitant's Account Value in each Investment Option bears to the Annuitant's total Account Value. The minimum withdrawal permitted is $300.

Reduction or Elimination of the Contingent Withdrawal Charge

We may reduce or eliminate the contingent withdrawal charge when sales of the contracts are made to individuals or to a group of individuals in such a manner that results in savings of expenses. The entitlement to such a reduction in the contingent withdrawal charge will be based on the following:

1. The size and type of the group of individuals to whom the contract is offered.

2. The amount of expected contributions.

Any reduction or elimination of the contingent withdrawal charge will not unlawfully discriminate against any person.

Transfer Charge

No charge is made for your first 12 transfers among the Variable Account Options or the GROs during a contract year. We are, however, permitted to charge up to $20 from the amount transferred for each additional transfer during that contract year. However, no transfer charge will apply to transfers under (1) Dollar Cost Averaging, (2) Customized Asset Rebalancing, (3) Asset Allocation and Rebalancing, or (4) systematic transfers from the STO, nor will such transfers count toward the 12 transfers you may make in a contract year before we may impose a transfer charge. Transfers from a GRO may be subject to a Market Value Adjustment.

Hardship Waiver

Withdrawal Charges may also be waived on full or partial withdrawal requests of $1,000 or more under a hardship circumstance.

The Market Value Adjustment may also be waived on any amounts withdrawn from the GRO Accounts. Such hardship circumstances include the Owner's (1) confinement to a nursing home, hospital, or long-term care facility, (2) diagnosis of terminal illness with any medical condition that would result in death or total disability, and (3) unemployment. We reserve the right to obtain reasonable notice and documentation including, but not limited to, a physician's certification and Determination Letter from a State Department of Labor. Some of the hardship circumstances listed above may not be applicable in some states and, in other states, may not be available at all.

Tax Reserve

We have the right to make a charge in the future for taxes or for reserves set aside for taxes, which will reduce the investment experience of the Variable Account Options.

Terms of Your Variable Annuity

Contributions under Your Contract

You can make contributions of at least $100 at any time up to the Annuitant's Retirement Date. Your first contribution, however, cannot be less than $1,000. We will accept contributions of at least $50 for salary allotment programs. We have special rules for minimum contribution amounts for tax-favored retirement programs.

We may limit the total contributions under one contract to $1 million if you are under age 76 or to $250,000 if you are over age 76. Once you reach eight years before your Retirement Date, we may refuse to accept any contribution made for you. Contributions may also be limited by various laws or prohibited for all Annuitants under the contract. If your contributions are made under a tax-favored retirement program, we will not measure them against the maximum limits set by law.

Contributions are applied to the various Investment Options selected by you and are used to pay annuity and death benefits.

Each contribution is credited as of the date we *receive* (as defined below) at our Administrative Office both the contribution and instructions for allocation among the Investment Options, *provided that at any time you may have amounts in not more than nine Investment*

Options. For purposes of calculating the nine Investment Options, each of your GRO Accounts counts as one Investment Option. Wire transfers of federal funds are deemed received on the day of transmittal if credited to our account by 3 P.M. Eastern Time; otherwise they are deemed received on the next Business Day. Contributions by check or mail are deemed received not later than the second Business Day after they are delivered to our Administrative Office. A *Business Day* is defined as any day that the New York Stock Exchange is open.

You can change your choice of Investment Options at any time by writing to the Administrative Office. The request should indicate your contract number and the specific change, and you should sign the request. When it is received by the Administrative Office, the change will be effective for any contribution that accompanies it and for all future contributions.

Your Account Value

Your Account Value reflects various charges. Annual deductions are made as of the last day of each contract year. Withdrawal charges and Market Value Adjustments, if applicable, are made as of the effective date of the transaction. Charges against our Separate Accounts are reflected daily. Any amount allocated to a variable Account Option will go up or down in value depending on the investment experience of that Option. For contributions allocated to the Variable Account Options, there are no guaranteed values. The value of your contributions allocated to the Fixed Accounts is guaranteed, subject to any applicable Market Value Adjustments.

Your Purchase of Units in Our Separate Accounts

Allocations to the Variable Account Options are used to purchase units. On any given day, the value you have in a Variable Account Option is the unit value multiplied by the number of units credited to you in that Option. The units of each Variable Account Option have different unit values.

The number of units purchased or redeemed (sold) in any Variable Account Option is calculated by dividing the dollar amount of the transaction by the Option's unit value, calculated after the close of business that day. The number of units for a Variable Account Option at any time is the number of units purchased less the number of units redeemed. The value of units of Separate Account II fluctuates with the investment performance of the corresponding Portfolios of the Funds, which in turn reflects the investment income and realized and unrealized capital gains and losses of the Portfolios, as well as the Funds' expenses. The value of units of Separate Account Ten varies with the performance of the securities held by the Divisions. The unit values also change because of deductions and charges we make to our Separate Accounts. The number of units credited to you, however, will not vary because of changes in unit values. Units of a Variable Account Option are purchased when you allocate new contributions or transfer prior contributions to that Option. Units are redeemed when you make withdrawals or transfer amounts from a Variable Account Option. We also redeem units to pay the death benefit when the Annuitant dies and to pay the annual administrative charge. Please note that special rules apply to the timing of allocations to the Select Ten Plus Divisions.

How We Determine Unit Value

We determine unit values for each Variable Account Option on the Valuation Date. The Valuation Date for purposes of determining unit values is 4 P.M. Eastern Time on each day the New York Stock exchange is open for business.

The unit value of each Variable Account Option in Separate Account II for any day on which we determine unit values is equal to the unit value for the last day on which a unit value was determined multiplied by the net investment factor for that Option on the current day. We determine a *net investment factor* for each Option in Separate Account II as follows:

- First, we take the value of the shares belonging to the Option in the corresponding Portfolio at the close of business that day (before giving effect to any transactions for that day, such as contributions or withdrawals). For this purpose, we use the share value reported to us by the Funds.

- Next, we add any dividends or capital gains distributions by the Fund on that day.

- Then, we charge or credit for any taxes or amounts set aside as a reserve for taxes.

- Then, we divide this amount by the value of the amounts in the Option at the close of business on the last day on which a unit value was determined (after) giving effect to any transactions on that day.

- Finally, we subtract a daily asset charge for each calendar day since the last day on which a unit value was determined (for example, a Monday calculation will include charges for Saturday and Sunday). The daily charge is 0.00003721, which is an effective annual rate of 1.35%. This charge is for the mortality risk, administrative expenses, and expense risk assumed by us under the contract.

We determine a net investment factor for each Division as follows:

- First, we take the value of the assets in the Division at the end of the preceding period.

- Next, we add any investment income and capital gains, realized or unrealized, credited to the assets during the current valuation period.

- Then we subtract any capital losses, realized or unrealized, charged against the assets during the current valuation period.

- Next, we subtract any amount charged against the Division for any taxes.

- Then we divide this amount by the value of the assets in the Division at the end of the preceding valuation period.

- Then we subtract the daily charge for management and investment advice for each day in the valuation period and a daily charge for estimated operating expenses for each day in the valuation period.

- Finally, we subtract a daily asset charge for each calendar day since the last day on which a unit value was determined (for example, a Monday calculation will include charges for Saturday and Sunday). The daily charge is 0.00003721, which is an effective annual rate of 1.35%. This charge is for the mortality risk, administrative expenses, and expense risk assumed by us under the contract.

Generally, this means that we adjust unit values to reflect what happens to the Funds and the Divisions, and also for the mortality and expense risk charge and any charge for administrative expenses or taxes.

Transfers

You may transfer your Account Value among the Variable Account Options and the GROs, subject to our then-current transfer restrictions. You may not make a transfer into the STO. Transfers to a GRO must be to a newly elected GRO (i.e., to a GRO that you have not elected before) at the then-current Guaranteed Interest Rate, unless Integrity otherwise consents. Transfers from a GRO other than within 30 days prior to the expiration date of a GRO Account are subject to a Market Value Adjustment. For amounts in GROs, transfers will be made according to the order in which monies were originally allocated to any GRO.

We reserve the right not to accept transfer instructions received less than two Business Days before any Investment Date.

The amount transferred must be at least $250 or, if less, the entire amount in the Investment Option. After 12 transfers have been made by you during a contract year, a charge of up to $20 may apply to each additional transfer during that contract year, except that no charge will be made for transfers under our dollar cost averaging or customized asset rebalancing or systematic transfer programs. Once annuity payments begin, transfers are no longer permitted.

Written transfer requests must be sent directly to the Administrative Office. Each Annuitant's request for a transfer must specify the contract number, the amounts to be transferred and the Investment Options to and from which the amounts are to be transferred. Transfers may also be arranged through our telephone transfer service provided you have established a Personal Identification Number (*PIN Code*). We will honor telephone transfer instructions from any person who provides correct identifying information, and we are not responsible in the event of a fraudulent telephone transfer that is believed to be genuine in accordance with these procedures. Accordingly, you bear the risk of loss if unauthorized persons make transfers on your behalf.

A transfer request will be effective as of the Business Day it is received by our Administrative Office, except for transfers to the Select Ten Plus Divisions (see Part II).

A transfer request does not charge the allocation of current or future contributions among the Investment Options. Telephone transfers may be requested from 9 A.M. to 5 P.M. Eastern Time on any day we are open for business. You will receive the Variable Account Options' unit values as of the close of business on the day you call. Accordingly, transfer requests for Variable Account Options that are received after 4 P.M. Eastern Time (or after the close of the New York Stock Exchange, if earlier) will be processed using unit values as of the close of business on the next Business Day after the day you call. All transfers will be confirmed in writing.

Transfer requests submitted by agents or market timing services that represent multiple policies will be processed not later than the next Business Day after the requests are received by our Administrative Office.

Withdrawals

You may make an unlimited number of withdrawals from your contract as frequently as you wish. Each withdrawal must be for at least $300. A withdrawal charge of up to 8% of the contribution amount withdrawn, as adjusted for any applicable Market Value Adjustment and the withdrawal charge itself, will be deducted from your Account Value unless one of the exceptions applies. Most withdrawals made by you prior to age 59½ are also subject to a 10% federal tax penalty. In addition, some tax-favored retirement programs limit withdrawals.

Assignments

You may not assign the contract as collateral or security for a loan, but an Owner whose contract is not related to a tax-favored program may otherwise assign the contract before the Annuitant's Retirement Date. An assignment of the contract as a gift may, however, have adverse tax consequences. We will not be bound by an assignment unless it is in writing and we have received it at the Administrative Office.

Death Benefits and Similar Benefit Distributions

We will pay a death benefit to the Annuitant's surviving beneficiary (or beneficiaries, in equal shares) if the last Annuitant dies before annuity payments have started. If the Annuitant dies at or over age 90 (or after the contract's 10th anniversary date, if later), the death benefit is the contract account value at the end of the business day on which we receive due proof of death. Similarly, if the contract was issued on or after the youngest Annuitant's 86th birthday, the death benefit is the contract account value at the end of the business day on which we receive due proof of death.

For contracts issued before the Annuitant's 86th birthday, if the Annuitant dies before age 90 (or the contract's 10th anniversary date, if later) and before annuity payments have started, the death benefit is the highest of the following (each reduced on a pro rata basis for prior withdrawals and after being adjusted for any applicable market value adjustments and/or charges):

1. The contract account value at the end of the business day on which we receive due proof of death.

2. The total of all contributions.

3. The highest contract account value on any contract anniversary that occurred prior to the annuitant's 81st birthday and prior to the Annuitant's death, plus any subsequent contributions.

The amount of the reduction will be determined by dividing the amount of the withdrawal by the annuity account value on the transaction date and multiplying this percentage by the then-current guaranteed minimum death benefit.

Death benefits (and benefit distributions required because of a separate Owner's death) can be paid in a lump sum or as an annuity. If no benefit option is selected for the beneficiary at the Annuitant's death, the beneficiary can select an option.

The beneficiary of the death benefit under a contract is selected by the Owner. An Owner may change beneficiaries by submitting the appropriate form to the Administrative Office. If no Annuitant's beneficiary survives the annuitant, then the death benefit is generally paid to the Annuitant's estate. No death benefit will be paid after the annuitant's death if there is a contingent annuitant. In that case, the contingent annuitant becomes the new Annuitant under the contract.

The maximum issue age for the Annuitant is 85 years old.

Annuity Benefits

All annuity benefits under your contract are calculated as of the Retirement Date selected by you. The Retirement Date can be changed by written notice to the Administrative Office any time prior to the Retirement Date. The Retirement Date may be no later than your 98th birthday, or earlier if required by law. The terms of the contracts applicable to the various retirement programs, along with the federal tax laws, establish certain minimum and maximum retirement ages.

Annuity benefits may take the form of a lump-sum payment or an annuity. Shortly after the Retirement Date, a lump-sum payment will provide the Annuitant with the Cash Value under the contract. The amount applied for the purchase of an annuity benefit will be the Adjusted Account Value, except that the Cash Value will be the amount applied if the annuity benefit does not have a life contingency and either the term is less than five years or the annuity can be commuted to a lump-sum payment without a withdrawal charge applying.

Annuities

Alternative forms of annuity benefits can provide for fixed or variable payments, to be made monthly, quarterly, semiannually, or annually. Variable payments will be funded through one or more Variable Account Options. For any annuity, the minimum amount applied to the annuity must be $2,000, and the minimum initial payment must be at least $20.

If you have not already selected a form of annuity, we will send you, within six months prior to your Retirement Date, an appropriate notice form on which you may indicate the type of annuity you desire or confirm to us that the normal form of annuity, as defined below, is to be provided. However, if we do not receive a completed form from you on or before your Retirement Date, we will deem the Retirement Date to have been extended until we receive your written instructions at our Administrative Office. During such extension, the values under your contract in the various Investment Options will remain invested in such options and amounts remaining in Variable Account Options and will continue to be subject to the investment risks associated with those Options. However, your Retirement Date cannot be extended beyond your 98th birthday, or earlier if required by law. You will receive a lump-sum benefit if you do not make an election by such date. We currently offer the following types of annuities:

A *period-certain annuity* provides for fixed or variable payments, or both, to the Annuitant or the Annuitant's beneficiary (the *payee*) for a fixed period. The amount is determined by the period selected. The Annuitant, or if the payee dies before the end of the period selected, the payee's beneficiary, may elect to receive the total present value of future payments in cash.

A *period-certain life annuity* provides for fixed or variable payments, or both, for at least the period selected and thereafter for the life of the payee or the payee and another annuitant under a joint and survivor annuity. You may not change or redeem the annuity once payments have begun. If the payee (or the payee and the other annuitant under a joint and survivor annuity) dies before the period selected ends, the remaining payments will go to another named payee who may have the right to redeem the annuity and secure the present value of future guaranteed payments in a lump sum. The *normal form of annuity* is a fixed life income annuity with 10 years of payments guaranteed, funded through our General Account.

A *life income annuity* provides fixed payments for the life of the payee or the payee and another annuitant under a joint and survivor annuity. Once a life income annuity is selected, the form of annuity cannot be changed or redeemed for a lump-sum payment by the Annuitant or any payee.

Annuity Payments

Fixed annuity payments will not change and are based upon annuity rates provided in your contract. The size of payments will depend on the form of annuity that was chosen and, in the case of a life income annuity, on the payee's age (or payee and a joint annuitant in the case of a joint and survivor annuity) and sex (except under most tax-favored retirement programs). If current annuity rates then in effect would yield a larger payment, those current rates will apply instead of the tables.

Variable annuity payments are funded only in the Variable Account Options through the purchase of annuity units. The Variable Account Option or Options selected cannot be changed after annuity payments begin. The SAI provides further information concerning the determination of annuity payments. The number of units purchased is equal to the amount of the first annuity payment divided by the new annuity unit value for the valuation period which includes the due date of the first annuity payment. The amount of the first annuity payment is determined in the same manner for a variable annuity as it is for a fixed annuity. The number of annuity units stays the same for the annuity payment period, but the new annuity unit value changes to reflect the investment income and the realized and unrealized capital gains and losses of the Variable Account Option or Options selected after charges made against it. Annuity unit values assume a base rate of net investment return of 5%, except in states that require a lower rate, in which case 3.5% will be used. The annuity unit value will rise or fall depending on whether the actual rate of net investment return is higher or lower than the assumed base rate. If the age or sex of an annuitant has been misstated, any benefits will be those that would have been purchased at the correct age and sex. Any overpayments or underpayments made by us will be charged or credited with interest at the rate of 6% per year. If we have made overpayments because of incorrect information about age or sex, we will deduct the overpayment from the next payment or payments due. We add underpayments to the next payment.

Timing of Payment

We normally make payments from the Variable Account Options or apply your Adjusted Account Value to the purchase of an annuity within seven days after receipt of the required form at our Administrative Office. Our action can be deferred, however, for any period during which (1) the New York Stock Exchange has been closed or trading on it is restricted; (2) sales of securities or determination of the fair value of Separate Accounts assets is not reasonably practicable because of an emergency; or (3) the SEC, by order, permits such action in order to protect persons with interests in the Separate Accounts. We can defer payment of your Fixed Accounts for up to six months, and interest will be paid on any such payment delayed for 30 days or more.

How You Make Requests and Give Instructions

When you communicate in writing with our Administrative Office, use the address on the first page of this prospectus. Your request or instruction cannot be honored unless it is in proper and complete form. Whenever possible, use one of our printed forms, which may be obtained from our Administrative Office.

Additional Information

Systematic Withdrawals

We offer a program for systematic withdrawals that allows you to pre-authorize periodic withdrawals from your contract prior to your Retirement Date. You may choose to have withdrawals made monthly, quarterly, semiannually, or annually and may specify the day of the month (other than the 29th, 30th, or 31st) on which the withdrawal is to be made. You may specify a dollar amount for each withdrawal or an annual percentage to be withdrawn. The minimum systematic withdrawal currently is $100. You may also specify an account for direct deposit of your systematic withdrawals. To enroll under our systematic withdrawal program, you must deliver the appropriate administrative form to our Administrative Office. Withdrawals may begin not less than one business day after our receipt of the form. You or we may terminate your participation in the program upon one day's prior written notice, and we may terminate or amend the systematic withdrawal program at any time. If on any withdrawal date you do not have sufficient values to make all of the withdrawals you have specified, no withdrawals will be made and your enrollment in the program will be ended.

Amounts withdrawn by you under the systematic withdrawal program may be within the free withdrawal amount, in which case neither a contingent withdrawal charge nor a Market Value Adjustment will be made. *Amounts withdrawn under the systematic withdrawal program in excess of the free withdrawal amount will be subject to a contingent withdrawal charge, an administrative expense charge, and a Market Value Adjustment if applicable. Withdrawals also may be subject to the 10% federal tax penalty for early withdrawals under the contracts and to income taxation.*

Income Plus Withdrawal Program

We offer the Income Plus Withdrawal Program that allows you to pre-authorize substantially equal periodic withdrawals, based on your life expectancy, from your contract prior to your reaching age 59½. Income Plus Withdrawals are exempt from the 10% penalty tax, normally applicable to early distributions made prior to age 59½, but remain subject to ordinary income tax. Once distributions begin they should not be changed or stopped until the later of age 59½ or five years from the date of the first distribution. If you change or stop the distribution or take an additional withdrawal, you may be liable for the 10% penalty tax that would otherwise have been due on all prior distributions made under the Income Plus Program and for any interest thereon.

The Income Plus Withdrawal Program may be elected at any time if you are below age 59½. You can elect this option by submitting the proper election form to our Administrative Office. You may choose to have withdrawals made monthly, quarterly, semiannually, or annually and may specify the day of the month (other than the 29th, 30th, or 31st) on which the withdrawal is to be made. We will calculate the amount of the distribution under a method selected by you. The minimum Income Plus Withdrawal currently is $100. You must also specify an account for direct deposit of your Income Plus Withdrawals.

To enroll under our Income Plus Withdrawal Program, you must deliver the appropriate administrative form to our Administrative Office. Withdrawals may begin not less than one Business Day after our receipt of the form. You or we may terminate your participation in the program upon seven business days' prior written notice, and we may terminate or amend the Income Plus Program at any time. If on any withdrawal date you do not have sufficient values to make all of the withdrawals you have specified, no withdrawals will be made and your enrollment in the program will be ended. This program is not available in concert with the Systematic Withdrawal Program, Dollar Cost Averaging, Systematic Transfer Option, or Asset Allocation and Rebalancing Program. Amounts withdrawn by you under the Income Plus Withdrawal Program may be within the free withdrawal amount, in which case neither a contingent withdrawal charge nor a Market Value Adjustment will be made. *Amounts withdrawn under the Income Plus Withdrawal Program in excess of the free withdrawal amount will be subject to a contingent withdrawal charge and a Market Value Adjustment if applicable.*

Dollar Cost Averaging

We offer a dollar cost averaging program under which allocations to the money market option are automatically transferred on a monthly, quarterly, semiannual, or annual basis to one or more other Variable

Account Options. You must specify a dollar amount to be transferred into each Variable Account Option, and the current minimum transfer to each Option is $250. No transfer charge will apply to transfers under our dollar cost averaging program, and such transfers will not count toward the 12 transfers you may make in a contract year before we may impose a transfer charge.

To enroll under our dollar cost averaging program, you must deliver the appropriate administrative form to our Administrative Office. You or we may terminate your participation in the program upon one day's prior written notice, and we may terminate or amend the dollar cost averaging program at any time. If you do not have sufficient funds in the money market option to transfer to each Variable Account Option specified, no transfer will be made and your enrollment in the program will be ended.

Systematic Transfer Program

We also offer a systematic transfer program under which contributions to the STO are automatically transferred on a monthly or quarterly basis, as selected by you, to one or more other Investment Options. Your STO contributions will be transferred in equal installments of not less than $1,000 over a one-year period. If you do not have sufficient funds in the STO to transfer to each Option specified, a final transfer will be made on a pro rata basis and your enrollment in the program will be ended. All interest accrued and any funds remaining in the STO at the end of the period during which transfers are scheduled to be made will be transferred at the end of such period on a pro rata basis to the Options previously elected by you for this program. No transfer charge will apply to transfers under our systematic transfer program, and such transfers will not count toward the 12 transfers you may make in a contract year before we may impose a transfer charge.

You may also instruct us to transfer approximately equal quarterly installments of at least $1,000 each over a one-year period from the STO to each of the four Divisions. We reserve the right to hold new contributions received less than five business days before any Investment Date in the STO until the next following Investment Date.

To enroll under our systematic transfer program, you must deliver the appropriate administrative form to our Administrative Office. We reserve the right to terminate the systematic transfer program, in whole or in part, or to place restrictions on contributions to the program. This program may not be currently available in some states.

Customized Asset Rebalancing

We offer a customized asset rebalancing program whereby you can select the frequency for rebalancing. Frequencies available include rebalancing monthly, quarterly, semiannually, or annually. The value in the Variable Account Options will be automatically rebalanced by transfers among such Variable Account Options, and you will receive a confirmation notice after each rebalancing. Transfers will occur only to and from those Variable Account Options where you have current contribution allocations. No transfer charge will apply to transfers under our customized asset rebalancing program, and such transfers will not count toward the 12 transfers you may make in a contract year before we may impose a transfer charge.

Fixed Accounts are not eligible for the customized asset rebalancing program.

To enroll under our customized asset rebalancing program, you must deliver the appropriate administrative form to our Administrative Office. You should be aware that other allocation programs, such as dollar cost averaging, as well as transfers and withdrawals that you make, may not work in concert with the customized asset rebalancing program. You should, therefore, monitor your use of such other programs, transfers, and withdrawals while the customized asset rebalancing program is in effect. You or we may terminate your participation in the program upon one day's prior written notice, and we may terminate or amend the customized asset rebalancing program at any time.

Asset Allocation and Rebalancing Program

We also offer an Asset Allocation and Rebalancing Program developed in consultation with an independent research and consulting firm specializing in the strategic asset allocation decision.

You may select one of five proposed Models: Conservative, Moderately Conservative, Moderate, Moderately Aggressive, or Aggressive. Your current contribution allocations will be initially allocated among the Options currently established for each Model. You and your financial representative also have the option to design a program that is tailored to your specific retirement needs.

When selecting this program, contributions will be allocated and your variable portfolios will be rebalanced at least annually as recommended by the Asset Allocation & Rebalancing Program. The program applies to all contributions made to your annuity contract. You will receive a confirmation notice after each rebalancing. No transfer charge will apply to transfers under the Asset Allocation and Rebalancing Program, nor will such transfers count toward the 12 transfers you may make in a contract year before we may impose a transfer charge.

In each investor profile, a portion of all contributions is allocated to a five-year Guaranteed Rate Option (GRO). The amount allocated to the GOR will not be reallocated or rebalanced while participating in a specific investor profile. You may cancel or change the investment profile you have selected at any time. However, the GRO funds may be subject to a market value adjustment (MVA) that may increase or decrease your account value.

To enroll under the Asset Allocation and Rebalancing Program, complete the Dollar Cost Averaging/Asset Allocation and Rebalancing form (Catalog #1814) found in the back of this prospectus. You should be aware that other allocation programs, such as dollar cost averaging, as well as additions, transfers, and withdrawals that you make, may not work in concert with the Customized Asset Rebalancing program. If, after selecting one of the five Models, you initiate a transaction that results in a reallocation outside one of the Models, your participation in the Model program is automatically terminated. You should, therefore, monitor your use of such other programs, transfers, and withdrawals while the Customized Asset Rebalancing program is in effect. This program is not available in concert with the Customized Asset Rebalancing program. We reserve the right to terminate or amend this program, in whole or in part, or to place restrictions on contributions to the program. This program may not be available in all states.

You may terminate participation in this program upon one day's prior written notice.

Systematic Contributions

We offer a program for systematic contributions that allows you to pre-authorize monthly, quarterly, or semiannual withdrawals from your checking account for payment to us. To enroll under our program, you must deliver the appropriate administrative form to our Administrative Office. You or we may terminate your participation in the program upon 30 days' prior written notice. Your participation may be terminated by us if your bank declines to make any payment. The minimum amount for systematic contributions is $1,000 per month.

Performance Information

Performance data for the Variable Account Options, including the yield and effective yield of the Money Market Option, the yield of the other Options, and the total return of all the Options, may appear in advertisements or sales literature. Performance data for any Option reflects only the performance of a hypothetical investment in the Option during the particular time period on which the calculations are based. Performance information should be considered in light of the investment objectives and policies of the Portfolio in which the Option invests and the market conditions during the given time period, and it should not be considered as a representation of performance to be achieved in the future.

Total returns are based on the overall dollar or percentage change in value of a hypothetical investment in an Option. Total return quotations reflect changes in Fund share price, the automatic reinvestment by the Option of all distributions, and the deduction of applicable contract charges and expenses, including any contingent withdrawal charge that would apply if an Owner surrendered the contract at the end of the period indicated. Total returns also may be shown that do not take into account the contingent withdrawal charge or the annual administrative charge applicable where the Account Value is less than $50,000 at the end of a contract year.

A *cumulative total return* reflects an Option's performance over a stated period of time. An average annual total return reflects the hypothetical annually compounded return that would have produced the same cumulative total return if the Option's performance had been constant over the entire period. Because average annual total returns tend to smooth out variations in an Option's returns, you should recognize that they are not the same as actual year-by-year results.

Some Options may also advertise *yield*. These measures reflect the income generated by an investment in the Option over a specified period of time. This income is annualized and shown as a percentage.

Yields do not take into account capital gains or losses or the contingent withdrawal charge.

The Money Market Option may advertise its current and effective yield. *Current yield* reflects the income generated by an investment in the Option over a specified seven-day period. *Effective yield* is calculated in a similar manner, except that income earned is assumed to be reinvested. The Bond Option may advertise a 30-day yield that reflects the income generated by an investment in such Option over a specified 30-day period.

Illustration of a Market Value Adjustment

Contribution:	$50,000.00
GRO Account duration:	7 years
Guaranteed Interest Rate:	5% annual effective rate

The following examples illustrate how the Market Value Adjustment and the contingent withdrawal charge may affect the values of a contract upon a withdrawal. The 5% assumed Guaranteed Interest Rate is the same rate used in the example under "Table of Annual Fees and Expenses" in this Prospectus. In these examples, the withdrawal occurs three years after the initial contribution. The Market Value Adjustment operates in a similar manner for transfers. No contingent withdrawal charge applies to transfers. The GRO Value for this $50,000 contribution is $70,355.02 at the expiration of the GRO Account. After three years, the GRO Value is $57,881.25 It is also assumed, for the purposes of these examples, that no prior partial withdrawals or transfers have occurred. The Market Value Adjustment will be based on the rate we are then crediting (at the time of the withdrawal) on new contributions to GRO Accounts of the same duration as the time remaining in your GRO Account, rounded to the next-higher number of complete months. If we do not declare a rate for the exact time remaining, we will interpolate between the Guaranteed Interest Rates for GRO Accounts of durations closest to (that is, the next higher or lower to) the remaining period described above. Three years after the initial contribution, there would have been four years remaining in your GRO Account. These examples also show the withdrawal charge, which would be calculated separately.

EXAMPLE OF A DOWNWARD MARKET VALUE ADJUSTMENT

A downward Market Value Adjustment results from a full or partial withdrawal that occurs when interest rates have increased. Assume interest rates have increased three years after the initial contribution and we are then crediting 6.25% for a four-year GRO Account. Upon a full withdrawal, the Market Value Adjustment, applying the above formula would be:

$$-0.0551589 = [(1 = .05)^{48/12}/(1 + .0625 + .0025)^{48/12}] - 1$$

The Market Value Adjustment is a reduction of $3,192.67 from the GRO Value:

$$-\$3,192.67 = -0.0551589 \times \$57,881.25$$

The Market Adjusted Value would be:

$$\$54,688.58 = \$57,881.25 - \$3,192.67$$

A withdrawal charge of 5% would be assessed against the $50,000 original contribution:

$$\$2,500.00 = \$50,000.00 \times .05$$

Thus, the amount payable on a full withdrawal would be:

$$\$52,188.58 = \$57,881.25 - \$3,192.67 - \$2,500.00$$

If instead of a full withdrawal, $20,000 was requested, we would first determine the free withdrawal amount:

$$\$5,788.13 = \$57,881.25 \times .10$$

$$\text{Free amount} = \$5,788.13$$

The Market Value Adjustment, which is only applicable to the nonfree amount, would be:

$$-\$783.91 = -0.0551589 \times \$14,211.87$$

The withdrawal charge would be:

$$\$789.25 = [(14,211.87 + \$783.91)/(1 - .05)] - (\$14,211.87 + 783.91)$$

Thus, the total amount needed to provide $20,000 after the Market Value Adjustment and withdrawal charge would be:

$$\$21,573.16 = \$20,000.00 + \$783.91 + \$789.25$$

The ending Account Value would be:

$$\$36{,}308.09 = \$57{,}881.25 - \$21{,}573.16$$

EXAMPLE OF AN UPWARD MARKET VALUE ADJUSTMENT:

An upward Market Value Adjustment results from a full or partial withdrawal that occurs when interest rates have decreased. Assume interest rates have decreased three years after the initial contribution and we are then crediting 4% for a four-year GRO Account. Upon a full withdrawal, the Market Value Adjustment, applying the formula set forth in the prospectus, would be:

$$.0290890 = [(1 + .05)^{48/12}/(1 + .04 = .0025)^{48/12}] - 1$$

The Market Value Adjustment is an increase of $1,683.71 to the GRO Value:

$$\$1{,}683.71 = .0290890 \times \$57{,}881.25$$

The Market Adjusted Value would be:

$$\$59{,}564.96 = \$57{,}881.25 + \$1{,}683.71$$

A withdrawal charge of 5% would be assessed against the $50,000 original contribution:

$$\$2{,}500.00 = \$50{,}000.00 \times .05$$

Thus, the amount payable on a full withdrawal would be:

$$\$57{,}064.96 = \$57{,}881.25 + \$1{,}683.71 - \$2{,}500.00$$

If instead of a full withdrawal, $20,000 was requested, the free withdrawal amount and nonfree amount would first be determined as above:

$$\text{Free amount} = \$5{,}788.13$$

$$\text{Nonfree Amount} = \$14{,}211.87$$

The Market Value Adjustment would be:

$$\$413.41 = .0290890 \times \$14{,}211.87$$

The withdrawal charge would be:

$$\$726.23 = [(\$14{,}211.87 - \$413.41)/(1 - .05)]$$

$$- (\$14{,}211.87 - \$413.41)$$

Thus, the total amount needed to provide $20,000 after the Market Value Adjustment and withdrawal charge would be:

$$\$20,312.82 = \$20,000.00 - \$413.41 + \$726.23$$

The ending Account Value would be:

$$\$37,568.43 = \$57,881.25 - \$20,312.82$$

Actual Market Value Adjustments may have a greater or lesser impact than shown in the examples, depending on the actual change in interest crediting rate and the timing of the withdrawal or transfer in relation to the time remaining in the GRO Account. Also, the Market Value Adjustment can never decrease the Account Value below premium plus 3% interest (before any applicable charges). Account values of less than $50,000 will be subject to a $30 annual charge.

The preceding examples will be adjusted to comply with applicable state regulation requirements for contracts issued in certain states.

Appendix D Excerpts from Sample Modified Endowment Contract

Issue Ages

- Issued to clients 18 to 80 years old.

- Younger issue ages available by individual consideration.

Tax Advantages

- Tax-deferred account growth.

- Tax-free Death Benefit.

- Tax-free transfers available among the investment options.

- Tax-preferred access to account value through policy loans and withdrawals available for non-Modified Endowment Contracts.*

- Nontaxable 1035 Exchange privilege allowed.

Premium Payments

- Ages 0–70—minimum premium is $10,000.

- Ages 71–80—minimum premium is $50,000.

- 100% of each payment is applied to the investment options immediately after the free-look period.

*Loans and partial surrenders reduce the policy's cash value and lower the death proceeds available to your clients' beneficiaries.

When Your Client Purchases Modified Single-Premium Variable Life

Your clients' single-premium amount is deposited in the Money Market Portfolio until the end of the free-look period. The free-look period is the latter of:

- 10 days after the policy is received.
- 45 days after the application is signed.
- Within 15 days after a Notice of Right of Withdrawal.

Portfolio Options

- Multiple variable investment options. Please see the investment options chart insert for a listing of all the options available.
- Fixed Account guaranteed.
- Current Fixed Account minimum guaranteed rate is 3%. If the Company were to become insolvent, the principal amount may not be paid. Principal amounts may be reduced by withdrawals of the Contract Maintenance Charge and by the cost of insurance.
- At least 5% of premium must be allocated to an investment option.
- Percentages allocated to investment options must be in whole numbers and total 100%.
- Clients can invest in as many investment options as they want.
- See the investment options chart insert for more specific information about each fund.

Portfolio Transfers

- Transfers are nontaxable among the investment options.
- Allowed as often as once a day within the variable account.
- Can be made by telephone (subject to state regulations).
- Up to 100% of the cash value in the variable account can be transferred to the Fixed Account after the first policy anniversary.

- Free transfers from the Fixed Account to the variable account can be made within 30 days after the termination date of the guaranteed interest rate period.

Death Benefit

- As long as the policy is in force, the Death Benefit will never be less than the Specified Amount, regardless of performance of the investment options.

- 100% is passed income tax–free to the owner's beneficiary.

Investment Performance

Fund performance for Modified Single-Premium Variable Life investment options is produced monthly.

Account Statements

- Your clients will receive account statements on a quarterly basis.

- Confirmation statements are sent to clients and producers after transfers or premium deposits.

- Annually, your clients will receive a summary of the activity of their policy.

- The Broker of Record receives a copy of the annual and quarterly summary statements.

Partial Surrenders*

- Your clients can begin taking partial surrenders from their Modified Single-Premium Variable Life contract after the fifth policy year, without Surrender Charges.

- Partial Surrenders may be made at up to 10% of total premiums *or* at 100% of cumulative earnings (cash value less total premiums paid less policy indebtedness).

*Loans and partial surrenders from a Modified Endowment Contract will generally be taxable and, if taken prior to age 59½, may also be subject to a 10% IRS penalty.

- Partial Surrenders must not result in a reduction of the Cash Surrender Value below $10,000.

Loans*

- During the first year, your clients can borrow up to 50% of the Cash Surrender Value. Loans are also permitted in conjunction with indebtedness carried over from another contract exchanged in a 1035 transaction.

- Beginning in the second year, clients can borrow up to 90% of the Cash Surrender Value.

- Minimum loan amount is $1,000.

- Two-tiered loan structure is available, which consists of Preferred and Regular loans.

- Preferred status applies to any cumulative loan amount less than or equal to the Cash Value less the cost basis. Additional loaned amounts are treated as Regular loans.

Repaying Interest

- Your clients will pay an interest rate of 6% (interest is charged daily and is due at the end of each policy year).

- Preferred loans are credited at 6%.

- Regular loans are credited at 4%.

- Outstanding loan balance will be deducted from the Death Benefit when it is paid to your clients' beneficiaries.

Declining Surrender Charge

- Applies if the policy is surrendered within the first nine policy years.

- Consists of a Sales Surrender Charge and a Premium Tax Surrender Charge.

*Loans and partial surrenders from a Modified Endowment Contract will generally be taxable and, if taken prior to age 59½, may also be subject to a 10% IRS penalty.

- Expressed as a declining percentage of the initial Guideline Single Premium Payment.

Completed Policy Years	0	1	2	3	4	5	6	7	8	9+
Surrender Charge	10.0%	10.0%	9.0%	8.0%	7.0%	6.0%	5.0%	4.0%	3.0%	0.0%

Asset Charge

- A single Asset Charge will be assessed monthly for mortality and expense risk, administration, cost of insurance, and taxes.

- The breakdown of the annualized Asset Charge is as follows:

	Policy Years 1–10	Policy Years 11+
Mortality and Expense Risk Charge	.90%	.90%
Current Cost of Insurance*	.65%	.65% / .30%**
DAC Tax	.20%	.00%
Premium Tax	.30%	.00%
Administration***	.30%	.30% / .15%**
Total	2.35%	1.85% / 1.35%

*Not to exceed guaranteed COI.
**These charges are reduced starting with the eleventh policy year provided the Cash Surrender Value on each policy anniversary is at least $100,000 or more beginning in the eleventh year.
***A minimum of $10 per month.

Management Fees

- Assessed at the underlying fund level and are discussed in detail in the prospectus.

Dollar Cost Averaging

- Available from the Fixed Account, the Money Market Fund, and the Limited Maturity Bond Portfolio to any other subaccount in the variable account.

- Minimum total Cash Value minus policy indebtedness of $15,000 required.

- Minimum transfer is $100.

- Transfers are processed monthly.

- This strategy does not guarantee a profit or protect against loss in a declining market.

Asset Allocation

- Helps your clients develop an investment strategy to match their tolerance to risk.

- Investment options are categorized by volatility.

Asset Rebalancing

- Allows clients to designate a specific asset allocation strategy they want to maintain.

- Accounts are rebalanced quarterly, semiannually, or annually to maintain their asset allocation.

- This strategy does not guarantee a profit or protect against loss in a declining market.

How the Process Works

To facilitate the implementation of our Modified Single-Premium Variable Life, we have developed a two-tiered underwriting process. If certain requirements are fulfilled, the policy will be issued on a Simplified basis. Regular Underwriting will be required for those situations which fall outside the nonmedical limits.

Figure D.1 shows how the underwriting process of Modified Single-Premium Variable Life works.

Underwriting Guidelines

- Issue ages 0–80. Applicants under 18 years old will be underwritten by individual consideration.

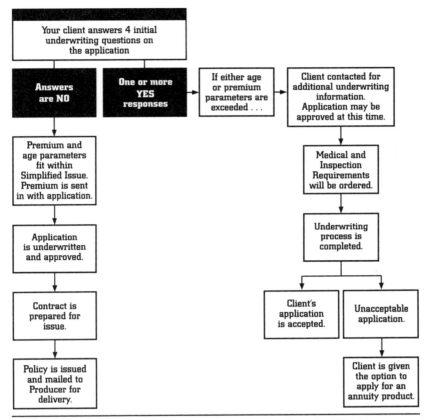

FIGURE D.1 Underwriting process for Modified
Single-Premium Variable Life.

- For Simplified Underwriting, issue age begins at 35.

- Minimum premium is $10,000 for ages 0–70; $50,000 for ages 71–80.

- Maximum face amount with which deposit is accepted is $1,000,000.

Types of Reports

- Personal history interview.

- Investigative consumer report.

Nonmedical Limits are based upon:
1. Net amount at risk applied for currently; and
2. Face amount in force issued since last exam was taken.

Medical Requirements are based upon:
1. Net amount at risk applied for currently; and
2. Any amount applied for within 90 days.

Financial Requirements Financial statements and related financial evidence of insurability will be routinely required on all net amounts at risk exceeding $1 million.

*** NOTE *** The Company reserves the right to request a Medical Examination or any medical test, Inspection Report, or Financial Statement on *any* Applicant, regardless of age or amount.

Single Premium	AGE						
	0–17	18–34	35–44	45–54	55–64	65–70	71–80
$ 10,000 – 15,000	IC	1	S I	S I	S I	S I	N/A
$ 15,001 – 30,000	IC	2 I	1 I	S I	S I	S I	N/A
$ 30,001 – 40,000	IC	2 I	1 I	2	S I	S I	N/A
$ 40,001 – 50,000*	IC	2 I	2 I	2 I	S I	S I	S I
$ 50,001 – 65,000	IC	2 I	2 I	2 I	3 I	S I	S I
$ 65,001 – 100,000	IC	2 I	2 I	2 I	3 I	S I	S I
$ 100,001 – 200,000	IC	3 I	3 I	3 I	4 I	3 I	4 I
$ 200,001 – 300,000	IC	4 I	3 I	3 I	4 I	4 I	4 I
$ 300,001 – 400,000	IC	4 I	4X I	4X I	4 I	4 I	4 I
$ 400,001 – 500,000	IC	4X I	4X I	4X I	4 I	4 I	4X I
$ 500,001 & up	IC	5X I	5X I	5X I	5X I	5X I	6 I

X   = Chest X-ray required if tobacco used in any form within the past five years or if Net Amount at Risk is $10 million up
IC = Individual Consideration – consult Underwriting
N/A = Coverage not available at these ages and amounts
*   = $50,000 Minimum Premium Required for Ages 71–80
†   = A signed informed consent must be obtained prior to arranging for a Blood Chemistry Profile
I   = Inspection Requirements

S I No Routine Underwriting Requirements. (Complete Simplified Issue sections of application.)

1
• Blood Chemistry Profile†
• Home Office Urine Specimen
• Height, Weight, Blood Pressure, Pulse

2
• Para-Medical Examination
• Blood Chemistry Profile†
• Home Office Urine Specimen

3
• Para-Medical Examination
• Blood Chemistry Profile†
• Home Office Urine Specimen
• EKG

4
• Physician Medical Examination
• Blood Chemistry Profile†
• Home Office Urine Specimen
• EKG

5
• Physician Medical Examination
• Blood Chemistry Profile†
• Home Office Urine Specimen
• Stress EKG (Treadmill)

6
• Physician Medical Examination
• Blood Chemistry Profile†
• Home Office Urine Specimen
• Stress EKG (Treadmill)
• Chest X-ray

FIGURE **D.2 MSPVL Nonmedical Limits and Medical Examination, Inspection, and Financial Requirements**

Inspection Requirements

- Broker should inform all applicants concerning inspection procedures and requirements.

- The Company will order all Inspection Reports.

- Inspection information is held in strict confidence as required by the Fair Credit Reporting Act.

Interviews

A representative may interview the proposed insured, spouse, neighbors, business associates, bankers, accountants, etc., to cover such areas as health, finances, hazardous sports, alcohol use, criminal activity, drug use, motor vehicle record, etc.

Medical Requirements

The Underwriting Department will routinely arrange for the medical requirements as well as attending physician reports.

Summary of the Policies

Variable Life Insurance

The variable life insurance Policies are similar in many ways to fixed-benefit whole life insurance. As with fixed-benefit whole life insurance, the Owner of the Policy pays a premium for life insurance coverage on the person insured. Also like fixed-benefit whole life insurance, the Policies may provide for a Cash Surrender Value which is payable if the Policy is terminated during the Insured's lifetime. (As with fixed-benefit whole life insurance, the Cash Surrender Value during the early Policy years may be substantially lower than the premiums paid.)

However, the Policies differ from fixed-benefit whole life insurance in several respects. Unlike fixed-benefit whole life insurance, the Death Benefit and Cash Value of the Policies may increase or decrease to reflect the investment performance of the Variable Account subaccounts or the Fixed Account to which Cash Values are allocated. There is no guaranteed Cash Surrender Value. If the Cash Surrender Value is insufficient to pay Policy Charges, the Policy will lapse.

The Variable Account and Its Subaccounts

The Company places the Policy's Cash Value in the Separate Account and/or the Fixed Account (the "Variable Account") at the time the Policy is issued. The Policy Owner selects the subaccounts of the Variable Account into which the Cash Value will be allocated. When the Policy is issued, the Cash Value will be allocated to the Nationwide Separate Account Trust Money Market Fund Subaccount (for any Cash Value allocated to a Subaccount on the application) or the Fixed Account until the expiration of the period in which the Policy Owner may exercise his or her short-term right to cancel the Policy. Assets of each subaccount are invested at net asset value in shares of a corresponding Underlying Mutual Fund option. The Policy Owner also can have Cash Value allocated to the Fixed Account.

The Fixed Account

The Fixed Account is funded by the assets of the Company's General Account. Cash Values allocated to the Fixed Account are credited with interest daily at a rate declared by the Company. The interest rate declared is at the Company's sole discretion, but may never be less than an effective annual rate of 3%.

Deductions and Charges

The Company deducts certain charges from the Cash Value of the Policy. These charges are made for administrative expenses, state premium taxes, federal taxes, providing life insurance protection, and assuming the mortality and expense risks.

The Company deducts a monthly charge for the cost of insurance, administrative charges, premium tax, and federal tax from the Policy's Cash Value attributable to the Variable Account and Fixed Account. The Company also deducts on a monthly basis from the Cash Value attributable to the Variable Account a charge to provide for mortality and expense risks. For Policies that are surrendered in the first nine Policy Years, the Company deducts a Surrender Charge not to exceed 10% of the initial Premium Payment. This includes a charge for deferred sales expenses and premium tax recovery. The sales surrender charge will never exceed 7.5% of the initial premium payments.

Underlying Mutual Fund shares are purchased at net asset value, which reflects the deduction of investment management fees and certain other expenses. The management fees are charged by each Underlying Mutual Fund's investment advisor for managing the Underlying Mutual Fund and selecting its portfolio of securities. Other Underlying Mutual Fund expenses can include such items as interest expense on loans and contracts with transfer agents, custodians, and other companies that provide services to the Underlying Mutual Fund.

Information about the Policies

Underwriting and Issuance

Minimum Requirements for Issuance of a Policy

Underwriting for these Policies is designed to group applicants into classifications that can be expected to produce mortality experience consistent with the actuarial structure for that class. The Company uses the following methods of underwriting: (1) simplified underwriting not routinely requiring a physical examination, and (2) medical or paramedical underwriting that requires such an examination.

The Company reserves the right to request a medical examination on any applicant where an affirmative response to one of the medical questions of the application requires additional underwriting by the Company.

The minimum amount of initial premium that will be accepted by the Company is $10,000 for issue ages 0 to 70 and $50,000 for issue ages 71 to 80. Policies may be issued to Insureds who are 80 or younger at the time of issue. Before issuing any Policy, the Company requires satisfactory evidence of insurability, which may include a medical examination.

Premium Deposits

The initial premium for a Policy is payable in full at the Company's Home Office. The minimum amount of initial premium required is $10,000 for issue ages 0 to 70 and $50,000 for issue ages 71 to 80. The Specified Amount of Death Benefit is determined by treating the initial premium as equal to 100% of the Guideline Single Premium. The effective date of permanent insurance coverage is dependent upon completion of all underwriting requirements, payment of the initial premium, and delivery of the Policy while the insured is still living.

The Policy is primarily intended to be a single-premium policy with a limited ability to make additional payments. Subsequent premium payments under the Policy are permitted under the following circumstances:

1. An additional premium payment is required to keep the Policy in force.

2. Additional premium payments of at least $1,000 may be made at any time provided the premium limits prescribed by the Internal Revenue Service to qualify the Policy as a life insurance contract are not violated.

Deposits of additional premiums, if accepted, may increase the Specified Amount of Insurance. However, the Company reserves the right to require satisfactory evidence of insurability before accepting any additional premium payment that results in an increase in the net amount at risk. The Company may require that any existing Policy indebtedness be repaid prior to accepting any additional premium payments.

Additional Premium Deposits, upon acceptance, will be allocated to the Nationwide Separate Account Trust Money Market Fund unless the Policy Owner specifies otherwise.

The Company will not accept a subsequent premium deposit which would result in total premiums paid exceeding the premium limitations prescribed by the Internal Revenue Service to qualify the Policy as a life insurance contract.

Allocation of Cash Value

At the time a Policy is issued, its Cash Value will be based on the Money Market Fund subaccount value or the Fixed Account as if the Policy had been issued and the premium invested on the date the premium was received in good order by the Company. When the Policy is issued, the Cash Value will be allocated to the Money Market Fund subaccount (for any Cash Value allocated to a Subaccount on the Application) or the Fixed Account until the expiration of the period in which the Policy Owner may exercise his or her short-term right to cancel the Policy. At the expiration of the period in which the Policy Owner may exercise his or her short-term right to cancel the Policy, shares of the Underlying Mutual Funds specified by the Policy Owner are purchased at net asset value for the respective subaccount(s). The Policy Owner may change the allocation of Cash Value or may transfer Cash Value from one subaccount to another, subject to such terms and conditions as may be imposed by each Underlying Mutual Fund and as set forth in the prospectus. Cash Value allocated to the Fixed Account at the time of application may not be transferred prior to the first Policy Anniversary.

The designation of investment allocations will be made by the prospective Policy Owner at the time of application for a Policy. The Policy Owner may change the way in which future premiums are allocated by giving written notice to the Company. All percentage allocations must be in whole numbers and must be at least 5%. The sum of allocations must equal 100%.

Short-Term Right to Cancel Policy

A Policy may be returned for cancellation and a full refund of premium within 10 days after the Policy is received, within 45 days after the application for insurance is signed, or within 10 days after the Company mails or delivers a Notice of Right of Withdrawal, whichever is latest. The Policy can be mailed or delivered to the registered representative who sold it or to the Company. Immediately after such mailing or delivery, the Policy will be deemed void from the beginning. The Company will refund the total premiums paid within seven days after it receives the Policy. The scope of this right may vary by state. The exact Policy provision approved or used in a particular state will be disclosed in any Policy issued.

Policy Charges

Deductions from Premiums

No deduction is made from any premium at the time of payment; 100% of each premium payment is applied to the Cash Value.

Monthly Deductions

On the Policy Date and on each Monthly Anniversary Date, the Company will deduct an amount to cover charges and expenses incurred in connection with the Policy. Generally, this Monthly Deduction will be deducted on a pro rata basis from the Cash Value in each subaccount and the Fixed Account. The amount of the Monthly Deductions will vary from month to month. If the Cash Surrender Value is not sufficient to cover the Monthly Deduction that is due, the Policy may lapse. The Monthly Deductions comprise the following charges.

Cost of Insurance Charge

Immediately after the Policy is issued, the Death Benefit will be substantially greater than the initial premium payment. While the Policy is in force, prior to the Maturity Date, the Death Benefit will always be greater than the Cash Value. To enable the Company to pay this excess of the Death Benefit over the Cash Value, a monthly cost of insurance charge is deducted.

Currently, this charge is deducted monthly and is equal to an annual rate of 0.65% multiplied by the Cash Value. On a current basis, for policy years 11 and later, this monthly charge is anticipated to be reduced to the Cash Value multiplied by an annual rate of 0.30% if the Cash Surrender Value is $100,000 or more.

In no event will this current monthly deduction for the cost of insurance exceed the guaranteed monthly cost of insurance charges. Guaranteed cost of insurance charges will not exceed the cost based on the guaranteed cost of insurance rate multiplied by the Policy's net amount at risk. The net amount at risk is equal to the Death Benefit minus the Cash Value. Guaranteed cost of insurance rates for standard issues are based on the 1980 CSO. Guaranteed cost of insurance rates for substandard issues are based on appropriate percentage multiples of the 1980 CSO. These mortality tables are sex-distinct.

Administrative Expense Charge

The Company deducts a monthly Administrative Expense Charge to reimburse it for expenses related to the issuance and maintenance of the Policies including underwriting, establishing policy records, accounting and record keeping, and periodic reporting to Policy Owners. This charge is designed only to reimburse the Company for its actual administrative expenses. In the aggregate, the Company expects that the charges for administrative costs will be approximately equal to the related expenses. This monthly charge is equal to an annual rate of 0.30% multiplied by the Policy's Cash Value. On a current basis, for Policy Years II and later, this monthly charge is anticipated to be reduced to an annual rate of 0.15% multiplied by the Cash Value, provided the Cash Surrender Value is greater than or equal to $100,000. This Administrative Expense Charge is subject to a $10 per month minimum.

Tax Expense Charge

During the first 10 policy years, the Company makes a Monthly Deduction to compensate for certain taxes that are incurred by the Company, including premium taxes imposed by various states and local jurisdictions and for federal taxes imposed under Section 848 of the Code. This monthly charge is equal to an annual rate of 0.50% multiplied by the Policy's Cash Value.

This charge is deducted monthly and includes a premium tax component equal to an annual rate of 0.30% and a federal tax component equal to an annual rate of 0.20%. The Company expects to pay an average state premium tax of approximately 2.5% of premiums for all states, although such tax rates can generally range from 0% to 4%. The Company does not anticipate making a profit from this monthly Tax Expense Charge.

The Company does not currently assess any charge for income taxes incurred by the Company as a result of the operations of the subaccounts of the Variable Account. The Company reserves the right to assess a charge for such taxes against the Variable Account if the Company determines that such taxes will be incurred.

Mortality and Expense Risk Charge

The Company assumes certain risks for guaranteeing the mortality and expense charges. The mortality risk assumed under the Policies is that the Insured may not live as long as expected. The expense risk assumed is that the actual expenses incurred in issuing and administering the Policies may be greater than expected. In addition, the Company assumes risks associated with the nonrecovery of policy issue, underwriting, and other administrative expenses due to Policies that lapse or are surrendered during the early policy years.

To compensate the Company for assuming these risks, a monthly charge for mortality and expense risks is deducted on a pro rata basis from the Cash Value in each Variable Account subaccount. This monthly charge is equal to an annual rate of 0.90% multiplied by the Cash Value attributable to the Variable Account. To the extent that future levels of mortality and expenses are less than or equal to those expected, the Company may realize a profit from these charges.

Surrender Charges

The Company will deduct a surrender charge from the Policy's Cash Value for any Policy that is surrendered during the first nine policy years. The surrender charge comprises two components: a sales surrender charge and a premium tax surrender charge.

The Company incurs certain sales and other distribution expenses at the time the Policies are issued. The majority of these expenses consist of commissions paid for the sale or these policies. Premium taxes are generally incurred by the Company at the time the Policies are issued. These surrender charges are designed to recover a portion of these expenses. The Company does not expect to profit from these surrender charges. Unrecovered expenses are borne by the Company's general assets, which may include profits, if any, from the monthly mortality and expense risk charges. Certain surrenders may result in adverse tax consequences. Maximum surrender charges are as follows:

Completed Policy Years	Surrender Charge as a Percent of Initial Premium Payment
0	10.0%
1	10.0%
2	9.0%
3	8.0%
4	7.0%
5	6.0%
6	5.0%
7	4.0%
8	3.0%
9+	0.0%

Approximately 75% of the total surrender charges are for the recovery of sales expenses and 25% for the recovery of premium taxes. In no event will the sales surrender charge exceed 7.5% of the total premium payments.

The amount of the sales surrender charge may be eliminated when the Policies are issued to an officer, director, former director, partner, employee, or retired employee of the Company or to an employee of the General Distributor of the Policies, an employee of an affiliate of the Company or the General Distributor, or a duly appointed representative of the Company who receives no commission as a result of the purchase. Elimination of the sales surrender charge Will be permitted by the Company only in those situations where the Company does not incur sales expenses normally associated with sales of a Policy. In no event will the elimination of any sales surrender charge be permitted where such elimination will be unfairly discriminatory to any person.

How the Cash Value Varies

On any date during the Policy Year, the Cash Value equals the Cash Value on the preceding Valuation Date plus any premium applied since the previous Valuation Date, plus or minus any investment results and less any Policy Charges.

There is no guaranteed Cash Value. The Cash Value will vary with the investment experience of the Variable Account and/or the daily crediting of interest in the Fixed Account and Policy Loan Account depending on the allocation of Cash Value by the Policy Owner.

How the Investment Experience is Determined

The Cash Value in each subaccount is converted to Accumulation Units of that subaccount. The conversion is accomplished by dividing the amount of Cash Value allocated to a subaccount by the value of an Accumulation Unit for the subaccount of the Valuation Period during which the allocation occurs.

The value of an Accumulation Unit for each subaccount was arbitrarily set initially at $10 when the Underlying Mutual Fund shares in that subaccount were available for purchase. The value for any subsequent Valuation Period is determined by multiplying the Accumulation

Unit value for each subaccount for the immediately preceding Valuation Period by the Net Investment Factor for the subaccount during the subsequent Valuation Period. The value of an Accumulation Unit may increase or decrease from Valuation Period to Valuation Period. The number of Accumulation Units will not change as a result of investment experience.

Net Investment Factor

The Net Investment Factor for any Valuation Period is determined by dividing a by b, where

a. is the net of:
1. the Net Asset Value per share of the Underlying Mutual Fund option held in the subaccount determined at the end of the current Valuation Period, plus
2. the per share amount of any dividend or capital gain distributions made by the Underlying Mutual Fund option held in the subaccount if the "ex-dividend" date occurs during the current Valuation Period.

b. is the net of:
1. The Net Asset Value per share of the Underlying Mutual Fund held in the subaccount determined at the end of the immediately preceding Valuation Period, plus or minus
2. the per share charge or credit, if any, for any taxes reserved for in the immediately preceding Valuation Period.

For Underlying Mutual Fund options that credit dividends on a daily basis and pay such dividends once a month, the Net Investment Factor allows for the monthly reinvestment of these daily dividends.

The Net Investment Factor may be greater or less than 1; therefore, the value of an Accumulation Unit may increase or decrease. It should be noted that changes in the Net Investment Factor may not be directly proportional to changes in the net asset value of Underlying Mutual Fund shares because of any charge or credit for tax reserves.

Valuation of Assets

Underlying Mutual Fund shares in the Variable Account will be valued at their Net Asset Value.

Determining the Cash Value

The sum of the value of all Variable Account Accumulation Units attributable to the Policy, amounts credited to the Fixed Account, and any associated value in the Policy Loan Account is the Cash Value. The number of Accumulation Units credited per each subaccount are determined by dividing the net amount allocated to the subaccount by the Accumulation Unit Value for the subaccount for the Valuation Period during which the premium is received by the Company. In the event part or all of the Cash Value is surrendered or charges or deductions are made against the Cash Value, generally an appropriate number of Accumulation Units from the Variable Account and an appropriate amount from the Fixed Account will be deducted in the same proportion that the Policy Owner's interest in the Variable Account and the Fixed Account bears to the total Cash Value.

The Cash Value in the Fixed Account and the Policy Loan Account is credited with interest daily at an effective annual rate which the Company periodically declares. The annual effective rate credited to the Fixed Account will never be less than 3%. The annual effective rate credited to the Policy Loan Account will never be less than 4%. Upon request, the Company will inform the Policy Owner of the then-applicable rates for each account.

Valuation Periods and Valuation Dates

A Valuation Period is the period commencing at the close of business on the New York Stock Exchange and ending at the close of business for the next succeeding Valuation Date. A Valuation Date is each day that the New York Stock Exchange and the Company's Home Office is open for business, or any other day during which there is sufficient degree of trading that the current net asset value of the Accumulation Units might be materially affected.

Surrendering the Policy for Cash

Right to Surrender

The Policy Owner may surrender the Policy in full at any time while the Insured is living and receive its Cash Surrender Value. The cancellation will be effective as of the date the Company receives a proper written request for cancellation of the Policy. Such written request must be signed and, where permitted, the signature guaranteed by a member firm of the New York, American, Boston, Midwest, Philadelphia, or Pacific Stock Exchange, or by a Commercial Bank or Savings and Loan that is a member of the Federal Deposit Insurance Corporation. In some cases, the Company may require additional documentation of a customary nature.

Cash Surrender Value

The Cash Surrender Value increases or decreases daily to reflect the investment experience of the Variable Account and the daily crediting of interest in the Fixed Account and the Policy Loan Account. The Cash Surrender Value equals the Policy's Cash Value, next computed after the date the Company receives a proper written request for surrender of the Policy, minus any charges, indebtedness, or other deductions due on that date, which may also include a Surrender Charge.

Partial Surrenders

Partial surrenders are permitted after the fifth policy year. Partial surrenders will be permitted only if they satisfy the following requirements.

1. The partial surrender request is in writing and the request is signed by the Policy Owner or an authorized party of the Policy Owner; and
2. The maximum partial surrender in any Policy Year, not subject to Surrender Charges, is limited to the maximum of:
   a. 10% of the total premium payments; and
   b. 100% of cumulative earnings (Cash Value less total premium payments less any existing policy indebtedness);
3. Such partial surrenders must not result in a reduction of the Cash Surrender Value below $10,000; and
4. After such partial surrender, the Policy continues to qualify as life insurance.

All partial surrenders will be next computed after the date the Company receives a proper written request. When a partial surrender is made, the Cash Value is reduced by the amount of the partial surrender. Also, the Specified Amount is reduced by the amount of the partial surrender unless the Death Benefit is based on the applicable percentage of the Cash Value. In such a case, a Partial Surrender will decrease the Specified Amount by the amount by which the Partial Surrender exceeds the difference between the Death Benefit and the Specified Amount. Partial surrender amounts must be first deducted from the values in the Variable subaccounts. Partial surrenders will be deducted from the Fixed Account only to the extent that insufficient values are available in the Variable subaccounts.

No Surrender Charges will be assessed against any such eligible partial surrenders. Certain partial surrenders may result in currently taxable income and tax penalties.

Maturity Proceeds

The Maturity Date is the Policy Anniversary on or next following the Insured's 100th birthday. The maturity proceeds will be payable to the Policy Owner on the Maturity Date provided the Policy is still in force. The Maturity Proceeds will be equal to the amount of the Policy's Cash Value, less any indebtedness.

Income Tax Withholding

Federal law requires the Company to withhold income tax from any portion of surrender proceeds that is subject to tax, unless the Policy Owner advises the Company, in writing, of his or her request not to withhold.

If the Policy Owner requests that the Company not withhold taxes, or if the taxes withheld are insufficient, the Policy Owner may be liable for payment of an estimated tax. The Policy Owner should consult his or her tax advisor.

In certain employer-sponsored life insurance arrangements, including equity split-dollar arrangements, Participants may be required to report for income tax purposes one or more of the following: (1) the value each year of the life insurance protection provided; (2) an amount equal to any employer-paid premiums; or (3) some or all of the amount by which the current value of the Contract exceeds the employer's interest in the contract. Participants should consult with the sponsor or the administrator of the Plan and/or with their personal tax or legal advisers to determine the tax consequences, if any, of their employer-sponsored life insurance arrangements.

Policy Loans

Taking a Policy Loan

The Policy Owner may take a loan using the Policy as security. During the first year, maximum Policy indebtedness is limited to 50% of the Cash Value less any Surrender Charge. Thereafter, maximum policy indebtedness is limited to 90% of the Cash Value less any Surrender Charge. The Company will not grant a loan for an amount less than $1,000. Should the Death Benefit become payable, the Policy be surrendered, or the Policy mature while a loan is outstanding, the amount of Policy indebtedness will be deducted from the Death Benefit, Cash Surrender Value, or the Maturity Value, respectively.

Any request for a Policy loan must be in written form satisfactory to the Company. The request must be signed and, where permitted, the signature guaranteed by a member firm of the New York, American, Boston, Midwest, Philadelphia, or Pacific Stock Exchange; or by a Commercial Bank or a Savings and Loan that is a member of the Federal Deposit Insurance Corporation. Certain Policy loans may result in currently taxable income and tax penalties.

Effect on Investment Performance

When a loan is made, an amount equal to the amount of the loan is transferred from the Variable Account to the Policy Loan Account. If the assets relating to a Policy are held in more than one subaccount, withdrawals from subaccounts will be made in proportion to the assets in each Variable Subaccount at the time of the loan. Policy Loans will be transferred from the Fixed Account only when insufficient amounts are available in the Variable Subaccounts. The amount taken out of the Variable Account will not be affected by the Variable Account's investment experience while the loan is outstanding.

Interest

Amounts transferred to the Policy Loan Account will earn interest daily from the date of transfer.

Total policy indebtedness includes two components: (1) Preferred Loans and (2) Regular Loans. The amount of the loan account will be treated as a Preferred Loan to the extent such amount is less than or equal to the Cash Value minus the result of: the premiums paid less any withdrawals not taxed as distributions plus any repaid loans previously taxed as distributions plus any amounts reported to the Company as cost basis attributable to exchanges under Section 1035 of the Code. Any additional loaned amounts will be treated as Regular Loans. Preferred and Regular Loan amounts will be determined once a year, as well as at any time a new loan is requested. On a current basis, preferred indebtedness will be credited interest daily at an annual effective rate of 6%, and Regular indebtedness will be credited interest daily at an annual effective rate of 4%. The credited rate for all policy indebtedness is guaranteed never to be lower than 4%. This earned interest is transferred from the Policy Loan Account to a Variable Account or the Fixed Account on each Policy Anniversary at any time a new loan is requested or at the time of loan repayment. It will be allocated according to the Fund Allocation Factors in effect at the time of the transfer.

The loan interest rate is 6% per year for all policy indebtedness. Interest is charged daily and is payable at the end of each Policy Year as well as at any time a new loan is requested. Unpaid interest will be added to the existing policy indebtedness as of the due date and will be charged interest at the same rate as the rest of the indebtedness.

Whenever the total loan indebtedness plus accrued interest exceeds the Cash Value less any Surrender Charges, the Company will send a notice to the Policy Owner and the assignee, if any. The Policy will terminate without value 61 days after the mailing of the notice unless a sufficient repayment is made during that period. A repayment is sufficient if it is large enough to reduce the total loan indebtedness plus accrued interest to an amount equal to the total Cash Value less any Surrender Charges plus an amount sufficient to continue the Policy in force for three months.

Effect on Death Benefit and Cash Value

A Policy loan, whether or not repaid, will have a permanent effect on the Death Benefit and Cash Value because the investment results of the Variable Account or the Fixed Account will apply only to the non-loaned portion of the Cash Value. The longer the loan is outstanding, the greater the effect is likely to be. Depending on the investment results of the Variable Account or the Fixed Account while the loan is outstanding, the effect could be favorable or unfavorable.

Repayment

All or part of a loan may be repaid at any time while the Policy is in force during the insured's lifetime. Any payment intended as a loan repayment, rather than a premium payment, must be identified as such. Loan repayments will be credited to the Variable Subaccounts and the Fixed Account in proportion to the Policy Owner's Premium allocation in effect at the time of the repayment. Each repayment may not be less than $1,000. The Company reserves the right to require that any loan repayments resulting from Policy Loans transferred from the Fixed Account must be first allocated to the Fixed Account.

How the Death Benefit Varies

Calculation of the Death Benefit

At issue, the Specified Amount is determined by treating the initial premium as equal to 100% of the Guideline Single Premium. Guideline Single Premiums vary by attained age, sex, underwriting classification, and total premium payments. The following table illustrates representative initial Specified Amounts.

Issue Age	$10,000 Single Premium		$25,000 Single Premium		$50,000 Single Premium	
	Male	Female	Male	Female	Male	Female
35	$62,031	$76,231	$155,077	$190,577	$310,154	$381,154
40	49,883	61,337	124,707	153,343	249,413	306,685
45	40,437	49,825	101,903	124,562	202,186	249,124
50	33,079	40,742	82,698	101,854	165,397	203,708
55	27,358	33,531	68,396	83,828	136,791	167,655
60	22,964	27,734	57,410	69,335	114,821	138,671
65	19,579	23,052	48,948	57,631	97,895	115,261

Generally, for a given premium payment, the initial Specified Amount is greater for females than males. The Specified Amount is shown in the Policy.

While the Policy is in force, the Death Benefit will never be less than the Specified Amount or the Applicable Percentage of Cash Value. The Death Benefit may vary with the Cash Value of the Policy, which depends on investment performance. The amount of Death Benefit will ordinarily not change for several years to reflect investment performance and may not change at all. If investment performance is favorable, the amount of Death Benefit may increase. The Applicable Percentage of Cash Value varies by attained age.

Applicable Percentage of Cash Value Factors

Attained Age	Percentage of Cash Value	Attained Age	Percentage of Cash Value	Attained Age	Percentage of Cash Value
0–40	250%	60	130%	80	105%
41	243%	61	128%	81	105%
42	236%	62	126%	82	105%
43	229%	63	124%	83	105%
44	222%	64	122%	84	105%
45	215%	65	120%	85	105%
46	209%	66	119%	86	105%
47	203%	67	118%	87	105%
48	197%	68	117%	88	105%
49	191%	69	116%	89	105%
50	185%	70	115%	90	105%
51	178%	71	113%	91	104%
52	171%	72	111%	92	103%
53	164%	73	109%	93	102%
54	157%	74	107%	94	101%
55	150%	75	105%	95	101%
56	146%	76	105%	96	101%
57	142%	77	105%	97	101%
58	138%	78	105%	98	101%
59	134%	79	105%	99	101%
				100	100%

Proceeds Payable on Death

The actual Death Proceeds payable on the Insured's death will be the Death Benefit as described above, less any outstanding Policy loans and less any unpaid Policy Charges. Under certain circumstances, the Proceeds may be adjusted.

Right of Conversion

The Policy Owner may at any time, upon written request to the Company within 24 months of the Policy Date, make an irrevocable, one-time election to transfer all subaccount Cash Values to the Fixed Account. The Right of Conversion provision is subject to state availability.

Changes of Investment Policy

The Company may materially change the Investment Policy of the Variable Account. The Company must inform the Policy Owner and obtain all necessary regulatory approvals. Any change must be submitted to the various state insurance departments which may disapprove it if deemed detrimental to the interests of the policyholders or if it renders the Company's operations hazardous to the public. If a Policy Owner objects, there is an unconditional right to transfer all of the Cash Value in the Variable Account to the Fixed Account. The Policy Owner has the later of 60 days from the date of the Investment Policy change or 60 days from being informed of such change to make this transfer.

Grace Period

If the Cash Surrender Value in the Policy is insufficient to pay the monthly deductions, Policy loan interest, or other charges which become due but are unpaid, a grace period of 61 days will be allowed for payment of sufficient premium to continue the Policy in force. The Company will notify the Policy Owner of the amount required to continue the Policy in force. If the required amount is not received within 61 days of the notice, the Policy will terminate without value. If the

Insured dies during the Grace Period, the Company will pay the Death Proceeds.

Reinstatement

If the Grace Period ends and the Policy Owner has neither paid the required premium nor surrendered the Policy for its Cash Surrender Value, the Policy Owner may reinstate the Policy by:

1. Submitting a written request at any time within three years after the end of the Grace Period and prior to the Maturity Date.

2. Providing evidence of insurability satisfactory to the Company.

3. Paying sufficient premium to cover all policy charges that were due and unpaid during the Grace Period.

4. Paying additional premiums at least equal to three times the guaranteed cost of insurance charges.

5. Repaying any indebtedness against the Policy that existed at the end of the Grace Period.

The effective date of a reinstated Policy will be the Monthly Anniversary Day on or next following the date the application for reinstatement is approved by us. If your Policy is reinstated, the Cash Value on the date of reinstatement, but prior to applying any premiums or loan repayments received, will be set equal to the appropriate Surrender Charge. Such Surrender Charge will be based on the length of time from the date of premium payments to the effective date of the reinstatement. Unless the Policy Owner has provided otherwise, the allocation of the amount of the Surrender Charge, additional premium payments, and any loan repayments will be based on the Underlying Mutual Fund Allocation factors in effect at the start of the Grace Period.

The Fixed Account Option

Under exemptive and exclusionary provisions, interests in the General Account have not been registered under the Securities Act of 1933, and the General Account has not been registered as an investment company under the Investment Company Act of 1940. Accordingly, neither the General Account nor any interests therein is subject to the provisions of these Acts, and Nationwide has been advised that the staff of the Securities and Exchange Commission has not reviewed the disclosures in this prospectus relating to the Fixed Account option. Disclosures regarding the General Account may, however, be subject to certain generally applicable provisions of the federal securities laws concerning the accuracy and completeness of statements made in prospectuses.

As explained earlier, a Policy Owner may elect to allocate or transfer all or part of the Cash Value to the Fixed Account, and the amount allocated or transferred becomes part of the General Account. The General Account consists of all assets of the Company other than those in the Variable Account and in other separate accounts that have been or may be established by the Company. Subject to applicable law, the Company has sole discretion over the investment of the assets of the General Account, and Policy Owners do not share in the investment experience of those assets. The Company guarantees that the part of the Cash Value invested under the Fixed Account option will accrue interest daily at an effective annual rate that the Company declares periodically. The Fixed Account crediting rate will not be less than an effective annual rate of 3%. Upon request and in the annual statement the Company will inform a Policy Owner of the then-applicable rate. The Company is not obligated to credit interest at a higher rate.

Other Policy Provisions

Policy Owner

While the Insured is living, all rights in this Policy are vested in the Policy Owner named in the application or as subsequently changed, subject to assignment, if any.

The Policy Owner may name a Contingent Policy Owner or a new Policy Owner while the Insured is living. Any change must be in a written form satisfactory to the Company and recorded at the Company's Home Office. Once recorded, the change will be effective when signed. The change will not affect any payment made or action taken by the Company before R was recorded. The Company may require that the Policy be submitted for endorsement before making a change.

If the Policy Owner is other than the Insured, and names no contingent owner, and dies before the Insured, the Policy Owner's rights in this Policy belong to the Policy Owner's estate.

Beneficiary

The Beneficiary(ies) shall be as named in the application or as subsequently changed, subject to assignment, if any.

The Policy Owner may name a new Beneficiary while the Insured is living. Any change must be in a written form satisfactory to the Company and recorded at the Company's Home Office. Once recorded, the change will be effective when signed. The change will not affect any payment made or action taken by the Company before it was recorded.

If any Beneficiary predeceases the Insured, that Beneficiary's interest passes to any surviving beneficiary, unless otherwise provided. Multiple beneficiaries will be paid in equal shares, unless otherwise provided. If no named Beneficiary survives the Insureds, the proceeds shall be paid to the Policy Owner or the Policy Owner's estate.

Assignment

While the Insured is living, the Policy Owner may assign his or her rights in the Policy. The assignment must be in writing, signed by the Policy Owner, and recorded by the Company at its Home Office. The Company is not responsible for any assignment not submitted for recording, nor is the Company responsible for the sufficiency or validity of any assignment.

The assignment will be subject to any Indebtedness owed to the Company before it was recorded.

Incontestability

The Company will not contest a Death Benefit based on representations in any written application when such benefit has been in force, during the lifetime of the Insured, for two years.

Error in Age or Sex

If the Insured's age, sex, or both, as stated in the application, are incorrect, the affected benefits will be adjusted to reflect the correct age, sex, or both.

Suicide

If the Insured dies by suicide within two years from the Policy Date, the Company will pay no more than the sum of the premiums less any unpaid loan. If the Insured dies by suicide within two years from the date an application is accepted for an increase in the Specified Amount, the Company will pay no more than the amount paid for such additional benefit.

Nonparticipating Policies

The Policies are nonparticipating. This means that they do not participate in any dividend distribution of the Company's surplus.

Riders

A rider may be added as an addition to the Policy. Riders currently include:

1. Maturity Extension Endorsement
2. Accelerated Death Benefit Rider

Rider availability varies by state.

Glossary

Attained Age   The Insured's age on the Policy Date, plus the number of full years since the Policy Date.

Accumulation Unit   An accounting unit of measure used to calculate the Cash Value of the Variable Account.

Beneficiary   The person to whom the proceeds are due on the Insured's death.

Cash Value   The sum of the value of Policy assets in the Variable Account, Fixed Account, and any associated value in the Policy Loan Account.

Cash Surrender Value   The Policy's Cash Value less any indebtedness under the Policy less any Surrender Charge.

Code   The Internal Revenue Code of 1986, as amended.

Death Proceeds   Amount of money payable to the Beneficiary if the Insured dies while the Policy is in force.

Fixed Account   An investment option that is funded by the General Account of the issuing Company.

General Account   All assets of the Company other than those of the Variable Account or those of other separate accounts that have been or may be established by the Company.

Guideline Single Premium   The amount of single premium calculated in accordance with the provisions of the Code. It represents the single premium required to mature the Policy under guaranteed mortality and expense charges and an interest rate of 6%.

Insured   The person whose life is covered by the Policy and who is named on the Policy Data Page.

Maturity Date   The Policy Anniversary on or following the Insured's 100th birthday.

Monthly Anniversary Date   The same day as the Policy Date for each succeeding month.

Net Asset Value   The worth of one share of a Mutual Fund as calculated at the end of each business day. Net Asset Value is computed by adding the value of all portfolio holdings, plus other assets, deducting liabilities, and then dividing the result by the number of shares outstanding.

Policy Anniversary   An anniversary of the Policy Date.

Policy Charges   All deductions made from the value of the Variable Account or the Policy Cash Value.

Policy Date   The date the provisions of the Policy take effect, as shown on the Policy Owner's Policy data page.

Policy Loan Account   The Portion of the Cash Value that results from policy loans.

Policy Owner   The person designated in the Policy application as the Owner.

Policy Year   Each year commencing with the Policy Date and each Policy Date anniversary thereafter.

Specified Amount   A dollar amount used to determine the Death Benefit under a Policy. It is shown on the Policy Data Page.

Surrender Charge   An amount deducted from the Cash Value if the Policy is surrendered.

Underlying Mutual Funds   The Underlying Mutual Funds that correspond to the subaccounts of the Variable Account.

Valuation Date   Each day that both the New York Stock Exchange and the Company's Home Office are open for business or any other day during which there is a sufficient degree of trading such that the current net asset value of the Accumulated Units might be materially affected.

Valuation Period   A period commencing with the close of business on the New York Stock Exchange and ending at the close of business for the next succeeding Valuation Date.

Index